Clown

About the Author

Figure 0.1 Author Joe Dieffenbacher.
Photo credit: Matilda Dieffenbacher.

Joe Dieffenbacher is a teacher, director, actor, designer, and author known for his theatre, circus, and cabaret work under the name nakupelle.

He was Physical Comedy Director for *Taming of the Shrew* (2016) at Shakespeare's Globe, London, and Regent's Park Open Air Theatre's Production of *Oliver!* He worked as Physical Theater Director for *Woman & Scarecrow* at RADA, London, and served as Circus Skills Director for the Scottish National Opera's, *Ariadne auf Naxos*. He was playwright, director, and prop designer for *Servant of Two Masters* at Coastal Carolina University and for numerous productions with the Dell'Arte Players, California.

As director of Clown Conservatory at Circus Centre-San Francisco, he developed an extensive pedagogy combining Clown, Circus, Theatre, Slapstick, and Commedia. His work was featured on ABC News: *Clown School: Day in the Life*, and as part of the documentary, *Bizarre, A Circus Story*.

Joe served as lead instructor for Clown, Physical Theatre, Mask Performance, and Slapstick at Dell'Arte International, and has been a guest teacher at the Belfast Community Circus, Teater Studion in Stockholm, Wuqiao International Circus Festival, Shijiazhuang, China, and Actor's Conservatory Theatre in San Francisco. He's worked with solo artists and ensembles all over the world developing original material for theater, circus, cabaret, dance theatre, and outdoor spectacles.

As a clown and physical comedian, Joe has collaborated on six productions with British pop sensations Take That, co-created sequences for the Closing Ceremonies of the London 2012 Olympics and Paralympics, was a clown and elephant jumper with the Ringling Bros. and Barnum & Bailey Circus, and has collaborated on shows for Disney in California and Florida. His own company, nakupelle, has featured in theater seasons, outdoor festivals, circuses and cabarets in Europe, Asia, and North America.

www.joedieffenbacher.com

Clown

The Physical Comedian

Joe Dieffenbacher

methuen | drama
LONDON · NEW YORK · OXFORD · NEW DELHI · SYDNEY

METHUEN DRAMA
Bloomsbury Publishing Plc
50 Bedford Square, London, WC1B 3DP, UK
1385 Broadway, New York, NY 10018, USA

BLOOMSBURY, METHUEN DRAMA and the Methuen Drama logo are trademarks of Bloomsbury Publishing Plc

First published in Great Britain 2021

Copyright © Joe Dieffenbacher, 2021

Joe Dieffenbacher has asserted his right under the Copyright, Designs and Patents Act, 1988, to be identified as author of this work.

For legal purposes the Acknowledgments on pp. xvi–xvii constitute an extension of this copyright page.

Cover design: Eleanor Rose
Cover image: Dan Griffiths in an orange suit. Photo by Eric Gillet.

All rights reserved. No part of this publication may be reproduced or transmitted in any form or by any means, electronic or mechanical, including photocopying, recording, or any information storage or retrieval system, without prior permission in writing from the publishers.

Bloomsbury Publishing Plc does not have any control over, or responsibility for, any third-party websites referred to or in this book. All internet addresses given in this book were correct at the time of going to press. The author and publisher regret any inconvenience caused if addresses have changed or sites have ceased to exist, but can accept no responsibility for any such changes.

A catalogue record for this book is available from the British Library.

Library of Congress Cataloging-in-Publication Data

Names: Dieffenbacher, Joe, author.
Title: Clown : the physical comedian / Joe Dieffenbacher.
Description: London ; New York : Methuen Drama, 2021. | Includes bibliographical references and index. | Summary: "Clown: The Physical Comedian is a detailed and comprehensive workbook for those interested in the art of clowning and physical theatre, including actors, directors, improvisers, stand-up comedians, circus artists, mask performers and devisers of new work. Offering an extensive and hugely diverse compilation of tried-and-tested exercises and games, the book is for students, teachers and practitioners to aid ensemble-building, character development, devising theatre, physicalising text and vocalising movement, plus creating cabaret acts, clown routines and adding physical play to scripted scenes. It offers advice on subjects such as developing presence onstage; increasing strength, flexibility and physical expression; developing partner and trio relationships; understanding the power of the mask; and working with an audience - in particular, turning a performance into a conversation with the audience and increasing the actor's ability to connect with a crowd. The exercises and teachings have been developed in classrooms, workshops and theatres all over the world and the book is packed with insights from the author, who has worked for over 35 years in a wide variety of venues, from intimate performance spaces to large-scale sports stadiums"– Provided by publisher. Identifiers: LCCN 2020038546 (print) | LCCN 2020038547 (ebook) | ISBN 9781350143098 (hardback) | ISBN 9781350141407 (paperback) | ISBN 9781350141414 (ebook) | ISBN 9781350141421 (epub)
Subjects: LCSH: Clowning–Handbooks, manuals, etc.
Classification: LCC PN1955 .D46 2021 (print) | LCC PN1955 (ebook) | DDC 791.3/3—dc23
LC record available at https://lccn.loc.gov/2020038546
LC ebook record available at https://lccn.loc.gov/2020038547

ISBN:	HB:	978-1-3501-4309-8
	PB:	978-1-3501-4140-7
	ePDF:	978-1-3501-4141-4
	eBook:	978-1-3501-4142-1

Typeset by RefineCatch Limited, Bungay, Suffolk

To find out more about our authors and books visit www.bloomsbury.com and sign up for our newsletters.

To my family, my first audience, and my biggest inspiration.
To my wife, who still finds me funny after all these years.

Contents

List of Illustrations xiv
Acknowledgments xvi
Preface xviii

Introduction 1
The Search 1
The Word 2
The Look 2
The Energy 4
The Mask 5

The Fundamentals 9
Terms Used 9
Roles Played 11
Clown Essentials 12
Lesson Plans 13
Defining Clown 15

Challenges and Obstacles 19
Technique—Commitment—Tactics—Story 20
Entrances and Exits—Discovery Moments—Success and Failure 23
The Right Way 24
Failure as a Choice, Accident as an Opportunity 24
The Ever-Changing Game 25
The Director and the Clown 26

1 Hello: A Pharmacist, Helium Balloons, and a Red Nose 29
Hello! 32
Birds and Bees 33

Group Loco Motion 34
Groups and Agreements 39
The Five Commandments 42
Wait, Watch, Jump, Play 43

2 Energy: The Telepathic Renaissance Fool 47
Walk This Way 49
Chase Me, Tag Me 50
The Solo and the Ensemble 52
Chair Games 54
Races 57
Relax 59

3 The Talking Body: Silence on the Streets 63
Dance! 65
Playing With the Breath 67
Where's My Center? 68
Sculptures 71
The Body Mask 72
Visualization 74
The Five Elements 76
Looking Out 80

4 Prop Play: The Prop Whisperer 87
Prop Around 89
Prop Improv 91
Prop Me 94
Prop and Status 96

5 Curiosity: Odd Fellows 101
Space Odyssey 104
Look, See, React 105
In and Out 109
Listen 111
Backstage Butting In 113

6 Clown Solos: Catching a Salad on Your Face 119

Pass It Around 121
The Real Thing 124
The Participating Audience 128

7 Clown Duos: The Wet Towel Intervention 137

Remember Me 139
Pushers 140
Mind Leading the Blind 142
Followed 144
Match My Mood 148
The Big Wind Up 150
Surprise, Surprise 152
Embrace 154

8 Clown Trios: Boss, Negotiator, Fool 157

Notes on Playing the Boss 159
Notes on Playing the Negotiator and the Fool 160
Get Rhythm 161
Paper and Balloons 163
Thumbs 165
Follow Your Leader 166
Status Snapshots 167
Get Up 170
Top That 171
Down the Line 173

9 Clown Ensembles: Fractious Fun 181

All Together Now 182
Follow Along 184
Follow Me 186
Support Staff 188
Caretakers 191
Eh? Oh 193

Add On 195
Run, Stop, Relax 196
Revealing 198
Misfits and Master 199
Chips and Stick 201
The Ridiculous Ensemble 203

10 The Rules, the Script, the Game, the Play: Welcome to the Playroom 207

The Evolution of a Game 208
Tail, Tag, Scene 211
Scene Tricks 213
Prop Journey 215
Blindfolded Experts 217

11 The Mask of the Clown 225

Makeup, Nose, Costume 225
The Painted Face 226
The Smallest Mask 229
The Body Mask 231

12 The Skillful Clown 235

The Dexterous Fool 235
Dance 236
Music 236
Mime/Movement 236
Tumbling 237
Partner Acrobatics 237
Slapstick 237
Skills, Tricks, Feats, and Stunts 240
Presentation 240

13 Getting Serious About Your Funny 243

Begin to Begin 243
Take Action 244
Get Serious 245

Make Progress Through Play 245
Own It 245
Stay Open 246
Make It Real 246
Tune In 246
Find Ways to Connect 246
Take Notes 247
Accumulate 247

14 Devising for Clown and Physical Comedy 249
Nuts and Bolts 249
Narrative, Plot, Arc, Through Line 252
Ensemble Devising: Developing Group Entrées, Scenes, and Routines 257
When It All Gets Too Confusing 260

Bibliography 263
Inspirations 267
Index 275

List of Illustrations

0.1	Author Joe Dieffenbacher	ii
0.2	Joe Dieffenbacher in *Icarus at the Office*	xiv
0.3	Clown and dolphin trainer Lars Adams	1
0.4	The author as Johnny Horrendezz	9
0.5	Paul Philion and friends	14
0.6	Clowns Tommy Toxic, Sydney Schwindt, Andrew Pulkrabek, Kate Brehm, and Ariel Speedwagon prepare for a show at the Clown Conservatory	16
0.7	Opera diva clown Crystal Philippi	19
0.8	Aeronautical Clown Carasue McClendon	22
1.1	Devin Shacket: Hello	28
1.2	The author's early days as a clown	29
2.1	Jonathan Rex: Energy	46
2.2	The Abbotts of Unreason, Mark Renfrow (seated) and Joe Dieffenbacher	47
3.1	Christian Schneider: The talking body	62
3.2	Joe Dieffenbacher as the janitor in nakupelle's *The Trap*	64
4.1	Windy Wynazz: Prop play	86
4.2	Michael Hayes meets the singing chicken	87
5.1	Mary Hicks: Curiousity	100
5.2	Wayward showgirl clown Sophia Knox-Miller	101
6.1	Ariel Speedwagon: Clown solos	118
6.2	Joe Dieffenbacher at Fiestas del Pilar, Zaragoza, Spain performing *Bon Appetit!*	119
7.1	Amica Hunter and David Cantor: Clown duos	136
7.2	A little bit off, Amica Hunter and David Cantor in *Bella Culpa*	137
8.1	Devin Shacket, Ariel Speedwagon, and Windy Wynazz: Clown trios	156
8.2	Clown trio Rebecca Hammond, Katrina Kroetch, and Paul Philion	157
9.1	Clown Ensembles: Amica Hunter, Carasue McClendon, Sophia Knox-Miller, Kate Brehm, Sydney Schwindt,	

	Christian Schneider, Windy Wynazz, Barbara Gonzalez, Tommy Toxic, Devin Shacket, Andrew Pulkrabek, Rebecca Hammond, Paul Philion, Ariel Speedwagon, Katrina Kroetch, Lars Adams, and David Cantor	180
9.2	Los Payasos Mendigos (the beggar clowns): Joe Dieffenbacher (Yahoo), Rudi Galindo (Lupita), Cosmo Kuzmick (El Excremente), and Dave Ferney (Guapo)	181
10.1	Kate Brehm: The rules, the script, the game, the play	206
10.2	Joe Dieffenbacher with clown, percussionist, and juggler Fuman	207
11.1	Devin Shacket: The mask of the clown	224
11.2	Paul Philion	225
11.3	The nose is a mask	229
12.1	Sophia Knox-Miller: The skilful clown	234
12.2	Joe Dieffenbacher aka nakupelle in *Bon Appetit!*	235
12.3	The crowd in Ludwigsburg, Germany enjoying nakupelle's *The Trap*	238
13.1	Amica Hunter: Get serious about your funny	242
13.2	Lars Adams and Carasue McClendon go on safari	243
14.1	Los Payasos Mendigos: Devising for Clown and physical comedy	248
14.2	Michael Hayes shows off the Emperor's new hat	249
14.3	Windy Wynazz flexes her mop	252
14.4	Sophia Knox-Miller, the balloon meditation	261

Acknowledgments

I'm eternally grateful to the teachers who inspired, challenged, and befriended me: John Creagh, Andrew Levitt, Tom Murphy, Randy Judkins, Bunni Thompson, Richard Ficke, Ruthie Chaddock, Frosty Little, Lou Jacobs, Donald Forrest, Bruce Marrs, Ralph Hall, Ronlin Foreman, Alex Ricca, Leira Satloff, Carlo Mazzone-Clementi, Mike 'Spike' Foster, John Rudlin, and Daniel Stein.

My various partners in Clown and Physical Theatre: Mark Renfrow and Bob Schiele of the Abbotts of Unreason, Rudi Galindo, Cosmo Kuzmick, and Dave Ferney of Los Payasos Mendigos, William Hall, Stephen Beuscher, Xiaohong Weng, Danielle Connover, and Master Lu Yi in San Francisco.

To my agents, directors and the festival organizers who have helped me spread the word (and pay my bills): Kent Huffman, Jo Burgess, Nicki Street, Carla Kogelman, Prisca Maas, Hanna de Mink, Gert Rudolph, Edit Hanscöck, Lieven Masschelein, Marc Romers, Ana Perez, Ana Lekube, Will Chamberlain, Jan Klompen, Charlie Bicke, Marion Künster, Henk Schoute, Barry Kendall, Kenny Ahern, Kim Gavin, and Caroline Byrne.

Many thanks to institutions I have trained and taught at, grateful that they keep the fire burning: Ringling Bros. and Barnum & Bailey Clown College, Clown Camp, the Dell'Arte School, Centre Sélavy, Clown Conservatory, Wuqiao International Circus Festival, Cork Circus Factory, In Your Space Circus, Derry, and the Belfast Community Circus. These places seek play in all its forms, from the silly to the serious, the skillful to the anarchic. They remind students not to lose their mischief, their imagination, their inventiveness, and their sense of adventure. They support a vast underground network of artistic gypsies, chameleons, builders, designers, dreamers, inventors, engineers, and healers.

Photos

Many of the photos in this book were taken by Eric Gillet of Shoot That Klown. His images helped inspire me to write this book and to show the variety of possibilities when it comes to the clown's "mask."

A Special Thanks

To Anna Brewer, Meredith Benson, Paula Devine, and the staff at Bloomsbury who helped me develop and clarify the structure of this book.

To the staff and students at the Dell'Arte School, Blue Lake, California, and Clown Conservatory at Circus Center-San Francisco where I worked for a number of years. They allowed me to experiment, challenge, and play with them and helped me to articulate so much of what is in this book. Much love and gratitude to them all!

Extra special thanks to Jane Hill, Bobbi Ricca, Joan Schirle, and Michael Fields at Dell'Arte, who took a chance on me in my early years of teaching, Ayla Agarwal, Katie Whitcraft, Erin Brothers, and Paoli Lacy who supported my work at Clown Conservatory, Nathaniel Justiniano who always got me thinking, and the best associate director and friend a clown could ever have, Dan Griffiths, a master teacher and wonderfully mischievous human being!

Preface

I've been performing as a clown and physical comedian for over thirty years. I've played in just about every kind of venue, and for every kind of audience imaginable: from house parties to nightclubs, intimate performances in black box theatres, to large crowds on the plazas of Europe, in 800-seat theaters for highbrow audiences, to European style one-ring circuses and three-ring American extravaganzas. I've performed as a clown at pop concerts at Radio City Music Hall and Wembley Stadium, as well as the London 2012 Olympics and Paralympics closing ceremonies. I learned valuable lessons from playing in each venue and the demands it made on me as a performer.

Over the years—out of curiosity or necessity—I've developed skills and acquired experience in four areas of theater: actor, director, teacher and

Figure 0.2 Joe Dieffenbacher in *Icarus at the Office*. *Photo credit: Matilda Dieffenbacher.*

Preface

designer. Because of this, I look at devised work and scripted plays from four different points of view: as an actor, I know the real struggles a working professional goes through when creating new work, and what it feels like presenting that to an audience for the first time. As a director, I understand how to shape devised material into a fully realized performance. As a teacher, I search for ways to translate what I learn from performing into exercises that will teach clown and physical comedy. As a designer, I see the power of the active use of props, sets and scenic elements in telling a story.

This book arose out of a desire to translate this wide-ranging experience into teaching clown and physical comedy. The problem when I sat down to write it was translating all that into a method. What's more, I was trying to create a method to teach something that openly thumbs its nose at methods! Even more frustrating, my own brain—conditioned over many years to think like a clown—constantly teased, challenged, and balked at my attempts to create a well-ordered approach to teaching clowning.

In my experience as a teacher, there is a certain amount of chaos inherent—and necessary—in clowning. Anyone teaching it must be comfortable with that and do their best to navigate between order and disorder, method and madness. The games and exercises in this book, and the text aiming to provide context, will help guide teacher, student and working professional, down this irregular road.

When I was director of the Clown Conservatory at Circus Center-San Francisco, I had to create a pedagogy that took the students on a 21-week journey through the world of clown and physical comedy. Because I was in constant conversation with the students, problem-solving, experimenting and evolving our understanding of the process, I saw myself as a collaborator, not someone standing outside the work and dictating a method. This collaborative approach is emphasized throughout this book.

I don't expect a student to get an exercise "right." I offer them a somewhat open format because I'm curious to see how they interpret my instructions. This makes the classwork more of a partnership between teacher and student rather than a memorization exercise. The games are meant to literally, "keep things in play." This is when true learning happens: the student realizes and embodies the objective of an exercise in the midst of their play, as well as discovering their own creative process. This is crucial to devised work: it's not just a matter of what you create but *how* you do it. Each player must explore and grapple with their own strengths and weaknesses, good and bad habits, how they deal with obstacles inside their head and those placed in front of them. Many devised clown pieces are elaborations of this very process transformed into performance material, so it's crucial that players understand the alchemy that is happening as they attempt to translate class work into stage play.

Teaching requires me to engage with each student where we both learn to listen to each other mentally, emotionally and physically; it's the same relationship the clown tries to create with the audience. Because of that listening, I noticed that the same problems were reoccurring, problems related to translating what students discovered in the classroom, to how it played for an audience. Rather than teach them traditional clown gags, or use games designed for actors, I invented variations on existing exercises drawing from theater, improv, and children's games, as well as creating new ones focusing on problems that were relevant to clown and physical comedy. I wanted to combine the traditional apprenticeship model of teaching—learning from someone who knows the real struggles a working professional goes through—with insights gained from years of teaching in a classroom setting.

This book doesn't go into a critical analysis of the clown, nor their role in history or various cultures. This is well covered in other books (see bibliography). While I feel the history of clowning is an important study, I also feel that to truly comprehend the art form, one must get on their feet and play. This deeper, *embodied* understanding of the clown is what I hope players will achieve via the discussions, games, and exercises in this book. My desire in writing *Clown: The Physical Comedian* is to offer the teacher, deviser, and performer ways of delivering practical information to students in the classroom, or partners in the rehearsal studio, while maintaining a healthy sense of mischief.

Some games and exercises have multiple variations. These can be expanded upon to create a scripted scene which retains the elements of a game (see Section 10: The Rules, the Script, the Game, the Play). This reflects my own process as a teacher: when I found or invented a new game, I would continually reimagine it in order to expand its possibilities. This same process happens when devising new material: you take a few ideas and decide on some rules, then you find variations on those rules in order to expand the potential for play, develop scenes, and deepen the connection with the audience.

It's my belief that no one can truly understand the significance of clowns—and why they are important figures in different cultures throughout history—until they rediscover and develop their own playful mind. They won't fully grasp the clown's reputation as a nonconformist, provocateur, shapeshifter, trickster and healer, until they challenge—and make fun of—their own habits, clichés, weaknesses, and prejudices, as well as those of the world around them. And, most importantly, take their discoveries and strike up a conversation with the audience in the form of a performance for them. It's a journey that has many twists and turns, many obstacles and many joys. I hope this book is a good friend and a knowledgeable guide.

Luck and laughter,
Joe

Introduction

The Search

I want to start by talking about the clown's look, the "mask" that is often associated with this comic type—the costume, makeup, and red nose. My first forays into clowning started with this mask. Like most people I associated the word "clown" with a particular look.

Do an online image search for clowns and you'll see costumes and makeup styles that we've come to associate with this comic type. After you scroll past the scary clowns, you'll find people wearing red, orange, or multi-colored

Figure 0.3 Clown and dolphin trainer Lars Adams. *Photo credit: Eric Gillet/Shoot That Klown.*

afro wigs, exaggerated face paint, frilly collars, oversized shoes, and brightly colored, pajama-like, one-piece costumes. Some pictures feature variations on the makeup and costume of Bozo, a popular children's entertainer who had his own TV show in America in the 1950s. Other images show people made up in the Ringling Bros. and Barnum & Bailey three-ring circus clown style. You have to scroll down quite a way to find anything other than scary clown, afro-wig-pajama-clown, or circus clown.

The Word

The word *clown* was initially used to describe a simpleton, usually someone from the countryside; clown was another word for a "rustic fool." Then it became a generic name for a type of character in the early commedia dell'arte (*zanni*). British actors in the seventeenth century—inspired by the commedia—called him "the clown" and he became a central figure in the British harlequinade of that era. In early plays he was still a country bumpkin, similar to the peasant fools in Shakespeare's works; a buffoon dressed in the ragged clothes of the lower classes. In time, he became a character in his own right. The Brits named him "Clown."

So, the word originally described a person who was foolish, incompetent, simple. It then became a descriptive term for a type of character—the unsophisticated country bumpkin—and then the name of the character himself, a satirist who used physical comedy, exaggeration, and ridicule to mock fashion, culture, politics, and society. I find it fascinating how the clown turned that around: first they were ridiculed by society for their incompetence, then they ridiculed society for its pretenses, urbanity, polity, and customs.

The Look

In the beginning there was no set costume for the clown, no specific makeup. The "definitive clown look" came about because an actor playing the clown dressed himself in a certain way, his portrayal became popular, and everyone agreed that *this* was how a clown dressed. That is, until another actor playing the clown came along with a different look and made *it* popular. Everyone copied this look and it became the new definitive look to represent the clown.

Different eras had different ways of defining the clown by their look: in the early 1600s it was the checkered costume and leather mask of Arlecchino, a zanni from the Italian commedia dell'arte. In the early 1800s, the brightly colored, frilly outfit of the English clown Joseph Grimaldi (whose whitened face with red triangles on the cheeks and thickly painted black eyebrows, was perhaps the biggest influence on the clown look in the West). In the early 1900s it was the French clown Albert Fratellini's red-nosed Auguste (the second biggest influence). The American hobo or tramp clown was popularized by Emmet Kelly and Otto Griebling of the Ringling Bros. and Barnum & Bailey Circus, along with Lou Jacobs' exaggerated Auguste, with a rounded cone fitted to the top of his head which enlarged his face, giving him a bigger "canvas" to paint on his makeup. In the 1980s and 1990s, American clowns such as Bill Irwin, Avner the Eccentric, and Russian clown Slava Polunin, all evolved different looks for their clowns. The first two kept it simple, Slava went for a more exaggerated look.

Both European and American circuses developed a number of variations on the clown's costume, makeup and nose. There was the *Classic Whiteface*, an elegant, glamorous clown, sharply dressed, his costume often covered with sequins. The *Whiteface* clown was similar to the Classic Whiteface, but less ostentatious, merrier, more animated. There was the *Grotesque Whiteface*, with painted features that were eccentric and exaggerated. There were the *Glitter Clowns* who wore a costume and makeup that were more ornamental than expressive. The lower half of the face of the *Tramp Clown* was a sooty black, with white around the eyes and mouth, and a round flesh-colored nose whose tip was a soft red, his costume a ragged mess. The look of the *Auguste Clown* was a mixture of Whiteface and Tramp: not as miserable looking as the Tramp Clown, but rougher than the Whiteface. The Auguste style popularized the red nose and ill-fitting, mismatched, costume bits: too-large neckties paired with tiny hats, big, long shoes below baggy pants. The look of the *Contra Auguste* was a mix of the Auguste and the Whiteface, the visual equivalent of neither being the boss nor the fool but somewhere in between. As clowns moved into theaters, nightclubs and hospitals, the *Character Clown* and *Clown Light* were created. They cherrypicked ideas from the other clown looks but toned them down, using a lighter base makeup with simple accents around the mouth and eyes, or no makeup at all, just a red nose, and costumes that were enhanced versions of everyday clothes. Russian clowning, which influenced such artists as Slava Polunin, Licedei, Aga-Boom and the KGB Clowns, created a unique evolution of the clown look, freely mixing Whiteface, Auguste, Tramp and Character makeups to create a mash up of costume elements.

The Energy

In my early years as a performer, I explored many of these popular clown looks. But as I did more research into the role of the clown in societies and cultures the world over, I saw that there was much more to them than a particular costume and makeup style; they had a larger, more important role that went beyond the mask. The popular look of the clown (in modern, Western societies) began to bother me: I wanted to know what a clown was underneath the costume. I felt trapped by the mask.

But what was a clown without their costume, makeup and red nose? How would you know someone was a "real clown" unless they dressed like one? But wasn't a costume just "an assortment of clothes worn by an actor or performer for a particular role?" So, was clown just a role? But some of my teachers talked about finding my *personal* clown. Others said clown is not a noun but a verb: a word used to describe an action, *to clown*. You can't *be* a clown, you can only, clown.

Because of my research, I began to question why I needed a particular look to define me as a clown. As I explored other forms of theater and comedy such as satire, agit-prop, silent film-style slapstick, sketch comedy, improv, stand up, monologues, object theater and puppetry, I began to shed the layers. Off came the makeup, then the nose, then the costume. I did away with the look but, I realized, the manner and the mindset of the clown still informed all my work. So, without the mask, how would I define the clown?

I came to the conclusion that the clown is energy. This energy is set in motion by an overwhelming curiosity, causing a person to engage with their environment in an inquisitive, immersive, playful way. This energy inspires them to want to relate, engage, and connect with, *everything* around them.

It's the energy of kids who discover, explore and reimagine their world through play (one of the reasons why clowns are often likened to children). Adults may dismiss play as frivolous, time wasting, but it's one of the most useful and important ways to truly understand the world. The playful mind is perhaps the best way to engage with the environment, enabling a person not only to experience what's in it and how it affects them mentally, emotionally, physically and socially, but also how they might contribute to the world and expand on what it offers them.

"Playful" is a good way to describe the clown's mindset and why there is a greater interest in the clown from modern theater makers and devisers. A mind closed to play sees a cardboard box as functional, something to put an object into, mail it, transport it or store it. But to the playful mind, it's those things and more: a hat, a car, a castle, a spaceship, a rabbit hole ... When children play (and adults rediscover this side of themselves through clowning), their energy and enthusiasm is concentrated, focused on what they're doing and the world they're creating. This is what kids strive for: play as a way to investigate, perceive and gain an understanding of the world. It's not a distraction; they don't do it just to "stay out of mommy's way," they don't indulge themselves in play now and then; their playful mind is *always* active. One could say that a child knows no other way to experience their environment but through play. They learn to express what's going on in their heads and hearts and try to make sense of the world around them, not in an analytical or theoretical way, but through *active engagement*. They discover new paths, learn to navigate them on their own or with friends, and in the process, develop their independence, self-confidence and potential. As they interact with the things in their environment—friends, strangers, parents, teachers, toys, objects, machinery, walls, floors, furniture, etc.—they learn about limits and possibilities, who to trust and who to avoid, what can be climbed, thrown, eaten, jumped over, what stinks, breaks easily, what can be wrestled with, bounced, or thrown against a wall, how to catch it when it comes back to you, how to avoid looking dumb when you miss the catch. Their spirit discovers what's possible with their body, and together they form relationships with the physical world around them. This is the same experience adults have when they interact with the world through play, and it is through play that they develop a true understanding of clowning.

The Mask

Through my explorations with makeup, red noses and various costumes, and later, my work with the neutral mask, full face character masks and the half masks of the commedia dell'arte, I began to see the clown's look as a *full body mask* that aided an artist in telling a story or engaging with the audience (see Section 3: The Talking Body). The clown look that I'd come to see as an obstacle, I now understood as a visual aid, used like an Elizabethan court dress or a three-piece suit to establish a setting, a world (see Section 11: The Mask of the Clown). When I removed this mask, what I had left was an inquisitive, irrepressible energy that desired to constantly transform itself; it wanted to be a king, a juggler, a housemaid, a policeman, a chef, a diva, an airplane, a lamp post, a prince of Denmark ... This energy could play any role, go off in any direction! This is why it kept turning up in my work and one of the reasons it intrigued me: good clowning has an edginess that's captivating, the audience always sensing that the clown's energy may erupt and the play could become chaotic, absurd, lyrical, grotesque, poetic, dark, magical. Why is this? Why is the clown's energy such a potentially disruptive force?

Stirred up by a playful mind, this energy recognizes no limits, sees all rules as malleable, all boundaries as porous. This can get the clown into trouble: they will readily jump from role to role, reality to reality, in the same scene. This annoys directors. Clowns will freely mix methods and styles. This pisses off purists. But unlike the medieval jester, the confrontational stand-up comic, or the lampooning satirist, the clown doesn't deliberately disobey a rule or push the button they're not supposed to push, it's just that their curiosity and their need to engage with the world are so powerful they can't help themselves! They're naive about the very idea of rules. "Why do we need them? If we really want to find out what's possible, we should just dive in and play!" Looked at this way, the clown is less an agitated rebel, more of an over-eager explorer.

Once I was able to fully comprehend the clown as energy and how it manifested itself in all the work I created, I let it take over. Whether in the classroom, rehearsal studio or in performance, approaching creative work with the mind of the clown—where anything is possible and everything has potential—opened me up to explore a whole range of skills, combine various styles of theater, play with eccentric ideas and connect things that I never thought to connect before. Could we put a shadow puppet play in a production of *Death of a Salesman*? Could Hamlet do a backflip during his famous soliloquy? The clown mind says "Let's try it! If the audience says yes, we'll keep it. If not, we'll take it out or try something else. Maybe he could tap dance."

This is one of the reasons why playwrights also have a problem with clowns: clowns see clearly that the world created onstage is make-believe—a big lie—and they may decide to point this out to the audience at any moment. In fact, they find it hard to resist pointing it out. A clown can play with all the focus and intensity of the most skillful thespian, have the audience enthralled by their performance, then suddenly break the illusion, turn to the crowd and say, "Isn't this a bit absurd? But we're enjoying ourselves, so let's carry on."

The playful mind isn't simply trying to undermine the seriousness of a performance but seeking other possibilities within it by acknowledging other realities. They see a script as an offer to explore and engage with the world the writer has created, to use it as a vehicle that takes everyone—

players, playwright, director, designers, and audience—on a journey. This approach acknowledges the creative potential of everyone involved in a production, their various talents, any performance skills they might have (the usual ones such as playing an instrument, acting, singing or dancing, as well as more eccentric skills such as playing the saw, doing a sloppy front flip, Tibetan throat singing ...). It can lead to the development of performance material that is unique to each individual or ensemble. It encourages a more thoughtful and provocative approach to the creative process. This is one of the reasons those devising new work often turn to clown training to help develop their plays: they want to learn to think outside the box, explore a greater range of possibilities, strengthen the ensemble, as well as surprise themselves and their audience.

Because this clown energy enters into everything with a spirit of curiosity and play, an audience is quicker to relate to and empathize with a clown. The crowd is reminded of the way they used to experience the world as kids and so they connect with the clown, playful mind to playful mind. United in this way, the clown gains the audience's trust, and this trust leads to a greater involvement with what's happening on stage, in the ring or on the screen, no matter how eccentric, dark, risky, or absurd. And because humor and wonder are inherent in the clown's approach, what is created is filled with the spirit of play, participation, and empathy.

So how would a person rediscover and develop this playful mind, this clown energy? How would they combine that with learning techniques and various performance skills? What sort of games or exercises would aid them in discovering the curiosity, the exuberance, the physical and visual humor that are the hallmarks of clowning? That's what this book is all about.

The Fundamentals

Figure 0.4 The author as Johnny Horrendezz.
Photo credit: Eric Gillet/ Shoot That Klown.

Terms Used

The book is divided into *sections*. At the start of each, I talk about my own experience as it relates to the various sections within (Ensemble Building, Prop Play, Devising, etc.), and why I think each section is necessary to understanding and progressing towards a greater comprehension of clown and physical comedy.

Games teach the fundamentals of clowning in a less structured way and involve the participation of all the players. *Exercises* are focused on specific aspects of clown and physical comedy and involve some of the players onstage while others observe. The first few games in each section introduce the main theme in a playful way. The exercises that follow explore the theme in more detail, requiring more of participants mentally, emotionally, and physically.

I use the words *student, actor, performer,* and *participant,* but mainly the term *player*. This is less a role and more a word to describe "a person at play." I sometimes use *teacher* but prefer *adviser*: I don't want to risk creating a status relationship with the student that might inhibit them (see comments below), so I prefer to advise or suggest a possible course of action to a student rather than dictate it to them. I alternate the use of the pronouns *he, she,* and *they,* and use *you* when addressing the reader, or the student when side coaching. The word *partner* can refer to a person, the ensemble, someone in the audience (or the audience as a whole), but also inanimate objects such as a chair, costume elements such as a coat or hat, or any part of the performance space such as the floor or walls. For a clown, everything in the room is a potential partner.

The name at the start of each game or exercise is an umbrella term for the *Variations* that follow. Under the name I describe the focus of a game or exercise and ways to use it. I also list any *props* that are needed. Under *room prep*, I suggest ways to prepare the space and address any safety issues, *physical prep* suggests ways of warming up for more vigorous games. *Advice* gives further insights into a game or exercise and can be used as side coaching by the adviser, or by the players doing an exercise on their own. *Notes* give further information about some aspect of a game or exercise. Some Notes can be used as side coaching.

The sections themselves follow a progression, from ensemble building games to those that encourage physical complicity, physical expressiveness, and how a player uses the performing space to reveal more about the clown and their world. I then continue with exercises to help the players develop material through the use of props. Curiosity is one of the fundamental traits of clowns, so there are exercises for inspiring a more inquisitive mind. This is followed by solo, duo, trio, and ensemble exercises that help the players create dynamic partnerships, as well as generate performance material. I close with sections on devising for clown and physical comedy that bring together all the previous sections.

In traditional circus clowning, the members of a trio were called Whiteface (highest status), Contra Auguste (middle status), and Auguste (lowest status).

A shorthand for this is #1, #2, #3. I use the terms, *boss, negotiator,* and *fool.* In duos, I use *boss* and *fool.* These are descriptive terms, but I'll sometimes use them to identify a role, for example, the *Boss.*

Sources for the games, exercises and variations are listed at the back of the book under *Inspirations.* There is also a *bibliography* for further reading.

Roles Played

In many orthodox learning situations, the teacher is seen as separate from the students. They're treated with a respect—and in some instances, a reverence—that can create a distance between student and teacher. While this respect is important—a teacher's experience should be acknowledged and deferred to—both teacher and student shouldn't let their roles get in the way of a shared learning experience. When teaching clown and physical comedy—especially when working with students devising new work—I feel the teacher is a collaborator first and foremost. They join in the games, participate in the exercises, improvise, explore, succeed and fail, along with everyone else. The main difference between teacher and student is the former's greater knowledge and experience. They're familiar with the rules and objectives of the exercises they introduce, how to use them to guide students and help them create their own work. But the teacher stays open to the group process, accepting that things will not always go according to plan, and willing to get their hands dirty when the "pudding turns to poop."

One of the most important roles the adviser can play is that of the Boss Clown. They represent the authority figure in the group, reminding the players to abide by the rules. I picked up this term from my time with the Ringling Bros. and Barnum & Bailey Circus: we called the leader of clown alley (the place where we got dressed and hung out during the show), Boss Clown. I love the contradiction: Boss usually refers to the person who knows the rules, tells others what to do—they're the smart one. But the word Clown signifies the opposite of that, so putting the two together creates a useful contradiction.

The adviser enacts the role of the Boss Clown in an insistent but playful way to such a degree that sometimes their side coaching comes across as a performance in itself. The adviser starts to blur the conventional interpretation of teacher/leader, exercise/performance, until everyone becomes a player, constantly exploring variations in their roles, their status, different ways of learning and devising. Like clowns, the players realize and develop games within games, introduce roles that are malleable. No one is quite sure who they are or what their role requires of them, so they decide moment-to-moment how they'll play (the boss can easily become the fool, a low-status character can use insights gained from serving a master to achieve a higher status, a player can be a traffic cop then suddenly become a traffic light). This may sound like it will lead to chaos and anarchy—and at times it does—but the players are constantly reminded to adhere to the rules in order to engage with the tension between discipline and freedom, improvisation and tightly choreographed routines. The best clown work lives on the edge between control and subversion, the audience entranced because they never know when things will fall apart, or suddenly coalesce, everything coming together in a giddy harmony. As they work this way—seeing their roles toyed with and reimagined—students begin to see that everything in the clown's world is in flux and always in play. The clown becomes the ultimate agent of creation and transformation.

The adviser's role of Boss Clown, the mutability of roles within the classroom and onstage, and the playing of games within games, are not revealed right away. The adviser stays open to improvising with the players (including altering rules now and then), in the hope that they will realize that she is playing the role of Boss Clown, and that the game or exercise is also a staged performance (one that is open to change). The adviser and the players work together to let go of ego-based interaction, they propose ideas and decide on rules but don't cling to anything (though they may fight for a rule or an idea). If something more intriguing comes up or, if in conversation with the audience, the players discover they prefer one thing to another, they'll go with that. But they don't pander; they suggest, converse, debate, and at times argue with their audience (and each other). The players offer their rules at the outset, but if at any point they get in the way of connecting with the audience and evolving the game (or their performance), the rules can be altered. Ultimately, the players seek to communicate, relate and connect.

Clown Essentials

Everything done in class aims to encourage and develop five Clown Essentials:

1 Deep and unlimited curiosity.
2 A desire to engage with the world in a provocative way.

3 Spontaneity and the welcoming of accidents.
4 Developing the playful mind, a way of interacting with the world that is mischievous, joyful, and open to learn.
5 Keeping a performance flexible, allowing the players to engage with the audience in an ongoing conversation.

Lesson Plans

I've used these games and exercises with a diverse range of people, all over the world, working in all sorts of settings and theater styles: one and three ring circuses, musical theater, cabaret, street theater, Shakespeare, commedia dell'arte, dance theater, hospital clowning, large-scale spectacle shows, puppet theater, Renaissance festivals, clown theater, opera, naturalistic theater, mask performance, and and improv. Some of the players have known each other for months, others have only met that day. I've worked with tight ensembles who've collaborated for years, and others struggling to find ways to connect. I've done three-day workshops, five-week intensives, and two-year courses exploring physical theater styles. As a teacher you may find yourself in similar situations. How do you know which exercises are best for a particular group?

I'd suggest starting with ensemble building games, letting participants get acquainted in playful ways, engaging with one another without having to think about learning concepts right away (see Section 1: Hello and Section 2: Energy). These games help build trust amongst the players making it easier for them to be more expressive and engaged with one another, and subsequently, the audience.

Exercises that involve physical contact and the handling of objects (see Section 4: Prop Play) are good to use early in the process as they focus the players' attention outside of themselves, get them engaging with each other and the world around them. For longer sessions, offer more technique, especially exercises that develop physical expression (see Section 3: The Talking Body). These should be practiced often so students are able to embody the skills and use them in the classroom.

Mix exercises where part of the class is sitting and observing (Sections 4–8), with games that get everyone on their feet and playing physically (all sections start with group games, but they're emphasized in Sections 1 and 2). This keeps their bodies warmed up and their minds flexible.

Setting a time restriction on some exercises is useful: the players can get lost jumping from one idea to the next, never committing to one thing and

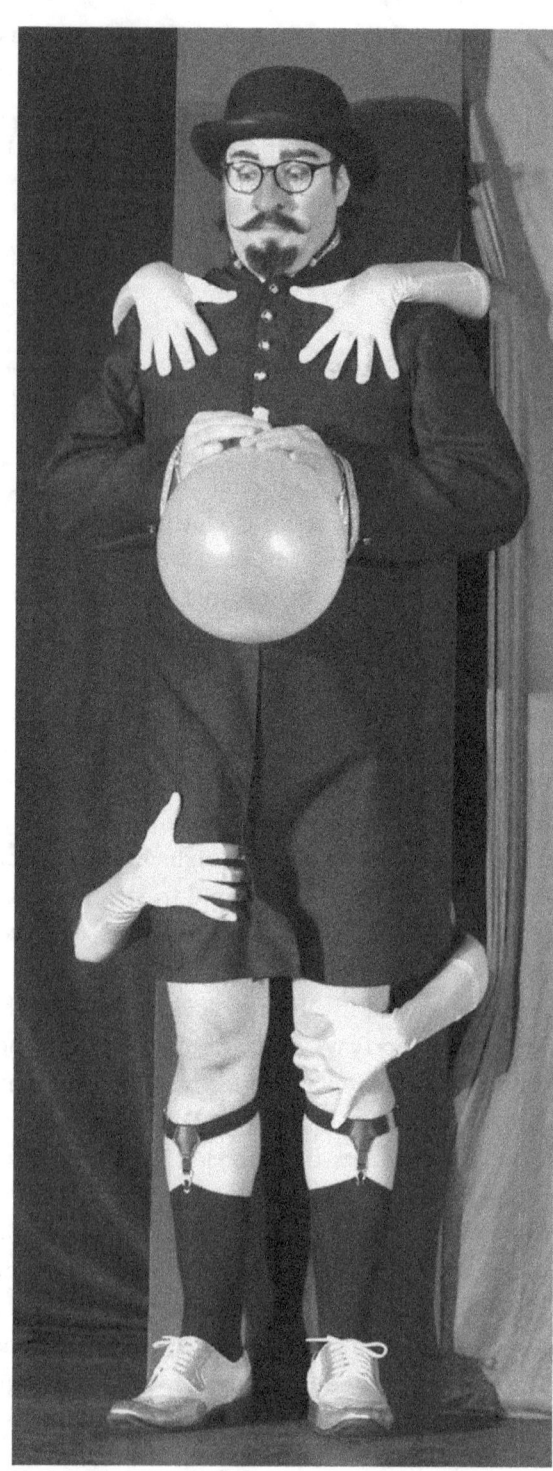

Figure 0.5 Paul Philion and friends. *Photo credit: Eric Gillet/Shoot That Klown.*

developing it. A dispassionate dictator like the clock has no opinion or critique to offer, it simply says, "your time is up." It teaches the players the value of self-editing and using their stage time wisely.

For some exercises, allow the players to explore on their own first, in order to become familiar with the rules and objectives, without the distracting pressure of improvising for others right away.

Get them working with partners as soon as possible so they associate play with relating and discover what collaborating and competing with others brings out of them. It makes them aware of the importance of using each other as foils, adversaries, and nurturers, as well as mirrors.

As participants understand the rules and get comfortable with each other, repeat games and exercises that focus on what the ensemble is exploring or needs to improve on. Repetition will help expand on any discoveries made in their first experiences with a game or exercise, give them insights into their own creative process, to partnering with others, and to ways of relating with an audience.

The games in each section can be used not only by teachers, but also by students sharing them with each other. Some exercises require a deeper understanding of clowning and performance, but even these can be explored by those new to the work; they may not get as much out of them as they would if they had a teacher's guidance, but they will gain from the experimentation and exploration. And the more familiar they get with an exercise, the more they will gain from it in when they explore it with an experienced teacher.

Experiment! Add new rules, develop new variations, bend a game to serve a concept, technique, or partner play. If played with commitment, the games and exercises should feel no different from a performance: the players carry the spirit of genuine play from the classroom right onto the stage.

Defining Clown

My training and experience has been influenced mostly by Western forms of clowning: European one-ring circus, the Ringling Bros. and Barnum & Bailey three-ring circus, street theater, the work of Jacques Lecoq and Philipe Gaulier, the silent film comedians and those they influenced during the so-called Golden Age of TV comedy in America (Sid Caesar, Imogen Coca, Bob Hope, Red Skelton, Dick Van Dyke, Lucille Ball, Carol Burnett, Tim Conway, etc.), British comedians Tommy Cooper, the members of the Monty

Figure 0.6 Clowns Tommy Toxic, Sydney Schwindt, Andrew Pulkrabek, Kate Brehm, and Ariel Speedwagon, prepare for a show at the Clown Conservatory. *Photo credit: Devin Shacket.*

Python troupe, Steve Coogan and Rowan Atkinson, as well as stand-up comics such as Lenny Bruce, George Carlin, Richard Pryor, and Bill Hicks. I also gained insights from my studies on the Native American Trickster, aboriginal shamanism, the teachings of Zen masters, the carnival tradition of various cultures worldwide, the Medieval Feast of Fools, and the Russian philosopher Mikhail Bakhtin.

There is not enough space in this book to cover different clown traditions from around the world, their masks, and their styles of performance, but in my experience, the essentials are the same. I've taught, directed and performed all over the world and much of what I do translates well: clown and physical comedy are universal, and what's in this book is applicable to most any style of clowning and theater performance.

So, what defines a clown? And what is the difference between a clown and a comedian? As stated in the Introduction, some define the clown as a performer who wears a red nose, makeup, and a garish costume. They do silly things, their antics are childish, their performances cartoon-like. But not all clowns perform in such a broad way: they can be understated, poetic. Some work without a nose, some perform in a three-piece suit. But if both clowns and comedians use humor as their main method of connecting with the audience, what's the difference between them? In my view, they approach devising and performing with different sets of tools.

A comedian works with the spoken word, their act is about their cleverness with ideas and how they express them in the form of jokes. Their humor is mostly verbal.

A clown is physical and visual. They may use words, but these are just another tool in their bag which they might utilize to engage with the audience. A clown will use their body more than a comedian; they'll work with props, employ visual jokes. Clowns play openly with the audience, engage them in their performance in a more direct way. A comedian may have some crowd interaction, use props and get physical, but it's more about getting the crowd to appreciate the comedian's verbal wit, the clever way they juxtapose different ideas, stimulate the mind with the spoken word.

Most of the exercises in this book eschew words in favor of developing a player's ability to express themselves physically and visually (visual play includes the use of props, costumes and scenic elements such as furniture, set pieces, doors, etc.). There are untapped riches of imaginative, comic play in the physical and visual worlds which, in my experience, most students rarely utilize. So, learning to be a comedian—while difficult—is easier than learning to clown because we're used to communicating with words. When we converse, we rarely look at what someone is saying with their so-called "body language" nor do we use objects to make a point or elaborate a thought in daily conversation. And rarely do we speak in a direct or forceful way: our use of words is chatty, unfocused; all sound, but little force or fury. This informal "training" in using words in a casual, reflexive way, teaches habits that don't serve us when it comes to clowning. When the clown wants to go on a mad flight into the surreal or the absurd, most of us lack the ability to express that leap. That's why clown training is important: it offers the opportunity to develop the imaginative, unconventional mind, and to find greater possibilities in the physical, the visual, and the verbal.

One of the objectives of this book is to remind the players that the world uses different ways of communicating to us but because we're so used to listening only to words, we're unable to "hear" with our eyes, or realize the potential of something through touch or sound alone. The physical and the visual are distinct languages and learning to hear them, respond to them, and use them in conversation, requires the same concentrated practice as learning Spanish or German. If a person working in the style of clown doesn't learn this idiom, they're cutting themselves off from a vast playground filled with rich comic and dramatic material. Stand-up comedy is a demanding and brilliant art form, but so much of it happens—is developed and shaped—in a person's head and expressed in words. What I love about clown and physical comedy is its willingness to utilize anything and everything in its play with the audience, in its efforts to open up lines of communication, create relationships and tell stories. It approaches devising and performing with the mindset that *everything* has potential – objects, colors, shapes, movement, words. For this reason, I believe it's the most inclusive and expansive of all the performing arts.

Because of this scope, I struggle with the popular notion that everyone has a unique, inner or personal clown. In my experience, it risks turning the clowning a student first uncovers into something precious. They become protective of it, they'll say "My clown wouldn't do that." Or they become nettled, even resentful, when asked to try something different; they'll say they've discovered their personal clown, they don't need to keep looking. Nor do I believe the clown has anything to do with rediscovering the inner child: it shouldn't lead to a regressed, infantile way of playing. The clown may be child-like but never childish. What I find more fascinating is the adult—with all their experience, emotional depth and power—playing with the openness and abandon of a child, honestly responding to the world around them and expressing that physically and visually. It's this combination of the incredulous and the unguarded, with the perceptive and sagacious, that makes the adult clown a more compelling figure.

The clown sees no limits, they adhere to no set role. They approach creative work with the mindset that anything is possible, which encourages them to explore a whole range of skills, lets their imagination roam, inspires them to play with eccentric ideas and the creation of material that is unique to each player or ensemble. It encourages a greater responsibility to one's art and urges the players to be more thoughtful, sensitive, and provocative in whatever they do, for what drives the clown more than anything else is their desire to connect with the world around them and all that is in it.

Challenges and Obstacles

When exploring clown, physical comedy, and devising scenes, most of what the players struggle with can be narrowed down to four things: technique, commitment, tactics, and story.

Figure 0.7 Opera diva clown Crystal Philippi. *Photo credit: Eric Gillet/Shoot That Klown.*

Technique, Commitment, Tactics, Story

Technique can be obvious: "This is how you do a handstand." Or less obvious: dancing in a random way may appear rough and too loose to teach anything, but it encourages physical improvisation and complicity with others; a chance to explore movement with only a few rules and no particular style to adhere to, just responding to, and communicating with music, however you like.

Learning good technique requires constant repetition to own it and make it appear natural. This repetition can be boring: it takes real effort to focus, practice and repeat over and over again. One approach is to make the practice part of everyday activity. Waiting for a train? Find a wall and hold a handstand for one minute. Restless hands? Juggle or practice sleight-of-hand. When walking down the street try different body leads, practice head takes, work your trips and slips throughout the day. Make people nervous, make them laugh.

Commitment is about making a decision to do something and not fretting over whether it's the "right" decision. Clowns commit to the most absurd actions! The audience goes with them because of their commitment: to give over to something fully, gives any action or scene a dynamic power.

When the clown makes an emotional commitment to an object, a partner and the play, the audience will make a commitment too. Sometimes it's as simple as the clown giving something his absolute attention. This makes others curious about what has him so enthralled. It creates relationships between the clown and the audience and everything he gives his attention to.

To understand and manifest the clown as energy, the players must develop their ability to commit to things on an emotional level. This commitment opens up a flow that will bring in new possibilities for play that could never be experienced if the players only work from ideas, or just try to be clever. Commitment involves taking risks, opening up and relating directly with the world.

Don't get me wrong, ideas are important. Like the rules of a game or the first draft of a script, they're jumping off points for play and give shape to an act or scene. But I've seen students spend too much time talking and not enough time doing, sitting and discussing ideas instead of getting on their feet and exploring them in a physically interactive, playful way. Ideas should encourage a complicity that is not only mental, but also physical and emotional.

Tactics help clowns get what they want. The clown has an objective. She commits to it and uses various tactics to overcome obstacles, utilize her successes, bounce back from her failures. The audience wants to see how clever, resourceful, imaginative, and resilient the clown is, therefore, each obstacle should be seen as an *opportunity*, a chance for the clown to connect with the audience as they watch her play with various tactics to achieve her objective. One of the best ways to develop a clown routine is to create obstacles to overcome, with each one complicating the situation, building to a finale where the clown's tactics finally bring about success (in a foreseeable or totally unexpected way), or he fails yet life goes on (Charlie Chaplin walking into the sunset).

One important tactic is how a clown plays with *status*. Sometimes the hierarchy is overt: the audience can see by the clowns' costumes and actions who has high status and who has low. Other times it's less obvious and malleable; the status changes throughout a scene. How does the clown use status to get what she wants? How does the creator of a clown routine use status to reveal relationships, characters, tell a story? (For more on status see Sections 7–9.) And status is not limited to *human* relationships...

A man walks along, so full of himself he doesn't look where he's going and runs into a wall. His objective was to walk along proudly preening. Because the wall has thwarted that objective it now has higher status. He gets angry at the wall, vows to get revenge. The comedy comes first from the interruption by the obstacle, the slapstick of hitting the wall. The clown expands on that by having a status battle with an inanimate object: he strives to maintain his status over a wall. This creates another layer of comedy, a higher level of slapstick, a way of making fun of our pretenses, our overwhelming need to succeed and control. Status becomes a tactic both for the clown in the scene and the creator of the story, using status play as a way to develop relationships and reveal more about the clown.

Storytelling is what you do every time you step on stage. I refer to everything as a story, whether it's a juggling act, an absurd comic routine, or a scene with a straightforward plot. I like the idea that the clown is not coming out to show off tricks or demonstrate how funny they are, but to tell us a story about themselves and their world (which could involve showing off tricks and being funny).

Another way to think about story is what is the *shape* of a piece? It can help to draw it with a line:

Does it move on a straight trajectory to a crescendo? Or descend from a high point to chaos or an acquiescing to fate? Does it have many peaks and troughs, or move along without much happening then suddenly build in an explosive way to a denouement? Drawing its shape can be a useful simplification.

Almost anything can give a story shape: tactics, objectives, different skills, objects or colors introduced. For example, a sudden burst of red in a routine can change its shape. The speed of a clown's actions—fast, slow, staccato, flowing—affects the shape. How actual shapes are represented—a round-shaped clown, props that are all lines and angles, set pieces that tilt in different directions, big, soft curvaceous objects that fill the stage, narrow rectangular flats, etc. Clowning is a visual art form: the players should

Figure 0.8
Aeronautical clown Carasue McClendon. *Photo credit: Eric Gillet/Shoot That Klown.*

consider color, shape and pace in mind when thinking about how to create a dynamic story (see Section 14: Devising for clown and physical comedy).

So, the players should always keep in mind technique, commitment, tactics, and story. If a player's act is based on their coat antagonizing them, they must ensure that their *technique* is good enough to make the audience believe the coat is alive. If a player doesn't *commit* to what they do, neither will the audience. A clown show should be a game played with the crowd filled with amusing and inventive *tactics* to keep them engaged, ready to join in. And the clown's *story* needs to have plenty of twists and turns and a certain logic (even if it's a skewed logic), or they risk losing the audience or leaving them dissatisfied.

Entrances and Exits—Discovery Moments—Success and Failure

The other problem areas for budding clowns and physical comedians are entrances and exits, discovery moments, and understanding how to work with success and failure.

Dynamic *entrances* that introduce the clown to the audience, and *exits* that leave them satisfied, agitated, or excited, are crucial to this work. How a clown enters and exits can say a lot about them if they know how to use the in and out in a creative way (see Section 3: The Talking Body and Section 5: Curiosity).

It's vital that the players take time to *discover a moment*. It gives the audience a chance to witness what affects the clown so it can affect them. Discovery moments can include an object, another person, a change in energy, a transition from one idea to another—anything that moves the story along, changes its direction. The players often rush these moments, not realizing that connecting with an audience requires them to give more focus to an action than they normally would. A discovery moment invites the audience in, makes them curious. Discovery moments give variation to a story's rhythm in the same way music has rests and quieter passages that build suspense, diversity, and depth. It gives the players—and their audience—a chance to breathe, get their bearings, and go deeper (see Section 3: The Talking Body and Section 5: Curiosity).

We live in a world obsessed with *success* and terrified of *failure*. Learning how to play with the tension this creates can produce powerful and very funny scenes. It's one reason people are drawn to clowns: they don't travel in a vertical line to SUCCESS! They fall and fail again and again, taking us on a journey that doesn't always lead to victory. We enjoy the ride because the clown shows us our humanity, which includes our screw ups, losses, and disasters. A good clown gives us a chance to laugh at failure, spend time reveling in chaos. This is part of the joy the audience feels when watching a clown show: for a time; they're liberated from their need to control things, to compete and win, from their fear of failing. The performance becomes a *communal event*; there is no boundary, no fourth wall between the players and the audience. It is a shared experience, a true conversation.

The Right Way

After doing an exercise, students will often ask "Did I get it right?" I reply, "Did *you* feel that what you did was working? Did you connect with the audience? Or did you feel inhibited, unable to play?" Our task as collaborators (adviser and student) is to find out why. What keeps the players from going with their impulses, welcoming accidents, and playing off them? The fear of judgement, the internal critics? A lack of practice, not knowing the material?

The players must develop the ability to know when something is working, when it isn't, and how to act on that knowing *in the moment*. This is at the core of the self-exploration a player must undertake: what obstacles hold them back and how do they overcome them? An adviser's job is to discern what those obstacles are and help the players to find tactics that work for them—aggressively as well as joyfully. The exercises in this book can develop the players' insights into what holds them back, help quiet their inner critics, learn to trust their instincts, and bolster their courage to face any audience.

Failure as a Choice, Accident as an Opportunity

Failure works on us in sometimes harsh and incomprehensible ways; we must learn not to take it personally. Mistakes are inherent in all the work we will ever do: every time we walk we might trip, whenever we say something there's the chance it will sound awkward. The beauty of clowning is that it can transform failure—and our fear of it—into our greatest ally! Many of the exercises have this as a core lesson: learning to accept, play with, and transform failures, accidents, and disadvantages, into successes, opportunities, and advantages. To learn to lose or fail *on purpose* in order to make a game more dynamic, to play with the tension between success and defeat.

The Ever-Changing Game

Once they understand the rules of a game, the players should be allowed to alter them and invent variations. Bending, breaking, and suggesting new rules as a game progresses, is how it evolves and becomes a collaboration not only between the players and the adviser, but between anyone who's ever played the game anywhere in the world at any point in time. This mutability is one of the beauties of games. While it is important to establish rules and follow them at the outset, games should be treated as open formats, constantly changing and evolving (see Section 10: The Rules, the Script, the Game, the Play).

Every group will play a game differently. The adviser should consider who is playing—actors, circus artists, clowns, improvisers, business executives—how well they know each other, and what the group's been up to before the class. Games are about working with group energy; the adviser should stay aware of this and adjust his game plan accordingly.

The players should not only compete and collaborate, they should challenge themselves and each other in the midst of the play: be cunning and devious, helpful and subservient, mean and vengeful, kind and respectful. Or sacrifice themselves—deliberately lose—to see how that might change a game and their understanding of its rules. *It's important that the players expand the experience of a competitive game, that the play moves out in many directions, not just vertically towards winning.* When competing, the players often get tense and defensive; they'll protect themselves at all costs. They forget about playing *with* the game, *with* their partners, that they can collaborate with those they're competing against. When a player chooses only to defend himself until he can find an advantage and win, the game becomes one-dimensional: we watch him obstruct rather than create, retaliate rather than relate, withdraw rather than come forward and play.

Games where roles change quickly and the players get a number of chances to try again, give all involved the opportunity to explore their feelings about playing, winning and losing. They start to let go of their obsession with victory or getting things right and gain insights into true play and their own feelings about competition and correctness, creating an environment that encourages invention and collaboration.

The Director and the Clown

In order to achieve a balance between devising material and performing it, the players should approach all games and exercises with a dual mind. I call this split the director and the clown.

The clown revels in the game, plays with abandon, tries to disrupt it now and then. The director stays aware of how they and their partners play *in the midst of playing*. Not in an analytical or judgmental way but observing tendencies, taking notes, and consciously guiding the play.

The director follows the script, stays with what's rehearsed. They're concerned with technique and craft, structure and plot. The clown wants to improvise, go off on tangents, follow their instincts, damn the script! These two are often at odds yet are absolutely necessary to each other: if the director dominates, a performance risks looking formulaic, too stiff, predictable. If the clown dominates, the performance may come across as vague or self-indulgent. But by learning to play in two minds at once, the players find a healthy balance between structure and spontaneity. Their performance has a solid plot yet it's full of unexpected twists and turns. They can take material they've rehearsed and feel confident with and let the clown play, go with whatever happens in the moment, with the confidence that the director will steer them back to the solid ground of the scripted show.

The adviser should constantly emphasize this dual mindset for every game and exercise in this book, especially during improvisation; it's in these moments that director and clown work together to find dynamic, focused and inspired play.

Figure 1.1 Devin Shacket: Hello. *Photo credit: Eric Gillet/Shoot That Klown.*

1

Hello

A Pharmacist, Helium Balloons, and a Red Nose

One of my earliest and most memorable experiences as a clown started with a red nose. I was working for a place called Huffman's Alley, run by Kent Huffman, a pharmacist turned party supplier. No, it's not what you think. He rented and sold costumes and accessories, magic tricks and juggling props,

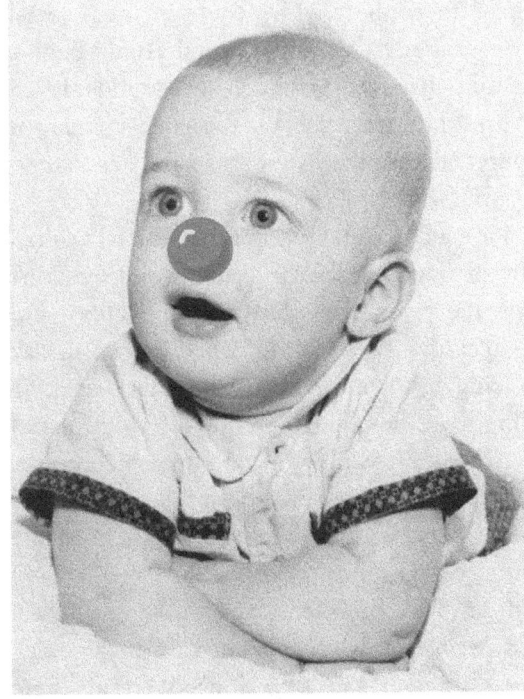

Figure 1.2 The author's early days as a clown.
Photo credit: Mary Dieffenbacher.

makeup and Halloween masks. He'd also cornered the local market on everything balloon: balloon bouquets, balloon releases, balloons for parties, weddings, corporate events—balloons of every color, shape, and style.

Two weeks into the job I was asked to help hand out balloons at an outdoor event. Kent asked me to dress as a clown to drum-up business. I hadn't done much in the way of performing—certainly not as a clown—but he reassured me. "Just put on some makeup, a colorful costume, and a red nose. It's a strong visual—it'll attract attention! And everybody loves clowns."

So, I found a red, ping pong ball-sized nose from the store's stock, and for the costume, chose a black-and-red-striped, 1920s-style bathing suit which ended just below the knees, black tights, white sneakers and a bowler hat. For the makeup, I covered my face with white, drew on black eyebrows, a bit of red around the mouth outlined in black. It was not the usual bright, colorful makeup and garish costume I'd seen on clowns, but I was an introverted kid being asked to draw attention to myself; black, red and white was as colorful as I wanted to get.

At the event, as I stood near a helium tank blowing up balloons, tying them to ribbons and handing them out, I was surprised at how open people were to my "clown." They were smiling, waving, engaging with me. Suddenly the introvert, who found it hard to connect with people in most social settings, was interacting with everybody! And my natural comic bent—which had always gotten me into trouble at school—was suddenly an advantage, a way for me to play with the crowd. I was the same shy person underneath the costume, makeup, and nose, so what was causing this change, not just in me but in everyone around me?

I chose not to talk. There was so much happening—and so much I wanted to play with—that my brain went into overdrive and my mouth couldn't keep up. I began to engage with the crowd using just my physicality—and whatever props were at hand—to express myself. This turned into an all-day improv session with me bouncing from one person to another, shaking hands, imitating people, dancing with them, hugging them, trying to steal their drinks, begging for a bite to eat then feeding the offer to someone else, showing off the six juggling tricks and four hat moves I'd mastered . . . It was a mad rush of emotion and performance as I transformed a space normally used for work and shopping into a playground.

At the end of that long, hot day, I was amazed that I wasn't exhausted. Instead, I felt invigorated! And perplexed: what happened to the shy kid? Why did I suddenly become so animated, so gregarious? Were all these people ready to play with me simply because I was *dressed* as a clown? Was that it, the costume and red nose made me a clown? And where had all those ideas, all those invented games come from? I had zero training, not much theater experience, no background in improvisation with an audience. What I did have was a burning need to connect with people, a deep curiosity, and a desire to play. The mask of makeup, costume, and red nose gave me—and the crowd—a license to do just that.

The crowd and I discovered—to use a word that is popular in theater—*complicité*. In the theater it refers to the ability of actors to come together as an ensemble, to connect with one another so there's a seamless flow of ideas, emotions, actions and reactions, amongst the members of the group. The dictionary describes it differently:

> **Complicity**   involved with others in an activity that is unlawful or morally wrong.

That's what it felt like that day: we were all engaged in activities that were normally wrong. Adults don't act that way in public! They don't get goofy, play games, embrace strangers, dance with people they don't know.

The feeling I had that day was so strong, I still remember it in my body some thirty-five years later. That day when the whole world (at least in my vicinity) opened up to me. That experience kick-started a lifelong fascination with the clown and led me to question why they encourage play and connection, how they overcome barriers internal and external, how they openly engage with the world around them with a fearlessness that borders on crazy. But are they fearless? Crazy? Or just curious?

Any artist who decides to teach has to spend a great deal of time figuring how to articulate what they've learned from experience or do instinctively. They then have to translate their insights into exercises, lesson plans and, ultimately, a method or pedagogy so they can teach what they know to others. When I started doing workshops on clowning, my first thought was "Don't just teach. Don't create exercises that students have to 'get right'. Don't show them things that only require them to imitate and parrot it back to me." What I needed to do was create an environment in the classroom that was as close to a live performance as possible. To try and recreate the experience I had on that first outing dressed as a clown.

The exercises in this first section are a combination of vocal and silent communication games that help the players get to know each other and the space they're working in. They begin the process of connecting the players to each other through vocal and physical play, helping to create and build the ensemble. They encourage complicité and, most importantly, they introduce participants to the open-minded play of the clown.

HELLO!

> In this game, the players introduce themselves to the group by name, accenting the introductions with gesture and movement. Participants present themselves in a playful manner; it's also a simple way to associate words with movement.

Variation 1—With moves The players stand in a circle. Starting player says her name then repeats it doing a movement or pose for each syllable. For example, "Tina Smith" is broken into three syllables and three movements. She repeats this, going slowly: as she does, the group imitates her movements and calls out the syllables of her name. They repeat this three more times, speeding up each repetition. This pattern continues around the circle, each player creating a movement sequence to go with the syllables of their name and leading the group through it.

Variation 2—With cheese The players roam. When they make eye contact with another person, they smile and say, "Hello!" to each other, come together and shake hands. First player who points at their partner starts the dialogue:

David   It's you!

Amica   Yes. It's me! Amica Punter.

David   Amica Punter! Good ol' Amica Punter.

Amica   Yeah, that's me. Good ol' Amica Punter. And you!

David   Yes. It's me! David Bantor.

Amica   David Bantor! Good ol' David Bantor. Great to see you David Bantor.

David   And *you*, Amica Punter! See *you* later Amica Punter!

Amica   Great to meet *you* David Bantor! See *you* later David Bantor!

The players repeat the dialogue with everyone they meet. The text doesn't have to be exact: the objective is to greet each other in an overly friendly way, introduce and repeat each other's name as often as possible.

Variation 3—With Tag This uses the game of Tag to help the players learn each other's names. One player is the Chaser. He tries to tag others. When he gets close to a player, she calls out the name of another player. The Chaser immediately runs after the player whose name has been called. If the Chaser tags any player before they yell another name, they become the Chaser.

BIRDS AND BEES

> This game gets the players moving and warmed up at the start of a class or rehearsal, or any time the focus or energy of the group is flagging. It requires that they learn specific movements then recall them accurately as variations are added and the game gets faster.

Variation 1—Chase The players form a circle. The adviser starts: she hops in the air and turns to her left, landing with her feet wide, as if a duck is running through her legs. She bends over as she watches the imaginary duck go through, does a hop so she's facing front again and looks to her right. This cues player to her right to do the same movement sequence. This continues around the circle.

When it gets back to the adviser, she lifts her left leg high, then her right (knee to chest), as if a goose is running under her legs. After she puts down her right leg, the adviser looks to her right. This cues player to her right to do the same sequence. This continues around the circle.

When it gets back to the adviser, she steps forward and does a three-quarter turn to her left as if watching a sparrow fly behind her, spinning in place as she watches it go until she's turned towards the player to her right. They do the same sequence. This continues around the circle, until all the players' bodies are turned to the right looking at the back of the next player in the circle.

When the movement goes all the way around the circle, the adviser looks over her left shoulder, quarter turns to her left so she's facing in towards the circle again and covers her face with both hands as if a swarm of bees is flying past chasing the sparrow. The adviser holds this for a second or two, removes her hands and looks to her right. This triggers the next player to do the same sequence. Continue around the circle. Run this a few times until the players learn the moves that go with each creature.

Variation 2—Fast chase Same as above, but when the duck reaches the third player from the adviser, she lifts her legs for the goose. When the goose reaches third player from the adviser, she turns for the sparrow, etc. In this variation, the players are constantly reacting to the birds and bees chasing each other rather than waiting for each one to go all the way around the circle. Run this a few times.

Variation 3—Duck! Goose! Sparrow! Bees! Same as Variation 2, but as the animals pass by, each player shouts the name of the creature going past, 'Duck! Goose! Sparrow! Beeeeeeees!' Run this a few times and see how fast the group can keep track of the creatures and do the choreography, amongst the playful chaos of movement and sound.

Note: Any type of creature can be used in this game as long as it's passage inspires movement. Try it with a fly, a cat, a dog, a horse, a vulture ...

GROUP LOCO MOTION

Any of these variations are good to use as a warm-up before any exercise or performance. They encourage interaction between the players and help them develop their kinesthetic awareness when moving in a group. Individuals learn how they might change the group energy, while at the same time seeking complicity with all involved. They'll make the players more aware of the space they're working in and how their partners move through it. They'll suggest ways of walking for a clown or character and can also be used in ensemble scenes as a way to inspire improvised group movement that could be developed into set choreography.

Props: Gym mats—thick ones that Velcro together not yoga mats—are helpful in some variations as they create a softer surface for the players to roll, crawl, lie down on, etc.

Physical prep: The first variations start easy with forward movement done at a normal to brisk pace, so it acts as a warm-up for the variations that follow. These add more vigorous movement, but the players are free to make choices on how they'll move based on their bodies and their training (those who have dance or acrobatic experience may try more agile moves in Variations 4, 7, and 8).

Variation 1—Feet first The players roam, walking around the room with their heads up and eyes forward. They walk tall, imagining a string attached to the top of their head drawing them upwards; their body hangs from this string without tension. They explore the feeling of buoyancy and support that this visualization can create. The players use this time to check in with their bodies, shake loose any tension, take note of places where they feel discomfort, and keep being aware of these places as they continue through the variations.

From this upright, neutral walk, they go up on the balls of their feet, a little at first, increasing the height as they feel the hamstrings and calves stretch. After walking up on the balls of the feet, the adviser tells them to switch and walk on the heels, lifting up the front of the feet so they're well back on their heels, adjusting their body to stay balanced. They then alternate from ball of foot to heel, switching every two steps. They then switch to walking on the outside edge of the feet, then switch to the insides (the players should progress in increments, gradually putting more weight on the outside and inside edges of the feet). They then alternate from inside to outside every two steps. Next, they turn their feet inwards—pigeon-toed—and walk this way. Then they walk with their feet splayed out, then alternate pigeon-toed to splayfoot every two steps. Then it's the rollout walk: the feet are splayed out, the players step right heel first, then roll along the sole of the foot and rise up on the ball. The knee bends out to the side, the hips sway side-to-side as they step the same way with the left foot (this is an exaggerated version of Charlie Chaplin's walk).

From the rollout, the players return to a neutral walk (this can be returned to after any step variation), then go into a lunge, taking a long step forward and bending the leg that steps out, keeping the knee in line with the ankle. After a few moments lunging, they stride, taking long steps without bending the forward leg as deeply. Then it's knee highs: they bring the knee up as high as they can towards the chest with every step, coming down with a flat-footed stomp (the players explore degrees of force to produce loud or soft sounds). They then do the same but open in the hips, so they raise the knee up on the side of their body not the front. Then it's the swing out: the knee comes up in front of the body, and while still up, is rotated at the hip socket to the side of the body then down to the floor. Repeat with other leg, alternating as they walk forward. From the swing out, the players do the fat tire walk, taking wide steps side-to-side as if stepping into large truck tires laid out on either side. Then they high step, kicking their legs up high while keeping them straight. They continue this but high step out to the side of their bodies.

They return to the neutral walk then turn sideways and step out wide with the right foot, bring the left foot up against it, and repeat as they progress around the room walking sideways, then switch and step out with the left foot first. Then they step sideways, always crossing the left foot in front of the right as they walk. Then switch with right crossing in front of left. Repeat both sides but stepping behind the leading foot. Then they alternate, stepping out sideways with the left foot, bringing the right foot in front of the left, side stepping out again with the left, then stepping behind the left with the right foot, repeating this pattern to move around the room (some call this step the Grapevine). Then repeat with the left foot crossing in front and behind the right foot. The players return to the neutral walk then speed up, progressing to the race walk, swinging, or swiveling their hips from side-to-side, their arms bent at the elbow, pumping forward and back. From this they break out into a full-on run, making quick shifts in direction and getting a good cardio workout. Gradually they slow down, imagining their body rolling to a stop like a ball coming to rest. They stand tall, imagining that string still attached to the top of their head drawing them upwards as they catch their breath and breathe deeply. They do another check over their body, taking note of any changes from when they started. The adviser gives them time to return to normal breathing, then they shake loose all parts of their body, and are given time to get a drink.

This first variation starts by warming up the feet and ankles, moving up to the legs and hips, and then the torso by increasing aerobic activity. It will improve mobility and balance, as well as agility.

Variation 2—Walking the dictionary The players roam. The adviser calls out dictionary definitions of ways of walking:

Amble   Walk leisurely, at ease, in no hurry to get anywhere.

Careen   Stumble side-to-side as if out of control.

Falter   Move with hesitation, weakly, as if about to collapse.

Flounder   Walk in a clumsy way, with the limbs flapping and the body flailing about as you move.

Limp   Walk as if you have a stiff leg. Alternate legs.

Lumber   Move as if the body is heavy and cumbersome.

Lurch Move suddenly in various directions as if unable to control your movements.

March Move as if you are in a parade being watched by spectators.

Meander Move in a laid-back way, in a winding pattern.

Prowl Move in a sneaky way, trying not to be seen but ready to pounce on someone.

Saunter Like meander but stronger, with a bit more attitude.

Sulk Move in a bad-tempered way, body drooping, head down between the shoulders.

Somnambulate Sleepwalk with your eyes open but as if still asleep.

Stiff Walk with all parts of the body tensed up.

Strut Walk as if you are the coolest, baddest person in the room (this one has a bit of dance in it).

Stumble With every few steps, nearly fall down but recover each time.

Swagger Walk proudly, full of yourself (more muscular than strut).

Trudge Walk as if making your way through thick mud.

Wade Walk as it moving through shallow water. Keep walking as the water gets higher.

While walking, using any of the definitions, the players should explore speed as well as style: walk faster, slower, in a subtle way, in an exaggerated way. Any of these ways of walking can be developed into a clown or character walk, a way of entering the stage, or to display changes in thought or emotion. They can also be used in ensemble improvisations: during a scene, someone in the group can call out "Swagger!" and everyone in the ensemble starts to walk proudly, full of themselves.

Variation 3—Size Always walking forwards, the players take up as much space as possible as they move: arms out, legs wide, a big, lively expression on their faces. They avoid colliding with others without stopping or changing their forward movement.

On a cue from the adviser, they walk forward, taking up as little space as possible, their bodies are contracted, arms and legs drawn in tight, they look at the floor, occasionally glancing up, the expression on their face is shy, retreating.

Variation 4—Variety The players mix it up, moving around the room in as many different ways as possible to increase their range of movement and level of energy—sideways, backwards, turns, length and speed of stride, jump, crawl, roll, etc. They can try a mix of the previous variations. The players avoid physical contact and find creative ways to move around each other.

Variation 5—Stops and stalls The players roam, keeping their heads up and eyes forward. Using the entire space, they weave around and in and out of the group *always walking forwards*. To this they add abrupt stops. Or they roll to a stop like a ball. They try slow stops, pause briefly, then a quick start, and vice-versa. Experiment with stalls, slowing down but not coming to a full stop. Try a gradual increase in energy and speed . . . or a sudden increase! Sync stalls and stops with different players without them knowing it.

Variation 6—Numbers The players count off, then walk. The adviser calls a numbers category—odd or even—and a command—speed up, slow down, hop, stop, crawl, duck walk, etc. For example, "Even, hopping!" Players with even numbers hop while those with odd numbers continue what they're doing. The adviser can call out "Walk" to bring them back to a normal walk or call out new commands—"Odd run! Even lie down! Even stop! Odd move in slow motion!"—and groups switch from hopping to running, to lying down, to stopping, to walking slowly, etc.

Variation 7—Blockers and movers The players roam. Half the group are designated as Blockers, the other half, Movers. The Blocker's objective is to step in front of a Mover, coming to a complete stop (stand, sit, kneel or lie down to block), while the Mover avoids them without stopping. *Important: Blockers must time their intervention so as not to cause collisions or trip up a Mover.* They can telegraph their intention through eye contact or make it obvious who they're going to block through gestures or movement. They play for an allotted time, then the adviser tells them to switch roles.

Variation 8—Stop and drop Same as Variation 7, but when a Blocker interrupts a Mover's trajectory, both players drop down and move around each other. For example, they squat and waddle past each other, do a forward roll, a crab walk, crawl on their bellies, etc. They can both do the same action or find two different ways of moving (they don't discuss it, just drop and go). Once past each other, they stand and continue walking. They play for an allotted time, then the adviser tells them to switch roles (gym mats are good to use with this one).

Variation 9—Stoppers One player is the Stopper. The game starts with everyone standing still. One player (not the Stopper) begins to move (if more than one player starts to move, they decide who keeps moving and who stops through eye contact or gestures). The Stopper goes after the lone Mover and grabs him by both shoulders from behind, stopping his movement. When this happens, another player starts to move (only one). The previous Mover becomes the new Stopper and takes off after the new Mover stopping him by grabbing him by the shoulders from behind. This pattern continues: the one who is stopped becomes the new Stopper for the next Mover.

Variations can be added as follows:

- The same person acts as the Stopper for each new Mover, the group playing the game with this one person responsible to stop any Mover. After they have stopped a few players, designate a new Stopper.
- Movers sound off: They make noise, hum, speak lines or sing as soon as they start moving, continuing sound and movement until the Stopper stops them.

Advice

- "It's not a competition: Movers don't try to get away. As soon as the Stopper grabs you, stop completely, wait, and when someone moves, you become the new Stopper and go after a new Mover."
- "Play with time: when one Mover is stopped, the next Mover can start right away, or the group waits awhile to see who will start the next movement."

GROUPS AND AGREEMENTS

These variations are for developing complicity and group play. They're absurd and a bit silly, so they're good for loosening the players up. I repeat them often: once the players learn them, they're a good way to get them focused at the start of a class, when energy is flagging, or to end the class on a playful note.

Props: Drum and drumstick.

Variation 1—Fish, bear, gorilla The players stand in a circle. Each one silently chooses an animal:

Fish: Place open hands against cheeks and flap them out and in like gills and say, "Blub blub."

Bear: Open arms wide, clench hands like big clawed paws and say, "Raaaarrrr!"

Gorilla: Pound chest with fists and say loudly, "OO-OO! OO-OO!"

The adviser hits a drum (or claps). Every player snaps into their chosen animal. The objective is for everyone to become the same animal right after the drum hit. Play a few times. Then play so the majority wins: animals that are in the minority step out. The game continues until all the players who are left snap into the same animal right after the drum hit.

Variation 2 – Dagger, baby, cat The players roam. The adviser calls the name of another player, points at him and says, "Whoosh!" while miming throwing a dagger. Catcher says, "Aaahhh!" on the catch. The dagger can be caught with the hand, between the knees, the armpit, etc. Or caught *in* the body, the catcher pulling it out of their shoulder, belly, thigh, etc. The Catcher becomes the new Thrower: they call out a name, point and hurl the dagger at a new Catcher, both players using the same movements and sounds that go with the prop and their roles. Continue this sequence, keeping movements and sounds clear for the throw and catch.

Now the adviser cradles a Baby in her arms, saying, "Waaah!" to represent a Baby crying. She gently passes the Baby to a Catcher. They coo "Ohhh" as they take it, then switch to "Waaah!" when they get it in their arms. The Baby is passed from player to player, keeping movements and sounds clear for the hand off and catch.

Now the adviser mimes holding an agitated Cat by the scruff of its neck, keeping it at arm's length as it thrashes about, causing her arm to jerk around. The adviser screeches, "Reehrrrr!" while she's holding the Cat. She hands it to a Catcher: They say "Noooo!" As they take it by the scruff of the neck, their arm starts jerking about. When the Catcher has the Cat in hand, they switch to saying, "Reehrrrr!" and carry it to another Catcher. The Cat is passed around, the movements and sounds clear for the hand off and the taking.

Now combine all three: if a player gets thrown a dagger, he catches it and can throw it to someone else. Or he can switch and pass the Cat, or the Baby. The players change the movements and sounds that represent the mime for each thing, keeping them distinct so each pass off is physically and vocally different.

Note: *Anything can be handed off as long as the movements and the sounds encourage different energies and ways of handling and receiving what is being passed. When creating a variation, make sure the movements and sound are distinctly different for each object or creature.*

Advice

- "When making the passes, use eye contact and/or pointing to another player make it clear who is to be the Catcher."
- "Play with speed: do the movements and sounds in slow motion. Do them quickly."
- "Try slowing down the exchanges: wait a little longer to throw or pass something on, play with it while holding it to build up the suspense. Or as soon as something is exchanged, throw or pass it off to someone else quickly!"

Variation 3—Height, age, sanity The adviser has the players line up shoulder-to-shoulder according to a criteria:

- Line up by height, tallest at the beginning, shortest at the end.
- Line up by age, oldest at the beginning, youngest at the end.
- Line up by how much red you're wearing. Most red at the beginning, least or no red, at the end.
- Line up by the color of your eyes, darkest eyes at the beginning, lightest eyes at the end.
- Line up by anger, most angry at the beginning, least angry at the end.
- Line up by happiness, most happy at the beginning, least happy at the end.
- Line up by how much you love chocolate, those who lust for it at the beginning, those who hate it at the end.

At some point, the criteria become absurd, for example, line up according to who is the most existential. When the players catch on, can they still come to an agreement and line up (rather than get in a long debate about who loves prunes more)? What matters is that the group makes decisions and agrees even when things get absurd.

THE FIVE COMMANDMENTS

> This works as both a physical and mental warm up. Each variation will require more concentration: The players must focus harder on what's said, and how that connects to what they do.

Variation 1—The commandments The players form a circle around the adviser. She explains: "There are five commands, Go, Stop, Clap, Jump, Turn. When I say Go, walk forward in a clockwise direction. When I say Stop, stop. When I say Clap, clap your hands. If you're walking, keep walking while you clap your hands, if stopped, stay still and clap. When I say Jump, jump up. If you're walking, jump, then keep walking. If stopped, jump, and stay still. When I say Turn, turn 180°. If you're walking, turn and keep walking in the other direction, if stopped, turn and stay still."

Play the game for a few rounds so the players know the commands, then call anyone out if they make mistakes; they take a seat inside the circle. Game continues until there is one left.

Variation 2—Eccentric commandments Same as above, but the adviser adds eccentric commands to the original five. For example, "When I say Boogie-Boogie, waggle your hands and say, 'boogie-boogie'. When I say Slo-Mo, move in exaggerated slow motion. When I say Back, walk backwards. When I say Skip, skip forwards." The adviser runs this for a few rounds then calls the players out when they make mistakes.

Variation 3—Inverted commandments In this variation, the adviser inverts the action that goes with the command. For example, "When I say Go, stop. When I say Stop, Go. When I say Clap, jump. When I say Jump, clap. Turn stays the same: turn 180°." The adviser runs this for a few rounds then calls the players out when they make mistakes.

Variation 4—Animal commandments Same as Variation 1, but along with Go, Stop, Clap, Jump, and Turn, the adviser calls out animals. The players imitate animals walking or standing depending on the previous command. For example, "Go! ... Roosters! ... Stop." For this sequence, the players walk clockwise then start imitating Roosters, then stop, holding a rooster-like pose. If the adviser next calls out "Dog!" they transition to a pose imitating a dog standing still. When he says "Turn. Go!" They turn and walk like a dog. The adviser runs this for a few rounds then calls the players out when they make mistakes.

Advice

- "Stay playful while focusing on following the commands. Perhaps being playful will help you stay focused."
- "Make remembering the commands a part of the game rather than trying to hide your struggle to remember the command or stopping altogether."

WAIT, WATCH, JUMP, PLAY

The beauty of this game is its simplicity. Variation 1 is subtle: All players lead the game without realizing it because they're so intensely focused on following their partner. This sometimes creates a laugh-inducing confusion: every player is suspended between the urge to do something, while obeying the rule of not forcing anything to happen. Variation 2 connects the players in a game that is part competition, part collaboration. It gets participants to play big, taking up space physically and vocally. Variation 3 is one of the best ways I know for uniting a group and getting them to instantly collaborate in a playful way. They give themselves over to the ensemble and join in with whatever the group chooses to do.

Variation 1—Watch and wait The players stand in a circle and count off. The adviser sets a pattern. For example, every third person. So if there are 12 in the group, the player who counted off 1 watches 4, 2 watches 5, 3 watches 6, 4 watches 7, 5 watches 8, 6 watches 9, 7 watches 10, 8 watches 11, 9 watches 12, 10 watches 1, 11 watches 2, 12 watches 3. The players are instructed to watch and wait. As they observe their partners, they mirror their physicality from head to toe: what is the expression on their face, are their shoulders hunched, their spine straight, their feet parallel or splayed? If a player's partner (the one they're observing) moves—even a raised eyebrow, a cough, a slight shift of the feet, moving a finger, etc.—the one watching mirrors their movement. This, of course, sets off a chain reaction as each observer reacts to the movement of their partner.

No-one tries to initiate an action deliberately; they simply respond to any subtle changes displayed by the one they're observing. Play for a minute or more, then count off again to observe and follow a new partner.

Variation 2—Hop HA! The players stand in a circle. Everyone inhales, then exhales with a long, "Haaaaaa …" They repeat, going up and down vocally, from a high pitch to a low. The adviser encourages the players to use their breath to release tension in the body, especially the face and throat.

Now the players try the sound with a hop: they take a deep breath, hop forward, land on both feet at the same time, flex at the knees and open their arms downwards towards the floor as if scooping up a big armful. The head is up, the eyes forward. The players exhale with their mouths open wide and say, "HA!" The sound is breathy, loud, and extended. They imagine the sound coming from the earth, through their feet, up their legs, filling the pelvis and the torso, exiting up through the neck and out the mouth. A sound that could move mountains …

Once the players run the hop and "HA!" a few times, the adviser says he will hop forward and say, "HA!" expecting everyone to do the same—at the exact same moment—then step back into the circle. The adviser leads the hop and "HA!" a few times, everyone focused on doing it together, then encourages anyone in the group to cue the hop and "HA!" with everyone prepared to jump forward at the same moment. The one leading the Hop HA! can choose to wind up and telegraph when they're going to do it, or not.

Advice

- "The energy from the hop goes down into the earth, back up through your body to be released in HA! You should feel heavy and grounded when you land."
- "Stay attentive to the group so you can hop and HA! *together*. It's not a competition."
- "Play with time: after the hop and HA! as soon as the group steps back, anyone can initiate a new jump. Or everyone pauses … makes eye contact, delays the hop and HA! watching each other closely to sense a cue when to go."

Variation 3—Who's got game The players stand in a circle and the adviser explains the rules. "I'll start the game by saying, OK. When I want us to stop, I'll cross my arms, we all reform the circle, and I'll say done." The players make eye contact with each other, relax their bodies and faces, stand in a neutral position, nothing moving but their eyes. The adviser says, "OK."

The game can be a player pursing his lips or sticking a tongue out, raising their arm or turning a foot outward, etc. The players see this first game, and everyone decides to copy it. For example, they all turn their left foot outwards. They can develop this game—turn both feet outwards, then both feet inwards—or another player introduces a new game such as singing "Happy birthday to you!" and the group decides to join in. The players vary the games: use words, sounds, or gibberish; move in exaggerated ways, or small and subtle. They can maintain the circle as they play or move about the room, but they must stay focused on the group to ensure they're all playing the same game, and to catch any new game that is adopted.

If two players introduce a game at the same time, they both keep at it until the group decides which game to play. The majority rules: any player who initiates a new game that isn't taken up by the group, lets it go and joins in with what the group decides; they don't cling to their idea and demand the group plays it.

To end the game, the adviser crosses her arms, the players return to the circle and the adviser says, "Done."

Summary

The objective of this section was to introduce the players to each other and start the process of uniting them through physical play and dynamic interaction. This starts to develop the trust needed for later sections when they're working together to devise ensemble pieces and taking more risks mentally and emotionally. This section also had the players moving through their workspace in dynamic ways, starting the process of getting them familiar with the room and finding simple ways to interact with it. This is crucial to clown performance and is further explored in Section 5: Curiosity. The next section continues to connect the players, encouraging and heightening their playful energy. Later sections will connect this to the clown's way of interacting with their environment.

Figure 2.1 Jonathan Rex: Energy. *Photo credit: Eric Gillet/Shoot That Klown.*

2

Energy

The Telepathic Renaissance Fool

Colorado. A Renaissance festival in a forested, mountainous region between Denver and Colorado Springs. The air is thin and crisp, filled with the scent of evergreens. On a wooden stage at the bottom of a low hill, the slapstick, acrobatic, comedy trio, the Abbotts of Unreason, are waiting for the crowd meandering down a shrubby, rocky incline towards the stage; they're coming to check out the Abbotts' fifth and final show of the day. The sun is low in the sky, some people carry mugs of ale, others have greasy turkey legs in hand,

Figure 2.2 The Abbotts of Unreason, Mark Renfrow (seated) and Joe Dieffenbacher. *Photo credit: Papa Renfrow.*

some munch on "medieval" egg rolls. They look happy: it's been a good day at the Colorado Renaissance Festival in Larkspur.

I'm standing onstage as Eoj (ee-o-juh)—the fool in this comic trio—sweeping the stage while my partners are getting ready. Some people readily take a seat on hay bales, others stand at the back unsure if they want to stay, wondering, who's the colorfully dressed janitor?

I'm clearing the stage of any debris that we might trip on, poke us in the back, dirty or tear our costumes; the Abbotts of Unreason are infamous for throwing each other around, knocking each other down, tripping and flipping across the stage—even crashing through wood floors and walls on some occasions. So, sweeping the stage has a practical purpose. But it also has an educational one: I'm learning about the crowd, their mood, gathering bits of info that might be useful later during the show. I discover it's someone's birthday and get the crowd to sing to them. I find a kid who knows how to balance a broom on his open palm and get the crowd to cheer him on. I talk to them but I don't tell jokes or try to be funny, I simply start a conversation, the humor coming out of the open, sometimes foolish, mostly simple nature of my character, and the playful dialogue.

In the midst of this leisurely approach to starting the show, I'm suddenly struck by the strangest feeling: as the crowd grows bigger and I engage with them, I have a feeling of telepathy, like I can read their minds. I've never felt a connection like this! Everything I say and do, connects with the crowd, warms them to the character, sets them at ease, but also gets them anticipating the show about to happen. And when my partners come on—one dressed as a squire, the other as a weird wizard in kabuki-style makeup—I see the audience lean forward, curious and ready to play. Complicity has become telepathy, an energetic connection with a crowd of a few hundred that came about through humor, play, and the open curiosity of the fool.

It started with a conversation that was both verbal and physical. It included play not only with a prop (the broom), but the space (not just our performance space but the audience's space as well). Me coming down to them, them coming onstage with me, built a bridge between the spaces, broke down the wall between their everyday reality and the Abbotts theatrical, imagined one.

This opening of the show—a man just sweeping the stage—that was not presented in any way as THE SHOW!—was played by me with the same back-and-forth, collaborative/competitive aspects of a game. And treating it as a game allowed me and the audience to open up to one another and create a flow that myself and my partners enjoyed for the next forty-five minutes. It was one of the best shows we had that year and opened my mind up to an understanding of clowning that went beyond jokes, gags, comic bits, or funny business. The clown's objective was not simply to satisfy his ego or seek approval by *making* the audience laugh, but to find ways of uniting them through play.

The games in this section aim to do just that. There isn't much on theory here, just games that get the players to be physical, competing and collaborating, and collaborating while they compete. This begins the process of understanding the paradox of ensemble clown play: it's a contest between individuals who, at the same, strive to cooperate to achieve a greater objective.

WALK THIS WAY

> This is a good physical warm-up game which also explores ways of moving that can be used for a clown or character walk, or to develop group movement. The suggested scenarios will encourage the players to explore different energies through physical play and how that is expressed when confined to movement done in place.

The players stand in a circle and begin walking in place. Their movements are casual, relaxed. The adviser then calls out a situation and they change the walking movement to reflect the scenario described.

Note: *The walking in place never stops, just the quality of the movement as it is affected by the scenarios.*

Here are some suggestions:
- Someone is stalking you from behind. You're nervous, scared. Your walk speeds up or slows down, you glance back now and then or keep looking back for longer stretches. You might even walk backwards.
- Walking along a beach as the sun rises, moving towards the one you love.
- A large scaly beast is following you, close behind. It's sweating, farting and drooling. Some of its bodily fluids fall on you as you walk and try to stay calm.

- A large, sweet, chocolate covered donut (or other desired confection) is dangling in front of you just above eye level. You walk along trying to grab it, but it remains out of reach.
- You're eating the sweet confection as you walk but are worried that someone is going to take it from you as you bite and chew on it.
- You're near the end of running a marathon walking race, sweaty and nearly dead from exhaustion. Then you see the finish line and the TV cameras turn to you. Your walk and your energy changes as you realize you're on TV.
- You're walking through a crowd with a letter you must deliver but you're not sure who it goes to, turning and looking in all directions as you walk.
- You're walking on a well-inflated bouncy castle.
- You're walking barefoot on hot coals.
- You're walking barefoot on a warm, soft, velvety surface, that brings you deep delight.

Note: *Play with speed. Any of these variations can be done in slow or fast motion. The adviser can also call out "Casual" to give the players a chance to rest, moving in a relaxed way before introducing a new scenario.*

CHASE ME, TAG ME

There are many variations on the game of Tag: it's one of the best ways to get everyone playing from a simple set of rules. The players challenge each other as well as help each other, run around frenetically, but also develop tactics for staying safe or gaining an advantage. Games of Tag are perfect to warm up the players at the start of a class or any time focus is drifting; they are immediately immersed in energetic, physical play, they're a good workout, and they inspire creative movement choices.

Props: Rope or masking tape to mark a playing area, or gym mats if available.

Room prep: The players often lose themselves in these games, so have everyone walk the space and ensure there's nothing that might be a hazard, making mental notes of raised levels, hard edges, corners, etc. Move any objects that might get in the way to the edges of the room.

Physical prep: Slow-motion variations are a good warm up for the more energetic games.

Note: *For slow-motion variations 1-3, mark off the area with ropes or tape so the players are confined to a smaller space.*

Variation 1—Slow-motion tag The players stand so they are just out of arms' reach of each other. One player is the Chaser. The adviser gives the signal to start. Everyone moves in slow motion as the Chaser tries to tag them. No one is allowed to speed up: they cannot make any sudden movements to escape the Chaser, nor can the Chaser reach quickly to tag them. When a player is tagged, he becomes the Chaser. During the game, the players also use their voices, using sounds and words to accent their slow movements.

Variation 2—Slow-motion melodrama tag Same as Variation 2, but with only one Chaser: when they tag someone, that person dies a slow-motion, melodramatic death—complete with vocals!—moving to the outskirts of the playing space as they lay down and die, and remaining dead until all are tagged.

Variation 3—Slow-motion ninja Same as Variation 2, but each player's left hand is a poisoned blade, their right arm is a shield. The players always move—as well as vocalize—in slow motion, matching sounds and words with movement. The adviser gives the signal to start: the players try to stab (touch) one another with their poisoned blade (left hand) anywhere on the torso or lower body (anywhere but the arms and hands, counts as a kill). They use their shield (right arm) to block others' poisoned blades. They can only use their right arm to defend themselves, never the left. This forces the players to twist their bodies to attack and defend. If a player is stabbed, they die a slow-motion, melodramatic death—complete with vocals - and remain dead until only one is left standing.

Variation 4—Circles tag One player is the Chaser another is the Chased. Half the class form a circle, arm's-length apart; the other half form a second circle standing a half meter behind the first (each player in the outer circle stands directly behind a player in the inner circle). The Chaser starts outside the circles, the Chased in the center. The Chaser tries to tag the Chased, pursuing her inside and outside the circles. If the Chased is tagged, the roles are switched. At any point in the pursuit, the Chased can stand at the front or the back of any of the pairs in the circle. This is a safe zone; he cannot be tagged. When the Chased steps in front of a pair, the person at the back becomes the Chased. If he seeks safety at the back, the player at the front becomes the Chased.

Variation 5—Human chain tag One player is the Chaser. When they tag someone, they join hands with her. Both are now the Chaser. They run about trying to tag others. Every time someone is tagged, they join the chain, with only the free hands at the ends of the chain able to tag. Other parts of the chain can try to block or corral those running about so they can be tagged by the ends. Continue until all have joined the Chaser's chain.

Variation 6—Everybody's it tag All the players are It. The adviser signals the start. The players try to tag each other while avoiding being tagged. If a player is tagged, he sits out. If two players tag each other at the same time, they're both out. Continue until there is one left.

Advice

- "If you're being chased, tease the Chaser! Play with the tension of nearly getting caught. Or beg to be tagged while you run away from the Chaser. Explore tactics for escaping or losing *theatrically*. Make it a scene with high stakes!"
- "If you're the Chaser, toy with those you're chasing! Play with the tension of *nearly* catching them, let them think they can escape then catch them off guard. Find inventive, dramatic tactics for capturing your prey."

THE SOLO AND THE ENSEMBLE

This exercise builds physical trust between players and focuses the group on moving as an ensemble. The variations also allow individual players to make choices that express their physical strengths and weaknesses, which are, in turn, supported by the group.

Props: Gym mats or thick towels may be used when the players are on their knees or lying on their backs.

Variation 1—The playful circle The players stand in a circle, holding hands, their feet just over shoulder-length apart. They lean towards the center of the circle as one, spines straight, not arching forwards or back nor bending at the waist, keeping their heels on the ground, and maintaining their balance (and the group's). They then lean back without lifting their toes, keeping their spines straight, still holding hands. They continue this back and forth, keeping the circle intact, all players moving in and out in sync.

Now they create a wave. Start with one player—we'll call her A—leaning forwards. As A starts to move back to upright, player to her right—we'll call her B—moves forward (as A leans back). Next player in the circle—C—starts to lean forward as B starts to move to upright and back. So, the movement of the circle is staggered, creating a wave pattern. Once they achieve this cleanly, the adviser tells them to come back to standing upright.

Now they all lean to the left—still holding hands, keeping their bodies straight and the soles of their feet on the ground, then right. They explore this side-to-side sway for a few minutes, then the adviser tells them to stand upright.

Now they move in tight together, sliding their hands up their partners' arms on either side of them until their hands are resting on each other's shoulders, their elbows bent. They make as tight a circle as they can without losing this shape, (no-one turns sideways or stands in such a way as it staggers the line of the circle). Once they are as close as they can be while maintaining a clean circle, they slowly move out, sliding their hands back down their partners' arms, continuing until they slide along each other's palms to the fingers, stopping when they achieve this light touch with just the four fingers (the pads of the fingers not the tips or thumbs). They then slide their hands up their partners' arms, reform the tight circle, then slide out again. Repeat until the group can do it smoothly. Try it faster.

The players must maintain contact with their partners' arms on either side of them as they step back in. Try to time it so all the players end with their fingers touching at the same moment.

Variation 2—The supporting circle Eight to ten players stand in a tight circle, their feet staggered so they are in a stronger position to catch the center player. Another player stands in the center of the circle with their eyes closed and their hands folded across their chest. Keeping their body straight and stiff the whole time, the player in the center leans in any direction and those in the circle reach out and catch them, then begin to gently pass them around the circle, everyone working together to support the center player. They try to do this smoothly, so the center player is not jostled or handled roughly.

Variations can be added as follows:

- Everyone on their knees, arms up. Keeping the circle tight, they pass the center player around.
- One player is on his knees, the one next to him standing. The next one kneeling, the next standing. Continue this alternating pattern around the circle. From these positions they pass the center player around.
- One player is on his knees, the one next to him standing, the next one lying on their back, feet up, to catch and shift the player with their feet. Alternate these positions around the circle. Pass the center player around.
- All the players are lying on their backs, feet up. Pass the center player around using only the feet.
- The players go from standing, then kneeling, ending with everyone on their backs, feet up, all while keeping the center player moving around the circle. When all are on their backs, they reverse the order, moving to the knees and then all standing. The movements can be staggered—some going on their knees while others are still standing—or the group can try to all go down on their knees at the same time (with one player holding the center player as she drops to her knees), then onto their backs as they pass the center player around the circle.

CHAIR GAMES

These variations with chairs combine both competition and cooperation. They get the players to explore the change in energy from sitting and waiting, to suddenly running about (this change in dynamic is important for physical comedy). They're good for ensemble building and I've used them to develop and enhance group scenes.

Props: Tape or rope to mark a finish line, enough chairs for everyone in the class, plus extras.

Room prep: Use sturdy chairs and check that none have splinters or weak parts, sharp points, or loose screws. Do this check every time the game is played.

Physical prep: Variations 1 and 2 require some fast moving, so do a short warm up such as a game of Tag or Group Locomotion from Section 1.

Variation 1—Caller in the middle The group is divided into three equal teams. Each team is given a name: Hoppers, Striders, Sidesteppers. The name signifies how they must move. Chairs are set in a circle with at least two meters between each chair. There are enough chairs for every player except one: she is the first Caller. She stands in the middle of the circle and calls out a team name: that team must switch chairs but move towards them according to their name. So, Hoppers hop to a new chair, Striders take long, striding-forward steps, Sidesteppers take long steps moving sideways only. The Caller must move the same way as they try to get to an empty chair before the team members do. If the Caller fails, she calls out another team (the Caller can do this immediately after stepping back into the middle or pause before calling). If they do get a chair, the person left standing becomes the new Caller (the former Caller becomes part of the group she called out).

Note: *The adviser can call the teams other names to force the players to move in other ways: Backers (players walk backwards), Flappers (players flap their arms as they walk like chickens), Little Steppers (players take small steps), etc.*

Variation 2—Numbered chairs Numbers are written on small sheets of paper, one for each player (start with the number 1). These are put into a hat and each player chooses a number, memorizes it, and keeps it secret. They put the papers back in the hat. Chairs are set in a circle as in Variation 1. One player—the Loner—stands in the middle of the circle. They call out any two numbers. The players with those numbers switch chairs. The Loner tries to beat them to one of the chairs. If they don't make it, they return to the middle and try again. If they do get a chair, the one left standing becomes the new Loner, goes to the middle and calls out two new numbers.

The Loner won't know who has what number at first, so it's a guessing game as to who will get up each time the numbers are called (one tactic for the Loner would be to deliberately lose in order to learn a player's number and take her chair when her number is called again). The players in chairs also don't know who has what number so there will be a moment when all are waiting to see who will move.

Variations can be added as follows:

- When the Loner manages to get a chair, the players choose a new number from the hat before resuming the game. This keeps everyone guessing on every turn.
- Have three of every number in the hat. So, with a group of twelve players, have three 1's, three 2's, three 3's, three 4's (if there is an odd number, have a group of four with the same number). When a number is called by the Loner, three people must switch chairs.

Advice

- "Play with time: You can move immediately when numbers are called so there is a mad scramble by all, or, sit calmly, make eye contact, covertly find out who has the numbers called and is ready to move...then run!"

Variation 3—Chair race The adviser tapes a finish line at one end of the room, far enough from the wall for four chairs in a line to cross over it (or just one if space is limited). The players set out two or more rows of four chairs each, one behind the other, at the other end of the room, facing the finish line. Three players sit in the first three chairs of each line (each row has an empty chair at the back end of the line). The players practice: the third player in each group reaches back and takes the empty chair behind him and passes it forward down the line to the front (everyone must stay seated while passing the chair). The players then move up one chair and begin again, with the third player grabbing the empty chair behind him and passing it forward each time. This continues until all chairs, in a straight line, cross the finish line (if there is not enough space, the winner is the group that gets one chair over the line and the group all shifted forward, the empty chair at the back). Once the players have practiced, they race. The adviser gives the signal and the first group to cross the line wins.

Note: *Make the rule that the players cannot lift their butts off the seats nor move forward until the chair is set in front. Nor can they stand and set the chair further forward to move the line along faster. The player in front must set the chair at arm's length in front of him, keeping his butt fully on the seat. Disqualify any who take shortcuts.*

RACES

Like Tag, there are dozens of variations on games that involve racing one another to a finish line. And like Tag, they'll help the adviser to get an idea of what sort of tactics the players gravitate towards in the midst of playing; useful information when they start working in duos, trios and ensembles. The players should take note of what sort of tactics they come up with; they could be used to develop relationships and status play within a scene or routine (more on this in Sections 7–10). Races are good for warming up the class, as well as teaching balance and body control.

Props: Three-meter strips of crêpe paper, two supports to hold crêpe paper finish line, 30cm long sticks or rolled up newspapers taped to create a baton for relay race, large sheets of newspaper.

Variation 1—Slo-mo race A finish line of crêpe paper is set at one end of the room between two supports. Divide the groups into teams of five. The first five go down into a runner's starting stance at the other end of the room from the finish line. All others stand on the sidelines as the cheering audience. The adviser calls out, "On your marks ... get set ... GO!"

Always moving in slow motion, the players run towards the finish line. They cannot stop moving, must lift their feet high with each step, and take long steps (this will help them cover distance as well as teaching body control). When the players reach the finish line, they mustn't speed up in order to break the paper tape, win or place. Anyone who does is disqualified. The slo-mo race continues until all the players cross the line.

While this is happening, the audience on the sidelines is cheering in slow motion, screaming out the name of their favorite runner, shouting encouragement.

Variation 2—Slo-mo cheaters Runners cheat, trying to trip, block and thwart the other racers to gain an advantage, all in slow motion, always moving forwards. The adviser should caution the players: "Don't get so lost in cheating that you forget to win the race!" The audience reacts on the sidelines as above.

Variation 3—Slo-mo relay Teams of three players do a relay race in slow motion. The players race to one end of the room, hand the baton to a teammate, who races back to where the first player started. They hand the baton to the third player who races back to the finish line.

Advice

- "Explore—*and enjoy*—moving in slow motion. It'll help you focus on the mechanics of moving, on articulation, balance and precision."
- "Keep the whole body—including the face—animated and moving, actively participating in the game."

Variation 4—Partners paper race The adviser lays down a rope to represent the finish line at one end of the room. The players partner up. Each pair is given two sheets of newspaper (the sheets need to be large enough for both players to stand on without their feet touching the floor). Pairs spread out at one end of the room, at least ten meters from the finish line. The adviser signals the start of the race.

One member of each pair sets down a sheet of paper, then both partners step onto it, taking care not to crumple or tear it. *No part of either partner's feet can make contact with the floor.* If they do, they're disqualified. The second sheet of paper is set down and both step onto it. They reach back to pick up the other piece, set it down in front of them and step forward. The adviser makes the rule that either both players have to pick up the paper together or that they alternate who picks it up. This continues until one pair reaches the finish line, both crossing over by stepping onto a sheet of paper and picking up the one behind them.

A variation can be added as follows:

- After all the players cross the finish line, papers are held up: the pair with the best-preserved papers—least crumpled or torn—wins, even if they were the last to cross.

Variation 5—Tear paper race The players work as solo racers: each one has a large sheet of newspaper. They spread out at one end of the room, at least ten meters from the finish line (this distance will be determined by the size of the newspaper sheet: how many pieces can be torn off to reach the finish line? See instructions below). The adviser signals the start of the race.

The players set a full sheet of paper down, step onto it, then tear away a piece large enough so when they set it down and step on it, no part of their feet will touch the floor. They place it ahead of them and step onto it. They pick up the larger piece behind them, set it down, step, tear off another piece and continue this pattern (they cannot carry forward any of the pieces they've torn off). This continues until one of them reaches the finish line, crossing over by stepping onto a sheet of paper.

Players can tear the pieces as large or small as they want as long as they maintain their balance and no part of their body touches the floor.

A variation can be added as follows:

- The players tear a sheet of paper off the larger piece, set it down, step on it, then tear off another piece, set it down, step, etc. This method is easier because the players don't have to keep reaching back to pick up the larger paper behind them; they are always moving forwards.

RELAX

A great way to end a class or after any vigorous game. These variations both relax the players and help build physical complicity and trust.

Variation 1—Slap down Three players. One person stands between the others with eyes closed, arms at their sides, feet parallel, body relaxed. He is the Receiver. Two players on either side of the Receiver inhale together and, starting at the top of the head, tap, pat, and slap the Receiver's body, working their way *together* to the person's feet, giving the Receiver a relaxing pat down. If the Receiver wants a more vigorous patting, they say "more." If the patting is too hard, they say, "less."

When their partners finish tapping the tops of their feet and toes with their fingertips, they inhale, raise their arms over head and, as they exhale, *ever-so-lightly* run their fingertips down the Receiver's body to their feet and then throw their hands outwards, finishing with a strong exhale, throwing away any tension and bad energy. The fingertip pass is done three times. The Receiver is given a moment to appreciate the experience, then another partner becomes the Receiver and they repeat the sequence until all have had a go .

Variation 2—Raft Six to seven players. One is a Raft; one is a Passenger. They stand back-to-back. Raft squats down so her butt is below the Passenger's.

She reaches back and grabs the Passenger's hips, then cantilevers her body and bends forward as the Passenger lays back; she lifts him up onto her back, lifting with her legs. Other players are Waves. They assist the Passenger onto the Raft's back, supporting him as he is lifted: one player takes the Passenger's head in her hands, one player on each arm, one on each foot, to support them in the lift.

The Raft begins to roll her spine, shifting her body from side-to-side, swaying, etc. Waves manipulate arms, legs and head and occasionally blow across the Passenger's body; it's a gentle, rolling, swaying motion, evoking a raft on calm waters with a gentle breeze blowing. The Passenger breathes deeply and enjoys the ride.

After a minute or so, the Raft and Waves gently lower the Passenger to his feet.

Switch roles until everyone has had a go.

Summary

How often do adults play like they did when they were kids, in an open-ended, inventive, imaginative way? In this section, children's and theater games were tweaked, and variations added. This introduces students to the clown's approach to play, one that is constantly seeking variety and new possibilities. In some variations, the players were encouraged to play at a heightened—*theatrical*—level, to imagine the game as a performance; this should be encouraged for all games (more on this in Section 10: The rules, the script, the game, the play).

The games are also a chance for the adviser to gather information, to get an idea of what sort of tactics the players gravitate towards in the midst of playing. Because people are less self-conscious when they're fully engaged in a game, an adviser can gain useful information about each player's tendencies, their physical, mental and emotional reactions to the games, and how they might work in a clown duo, trio, and in the ensemble as a whole. The players can also use this information when devising a clown scene or routine (Section 14: Devising for Clown and Physical Comedy). These games are also important physical warm-ups that teach agility and body control. This prepares them for the next section on physical expression.

Figure 3.1 Christian Schneider: The talking body. *Photo credit: Eric Gillet/Shoot That Klown.*

3

The Talking Body

Silence on the Streets

I've often worked in large venues where the body was the primary communicator: three-ring circuses, street theater, outdoor spectacles, stadium shows. Through training and experience I learned to express myself without the use of words. But when I found myself creating a new show for the street festivals of Europe, performing solo in large plazas, playing for hundreds, I began to doubt my silent communication skills.

The majority of the street performers I'd seen used words, and through my own outdoor work with the Abbotts of Unreason and Los Payasos Mendigos, I was led to believe that the only way you could gather and win over a crowd on the street was to talk to them.

This new show featured a silent character that had been a slapstick walk act for years, slipping, sliding, and tumbling down steps, off stages and down ladders. My body used whatever space I was in—and whatever was in the space—as a partner. But the thought of using this quiet character to gather and hold a large crowd on the street, intimidated me no end, despite my training and experience.

I did some tryouts with him talking but found that I was letting my voice dominate the conversation; once I opened my mouth, I paid less attention to communicating with my body and the audience focused on my words. So, I went back to silence, to the earlier experience I had as a clown handing out balloons; all the words in my head had to be expressed through my body and its play with the world around it.

The show had a tough learning curve. It was called—appropriately enough—*The Trap*. But as it evolved, my physical communication skills improved, my training was transmuted into play in the crucible of live performance, and I gained a greater appreciation of stillness, of letting the

Figure 3.2 Joe Dieffenbacher as the janitor in nakupelle's *The Trap*. Photo credit: Matilda Dieffenbacher.

shape of my body at rest speak to the audience. I became conscious of every little detail: the position of my head, the way I held my shoulders, the shape of my spine, how that affected my pelvis, and the position of my feet. All these things were speaking to the crowd whether they were conscious of it or not. But as the creator of the show, I had to be conscious of it.

The ability to carry comedy, character and story in the body and express it physically is crucial to clowning, but because we communicate verbally every hour of every day with everyone we meet, most of us lack a truly expressive body. We haven't built up the muscles to hold a strong pose or a facial expression that communicates a powerful emotion. We're "out of shape" in regards to physical expression. The exercises in this section aim to make the players conscious of the power their body has to express ideas, thoughts, and emotions. They're important not only for developing a greater emotional range and expressing that physically, they also help build the necessary muscles to do so.

This is technical work and it requires practice. I repeat these exercises in class as well as encouraging the players to do them on their own time. Training a body to be physically expressive to the degree necessary for clown and physical comedy can be a workout: the body is used in ways similar to an acrobat or dancer, as well as connecting with the audience on an emotional level the way an actor does. The players have to think about the scene, skills they may need to incorporate, staying aware of their partners, connecting with the audience ... It can be exhausting if they don't train well.

Instruction in any body-focused art form—acrobatics, dance, mime—is useful as long as a player doesn't pursue it to the point where their training becomes obvious, their muscles confined to a certain way of moving; they risk losing their body's natural expressive power. Skills training should serve to reveal the clown, not just as a way to show off: slapstick comedy is a perfect example of hiding acrobatic training in order to create comic play, a way of responding to the world that inspires not only laughter from the audience, but empathy (see Buster Keaton or Jacque Tati's use of slapstick).

Underneath the best clowning there is specificity and structure, technique, and skill. Training in technique may seem boring to those who just want to play and improvise, but like a pianist who has to practice scales over and over again so she can cut lose in performance, a clown must work the technical aspects of her craft in order to raise the standards of her art and enrich the experience for her audience.

The following exercises include elements of mime, acting, movement and dance, and use physical play to connect students to the space they're working in. Here I introduce the Five Elements: a way of breaking down a performance into its most basic actions. This begins the process of making the players more aware of their body in relation to the performing space, and how to use both body and space to introduce their clown to the audience. These exercises also explore ways to create scenes that have a stronger emotional and visual impact.

DANCE!

> When it comes to physical expressiveness, a lot can be learned about students by putting on some music and watching them move.

> Where do they hold tension? What parts of their bodies are more flexible, the most expressive? How do they respond to and play with the beat: do they treat the music as a partner or just something to move to?
>
> The clown is always dancing, even when standing still; something inside is always moving, flowing. Their dance is a way of communicating with the physical world in a way that is direct and integrating. It combines skill, kinesthetic awareness, physical improvisation and exploration, with a focus on exuberant play.
>
> I like to start classes by having the players dance any way they please, using it as a free-form warm up. I avoid music with vocals or songs that are well-known; dancers should respond directly to the music not their associations with the lyrics or a popular tune. I use music with strong beats, songs that are easy to follow but also those that are more complex, both fast and slow. I also use compositions that encourage flowing, expressive movement.

Props: A ball, hat, or other soft object, easily passed around. Have exercise balls, bedsheets, foam pool noodles or pipe insulation, costume bits—anything soft that dancers can play with—scattered about.

Room prep: Gym mats: spread them out for the players to roll over, lie down on, crawl on, etc.

Dance warm up: The players use free-form movement to loosen up the body for physical work. This one is good to start off any class.

Lone Dancer: Everyone dances in a subdued, controlled way. The adviser calls out a name. That player keeps on dancing as all others stop, cross their arms and stare at Lone Dancer, shocked by his display! Instead of being bothered, Lone Dancer is encouraged by their disgust to dance even more! Slowly the others dance again but in a subdued, controlled way. Lone Dancer tones it down, his dance becomes stiffer like the others. The adviser calls out a new name. This sequence is repeated until everyone gets a turn at being Lone Dancer.

Lone Watcher: Everyone dances in a loose, joyful way. The adviser calls out a name. That player stops dancing, crosses her arms and stares at the others as they continue dancing. Lone Watcher looks on, insulted by the display! The players dance around her, encouraging Lone Watcher to join in but she refuses at first. Slowly she loosens up, then joins in the dance. The adviser calls out a new name. This sequence is repeated until everyone gets a turn at being Lone Watcher.

Bad dancer: The players dance as awkwardly as possible: eccentric moves, off the beat, creating clunky shapes, odd shifts in their energy, like they just can't find the groove.

Follow the leader: The leader of the dance is chosen and given a prop: a ball, hat, or other soft object. They lead, all others mimic them. The leader moves in ways others can copy, repeating movements so followers have a chance to catch on. After 30 seconds or so, she passes the prop to someone and this new leader takes over, all following him. *The passing of the object has great importance!* Don't just toss it. The players should treat the hand off as if they're crowning royalty. They keep dancing until everyone has had a chance to be the leader.

In contact: Groups of three or more dance with some part of their bodies *always* in contact; all hands, or a palm against a forehead, back against a shoulder, etc. If they want to switch the point of contact they must do so in a way that maintains contact with their partners at all times. The adviser bangs a drum to signal the players to switch partners: they move towards another group, make a point of contact with a new partner, relinquish contact with their old one, and dance off.

PLAYING WITH THE BREATH

> These variations get the players using their breath in playful ways, connecting it to movement while exploring contraction and expansion (an important concept in physical comedy). They help to relax the players and are a good way to release tension. I've also used them in improvs and scripted scenes, getting all the players to react to a moment by deflating or inflating.

Variation 1—Deflate–inflate Everyone stands in a wide circle. They take a deep breath in, and on the exhale, deflate, their bodies collapsing to the floor (make it a controlled descent). The players can deflate at their own rate or the entire group works together and tries to all deflate in sync. Then, still deflated, they take a deep breath in and out, then a deep inhale which causes them to inflate. Their bodies expand and they float upwards until they're back on their feet, bodies full of air, spreading out to their limbs and on down to their toes (they can take more than one inhalation to inflate if needed). They bobble like a balloon, do another breathing cycle—inhale-exhale—then exhale and deflate, repeating the whole cycle a few more times.

Variation 2—The air doll The players partner up. One is a doll, the other DI (Deflator–Inflator). The doll puffs himself up so his whole body is expanded like a balloon full of air. DI pulls the plug (grabs a finger, nose, ear, toe, etc., and mimes pulling it out). The doll deflates all the way to the floor making a hissing-deflating sound. DI then mimes a bike pump, connects the hose to some part of the body, and pumps the doll full of air making hissing-inflating sounds in sync with her pumping action. The doll matches the sound of the inflating: a short pump might just expand a finger, a series of fast pumps might cause the body to expand in a jerky way, a long slow pump might expand the torso fully; the players work to connect their actions so we see the cause and the effect. DI can help the doll by lifting body parts so they are easier to inflate or pick the doll up so he can stand, expand and eventually, flow and bounce lightly around the room once DI detaches the pump. Switch partners or repeat the deflating/inflating.

WHERE'S MY CENTER?

A player's center in this exercise is the place in their body where they respond to the world and/or protect themselves from it. It's more an emotional center than a physical one, but in this exercise, it is exaggerated until it's obvious where a player leads from. Are they a head person, or do they lead with the heart? The belly or the pelvis? It could be the feet or the hands. In this exercise they locate their center, lead with it (extend it outwards), then shift it around to find variety in their movement choices, and more control over their physicality.

Props: Stage flats or curtains big enough for two people to hide behind, a chair, a half-meter long wooden club or other weapon (see Variation 7).

Variation 1—My center The players move about, searching for their natural center. They then exaggerate it, push it out in front of their bodies, leading with it. For example, if they think they're head-centered, they extend their neck forward, the head thrust out, and walk around the room leading with this. If they're not sure, they can try various parts of their body to see which one feels best.

Variation 2—Front centered The players walk, placing their center of gravity in front of them as if they have a stone hanging from their neck, sitting at chest level. The weight causes the players to lean forward, *pulling* them into walking. They imagine the weight increasing, pulling them forward and down. The players then walk without the lean: they feel the weight at their front without showing it in an obvious way. They return to a neutral walk.

Variation 3—Back centered The players imagine a stone hanging behind them, sitting between the shoulder blades. They imagine the weight increasing while walking forward, causing them to lean back as far as they can. The players then walk without the lean: they feel the weight at their back without showing it. They return to a neutral walk.

Variation 4—Side centered The players imagine a stone hanging off their right side. As they walk, the weight increases and they lean to the right as far as they can. The players then walk without the lean: they feel the weight at their right without showing it. Repeat on the left side. They return to a neutral walk.

Variation 5—Belly centered The players imagine a stone inside their belly. They explore ways of showing the belly weight, flexing in the knees, pushing the belly out, etc. The weight gets heavier, slows the player down, makes it hard to move. They then express the weight of the stone without showing it physically: it encourages a slower, more grounded way of moving. They return to a neutral walk.

Variation 6—Stone overhead The players mime throwing a fist-sized stone over their heads a few times, getting the feel and weight of the stone fixed in their minds, showing the weight and size by how they mime the throw and the catch. Once they have this, they toss it up three times. On the third throw, it stays hovering directly over their heads, slightly forward. The adviser reminds the players, "Don't look up. Just keep the awareness of the stone in your mind." The players do simple actions—walking, sitting in a chair, putting on a coat, etc.—while maintaining the image of the stone hovering overhead, placing their center in the stone above.

Now they imagine the stone dropping back into their hands. They toss it up again, let it hover, take a few steps, then let it drop. Repeat this a few times. The players mark the difference in their physicality when the stone is hovering above and when its in their hand. The players return to a neutral walk.

Variation 7—The threat A chair is set center stage. Two players stand behind a flat, one has a weapon (e.g. a wooden club) in her hand, the other enters, goes to the chair, sits in it, makes eye contact with the audience for a few moments, stands and exits. During this sequence, the player onstage keeps the image in their mind of someone behind them with a weapon. The player with the weapon allows herself and the weapon to be seen from behind the flat but does not attempt to do anything other than be seen; she doesn't make any threatening gestures or faces. The adviser can side coach, reminding the player about the person with the weapon, lurking behind them. The player onstage shouldn't look back at any time. They act out a simple scene with his center of focus outside themselves, on something threatening behind them. The players switch roles and repeat the exercise.

This can be done with any simple action: tying a shoe, putting on a coat, sweeping the stage, etc.

Advice

- "What energy, emotions or character does each version of the weight suggest?"
- "Can you use the shifts of the stone for comic effect? For example, play with shifting your center around your body to show drunkenness. You'll appear drunk as you tilt right, left, backwards and forwards, but have more control over how you move." (See Charlie Chaplin in *One A.M.*)
- "How does it feel to carry out a simple task while feeling threatened, your center of focus tinged with fear? Can you be conscious of it

without holding too much tension? Let the point of focus create a heightened awareness, an expressive apprehension in your body."

SCULPTURES

This exercise is a good combination of observation and ensemble play as participants learn to memorize and imitate the physicality of others; they encourage the players to find ways to consciously reshape their bodies. These impressions could be used to create tableaus in scenes, or a chorus effect, with a large group of the players all assuming similar poses. It's also good for duo, trio or ensemble clown scenes, using imitation to make fun of partners, develop complicity, as well as physical play.

Props: Enough sturdy chairs for all the players.

Variation 1—Chair sculptures The players form groups of five. Each group sets a circle of chairs separate from the other groups. They place themselves in a physical relationship to the chair. For example, sit on it, drape over it, lie under it, curl up in a ball on the seat, etc. They give these "sculptures" their names. For example, if Johnny stands on the chair with his arms open wide, that sculpture is, "the Johnny." Each player does their pose for their group, the others memorize it by imitating it, and remembering its name. Once all the sculptures have been learned, the players walk around the chairs. One person in each group is chosen to call out a name. "The Johnny!" The players choose any chair in their circle and strike the pose. If a player forgets the sculpture, he gets on a chair and adjusts his body as he gets visual clues from the rest of the group for the sculpture. When all have recreated the sculpture, the game begins again. The person whose name was called—Johnny in this case—now calls out the name of a different sculpture.

Variation 2—Body sculptures Same as above but without chairs and with the whole group. Each player creates a sculpture with their body only and names it. Once each player has shown their sculpture and they've been imitated and memorized by the group, they walk around the room. The adviser calls out a name, "The Jane!" and the players strike the pose created by Jane.

Advice

- "Don't stress if you can't recall each pose: make a choice and adjust as you pick up clues from the group. Enjoy the game of it, the play with the ensemble remembering together!"
- "Consciously choose to use the group to remember the pose not the originator."

THE BODY MASK

A body mask is a strong physical pose that creates a full body expression of an energy. For example, imagine you were going to sculpt the emotion jealousy, how would it look to you and how would you shape—sculpt it—with your body? Finding a strong body mask can help you fully inhabit an energy; you can return to the body mask at any moment if you feel you're losing the energy; you can use it to clarify the energy for the audience (especially when playing in a large venue or within a group); you can use it for comic effect, returning to the body mask after losing yourself in an emotional outburst.

Strong energies that are habitual for a clown can each have a body mask. They can be used to create strong visuals that are like still photos of the energy. These moments of stillness are crucial to good comic timing: it gives the audience—and the players—time to focus, attune their eyes to the action, gather and aim their energy towards the next moment. These body masks enable the players to effect pauses in the action without stopping the play: though still, the body masks are dynamic and revealing.

Props: Mirrors large enough to observe the entire body. Or have the players observe each other and give feedback.

Variation 1—Sculpted energy The players stand before the mirrors (or partners). The adviser calls out an energy. For example, fear, sadness, anger, joy, lust, greed, defeated, victorious, impatient, confused, suspicious, proud, awestruck, paranoid, etc. The players assume a strong pose that they feel best expresses the energy. The pose is not frozen but held: a player can make small adjustments, move their head or eyes, and use their breath. She holds a strong *attitude,* present but not overly animated. The adviser side coaches, encouraging the players to take note of all parts of the body, "Are your hands expressing pride as well as your face? What about your proud buttocks, your arrogant elbows, your conceited belly, your superior spine? Are all parts of your body working together to express the energy?" When the players have found a strong body mask, using all parts of their body (including their breath), the adviser tells them to let it go, gives them a moment to breathe and relax, then calls out a new energy.

The adviser reminds the players to think about their spine: how does its shape help to create a strong body mask? The players should work to keep the energy flowing when holding a pose, don't tense up or lock the limbs; stay alert and relaxed in the pose and remember to breathe. The players explore a number of body masks for different energies, then the adviser calls them out and claps after naming each one: the players go through each pose, switching to a new one with each clap.

The adviser can have the players try different body masks for the same energy. For example, how many different body masks can a player create to express joy? Is there one that expresses the energy best for their body type?

If mirrors aren't available, have the players partner up and the adviser calls out an energy: one player sculpts himself while the other gives suggestions to help make the body mask more expressive.

Variation 2—Energy variations Four people get up in front of the class. The adviser calls out an energy, for example, "Love!" The players assume a body mask of love, all at the same time. He says, "Let it go" and the players go back to a neutral stance. He calls out another energy, and the exercise continues. The benefit of this variation is that observers have a chance to see how the same emotion manifests itself on different faces, different bodies, and how they choose to sculpt it.

Variation 3—Levels and contrasts The players continue to explore body masks but play with contrasts. For example, be afraid but be tall and upright. Be proud but cower. Be angry while sitting down, etc. What do these contrasts feel like, for example, to be proud yet bent over, the body pulling inwards?

Variation 4—Outburst The players assume the body mask of an energy (the adviser can choose one for them if she feels there is something the class or an individual need to work on). The players imagine the energy building until their body explodes with it from the still pose to a series of expressive gestures and movements that convey the explosion of the energy in action. After a few seconds, they snap back into the same body mask/still pose they began with. The players explore this exchange between explosive, uninhibited movement expressing an energy, and then a still, subdued pose of the energy, for comic and dramatic effect. The adviser asks them to play with different energies, their body masks, and their outbursts. The outburst can be triggered by seeing another player, an object in the room, or for no reason other than the energy needs to express itself in action.

Advice

- "What is the strongest body mask of the energy that can be expressed with your body? Ask others for feedback."
- "Can you use your clothes to enhance the sculpture, to express the energy more effectively? Can you use your hair, the position of your feet, the shape of your spine, etc. Stay aware of all details including shape, color, and body line."
- "Beware of holding too much tension. *Support* yourself in the pose, don't lock into it."
- "Stay aware of your breath, how it's affected by the different energies and how it expresses itself in movement."

VISUALIZATION

Ringling Bros. and Barnum & Bailey veteran circus clown Frosty Little once had me walking around with gravel in my shoes because he wasn't satisfied with how I was miming walking on hot coals (thankfully he didn't make me walk on hot coals). Imagining environments you must pass through helps to develop physical expressiveness and encourages a more inventive use of the body. This can be used in scenes not only to evoke a setting but to create comic interaction between the players. For example, two clowns carry trays full of dishes in contrasting ways, one as if walking on ice, the other like they're trudging through mud. This exercise begins the study of consciously connecting the body and its movement with the playing space.

Props: Any props needed for Variation 3.

Variation 1—Environments The players move around the space imagining they are walking through different environments called out by the adviser. For example, on a slack rope, barefoot on hot sand or on gravel, slick shoes on an icy road, slogging through quicksand, lifting their feet out of sticky, heavy mud, pushing their whole body through Jell-O, walking through a bitterly cold landscape with the snow blowing around them, through a baking hot desert, through a strong, blustery wind at the edge of a hurricane, etc. They should be encouraged to use the entire space, along the walls, onto levels, down near the floor, etc. It's not charades: the environments are meant to inspire movement choices, not to enact a scene. For example, if the environment is a slack rope, the players don't need to walk in a straight line but should move as if they are trying hard to stay balanced.

Variation 2—Environments on a grid The players move through environments as above but in a designated area in a grid pattern, walking in straight lines. All changes in direction are taken at sharp 90° angles (e.g. even when walking on slippery ice).

Variation 3—Environments with a task Same as Variation 1, but the players perform a simple task. For example, walking towards a chair and sitting in it while barefoot on hot sand, sweeping during a strong, blustery wind at the edge of a hurricane, carrying a cup of water on an icy floor, carrying a cardboard box while walking through heavy mud, etc. The players should use actual props.

A variation can be added as follows:

- Take a scene—one that the players have devised or from a known play or story—and put it in a certain environment. Then play it in an environment on a grid, then give the players props to handle.

Advice

- "Stay aware of how the different environments affect the quality of your movement. Develop it, make it more eccentric, expressive."
- "How do the environments and the movement they inspire, affect your breathing?"
- "Does moving on a grid through the environments affect the quality of your movement and your breathing in ways different from moving

randomly as in Variation 1?"
- "How do each of the environments make you feel, and can you express that in movement?"
- "How can visualizing an environment help create eccentric movement and comic play, not just illustrate or mime a specific environment?"

THE FIVE ELEMENTS

Over the years, working as a teacher and director, I have witnessed too many students and actors simply walk onstage and move quickly to their act or scene, starting it before I had a chance to get to know who they were. I saw a huge wasted opportunity: their entrance, and the movement to the space where they would do their act or play their scene, was the perfect time to introduce themselves visually and physically, hint at what they were feeling (or playfully disguising it), and create suspense—or least an expectation—about what they were going to do.

Based on my reading of a number of physical theater practitioners, I developed the Five Elements, breaking down a scene or routine into five sections. I wanted to help the players clarify an act or scene, make them more aware of the physical space they were playing in, and how to use it as a partner. But most of all, to use the Five Elements to draw the audience in and expand on a player's performance, reveal something about their clown or character and the story they wanted to tell. Every part of the stage was treated as a living partner rather than just a space to move through quickly so a player could get to their act; interacting with the space is crucial to clown and physical comedy. Once the players learn the Five Elements, they should be reminded to use them any time an exercise calls for a presentation on stage.

The Five Elements are:

1 Enter
2 Move into the space
3 Present
4 Leave the space
5 Exit.

1. Enter This is the audience's first impression of the player. How they enter can make the difference between the audience being welcoming, curious, drawn to them (even if their entrance makes them uncomfortable), or uncertain, guarded or disinterested, forcing the player to work harder to connect with them once the act or scene kicks in.

A player shouldn't enter thinking, "My scene doesn't start until I hit my spot onstage." Entering starts backstage! A player doesn't enter from a void or without thought or emotion; their entrance expresses something about who they are, where they came from, and/or what they're about to do. The players should use their entrance to hint, suggest, generate interest, suspense, or tension, right from the start.

Note: A simple technique is to take four or more steps away from the point of entry onstage, so a player has time and space to get energized before they're revealed.

2. Move into the space The area between the place from where a player enters, to the spot where they'll present, is an opportunity to draw the audience towards them, tell them a bit about who they are and how they're feeling. For example, walking directly to center stage might suggest a confident player ready to put on a show! Moving in a series of straight lines and angles might suggest a regimented player who likes to follow rules. A player who sticks close to the curtain as she makes her way stage left, may strike the audience as shy, reluctant, secretive ... What would moving in wavy lines, diagonals, circles, or zigzagging hint at? Each shape will suggest a different story to an audience, so by the time a player starts the main act or scene, the audience already knows something about them.

Note: In the entrance and moving into the space the players can toy with the audience, using this time to get familiar with them, especially if they are offering an eccentric or surreal act. The time a player takes for this will depend on the act or scene, the style of the show and the performance space.

3. Present This is the main body of the act or scene. The players have introduced themselves with their entrance, given the audience a bit of info about who they are as they moved into the space, and now the crowd is sitting back (or on the edge of their seats) ready to get to know them better. The players usually rush to this moment—and sometimes that's for the best—but even in rushing to present, they should stay conscious of the elements before this and use them to their advantage.

The players should consider where they present as well. Performing at the front edge of the stage might appear desperate, begging for attention. A player who strides directly to center stage, may express that she's confident, ready to play. One who presents far upstage may appear suspicious or afraid of the crowd. The stage—and the scenic elements on it—should be imagined as a huge frame: where do the players place themselves in order to create the best stage picture and give the audience information about them and their scene?

4. Leaving the space This usually happens quicker than moving into the space. The act is over and the player wants to get offstage before the audience stops clapping. But they can use the leaving to play with the applause, starting to leave but coming forward for more. They could exit with the same movement pattern they entered with—their presentation or scene hasn't changed their energy. Or they could move off with a totally new pattern: She entered in straight lines, left in wavy ones. She went from regimented to loose and crazy!

In physical comedy, the players use their bodies in relation to the space, to tell a story visually. When we watch a performer onstage, we may think the information about her is all coming from her face or voice, but we're reading her body language as well – a body in conversation with the performing space—whether we realize it consciously or not. The players make it conscious by using the Five Elements in informative and intriguing ways.

5. Exit This is the goodbye, the last impression the audience will have of a player. I've heard it said, "Make a great entrance and a great exit, and the crowd won't care what you did in between." That's not completely true, but it says something about the importance of how the players bookend their presentation. Leave them wanting more! Or satisfied/happy/thrilled they got to spend time with the performer. Does the player pause before leaving, or race off? Do they take a running leap, cartwheel offstage, hurl the curtain aside as they exit, or slink off slowly, impishly, like they don't want to go but they must?

The following exercises use the Five Elements, explore variations, and encourage a deeper understanding of how to integrate them into an act or scene.

Props: Stage flats or curtains for entrances and exits, miscellaneous props.

Variation 1—Punctuation Three players wait backstage. The first player takes a deep breath, enters, then exhales. They inhale again, move into the space to where they will present, then exhale. They inhale, then exhale as they present (keep this simple—bow, wave, smile, clap, jump up, etc.). They inhale again, move towards where they will exit, exhale. Inhale, have a final moment with the audience, and exit on the exhale. The breathing will help with timing, separating each element (for player and audience), and act as punctuation. Each breath can be different – a fast inhale followed by a slow exhale; a series of short in-breaths followed by a long, full exhale, etc.

Variations can be added as follows:

- The punctuation could be a sound instead of the breath. For example, the player comes to a complete stop, then clicks her tongue, claps her hands or stomps her foot, to mark the end of each element.
- The punctuation could be marked with a word. For example, the player comes to a complete stop, and says, "Yo" or "Wow" at the end of each element.
- The punctuation could be marked with a movement. For example, the player comes to a complete stop, then crosses her arms, does a little dance, or does a karate kick, at the end of each element.

Each player's turn is short, simple, they don't make a scene out of it, or try to be clever or funny. It's a chance to practice these elements by separating them in a conscious way. The adviser may ask a player to pause a little longer in the present, letting the audience take her in, get to know her visually before leaving the space.

Note: *We all have a certain energy even when we are trying to be relaxed and nondescript—our version of normal. But our bodies tell a story even at rest and that story is brought into greater relief onstage. An audience will ask questions about a player, wonder who they are, what their history is: Why does he walk that way? Why does she hold so much tension in her shoulders? Why doesn't he swing his arms when he walks? Why is their face so open? A player needs to understand what he suggests to an audience when he is just "being himself." He needs to discover what impression his face and body give when he is making no effort. Much can be learned from having the players move through the Five Elements without pretense or performance. Observers should feel free to take notes, give feedback: what impressions did they get from their partner's simple scene?*

Variation 2—minimum-to-MAXIMUM The players go through the Five Elements expressing an energy. They build it—go from minimum-to-MAXIMUM—as they progress through the sequence. For example, the energy is frustration:

1. **Enter:** Player struggles to get through the curtain. Once past it he holds a body mask of frustration.
2. **Move into the space:** His frustration builds as he paces around the stage: he can't decide where to present.
3. **Present:** He tries to do a dance routine but can't recall the steps and gets more frustrated (the present becomes a dance of frustration).
4. **Leave the space:** He starts to go but things get in his way—he trips, can't find the opening in the curtain, can't believe he forgot the dance steps!
5. **Exit:** He gets tangled in the curtain, pulls it open further as he stumbles off. There's the sound of a crash backstage, a final shout of his frustration peaking.

Advice

- "How does the energy affect each element? A joyful person might throw aside the curtain to reveal himself when he enters, pull it downstage to get more play out of it as he moves into the space, open his arms wide as if to embrace the entire audience in the present. As he leaves the space, he does a cartwheel, rolls himself in the curtain, letting it embrace him as he exits."
- "In a minimum-to-MAXIMUM exercise, always increase the intensity and energy. Keep moving towards an explosion!"
- "Don't tense up in order to peak. As you move towards the explosion and get bigger, try to go deeper. You can choose to go BIG yet stay cool, become more focused and passionate about what you are doing. Escalate and *expand* the experience."
- "It does not have to get manic or panicky. It can also be quiet, tender, sad or rapturous. It just needs to build within the energy that's chosen."

LOOKING OUT

There are different schools of thought about when a clown makes eye contact with the audience. Some say the clown should always be looking at the audience; this keeps them connected to what the clown is doing. I prefer that the clown uses this technique sparingly, choosing her moment to bring the audience in with her eyes. For example, use the eyes to ask a question, "Did you see that?" Or to encourage a response from the audience at opportune moments. The eyes are used to share the clown's struggle, joy, mischief, curiosity, etc., either when those energies peak—a place in the scene when the clown experiences unbridled joy, for example—or glancing out as the energy builds to encourage the audience to join the clown on the journey.

If overused, the looking out risks distancing the clown from the world she's creating onstage. It may appear that she's not fully invested in what's going on in her world, too distracted by the audience, or too much in need of their attention. If the clown is fully engaged with what she's doing, if she commits to it, that commitment will draw the audience in. "What has her so enthralled?" they ask. "When will she share it with us?" This can build curiosity, suspense, and the pleasure of being let in on a secret once the clown finally does look out. The eyes then become a powerful tool to tease, charm and invite the audience in, rather than a constant call for attention or approval.

Below are a number of variations on using the eyes. Depending on the size of the class and the time available, you can let a few of the players try one of the variations then move on to another group, or choose to have everyone try each one. They are meant to be explorations, not scenes: the players observe the effect it has on an audience (both when they're onstage and while watching others) and consider how they'll use this technique in an act or scene.

The deliberate use of the eyes is a simple way to connect player to audience, and when used in conjunction with the Five Elements, connect the audience to the action and the playing space.

Props: Two stage flats or curtains to create wings with a gap of four meters between them, miscellaneous props (see Variations 3–5 for ideas).

Variation 1—Group rounds Three players wait backstage. They enter together, move across the stage and exit (use the Five Elements). As they run this, the trio *never makes eye contact* with the audience, from the moment they enter until they exit.

They enter again, this time *always looking out* at the audience. They enter with eyes looking out, make contact with the crowd right away, and keep looking at them until they're completely offstage (even if it means scrambling to find the exit because they must not look to see where it is).

They enter again, but the trio choose to make eye contact only once during the journey. They tune into each other, so they all look out at the same moment. It can be at any time—as soon as they enter, while crossing the stage, or just before they exit.

For the final round, the trio chooses a combination with the eyes. For example, two players looking out, the third never making eye contact with the audience. Or one player looking out, the others never making eye contact. One looking out, one choosing her moment, the third never making eye contact. They stay this way as they run the Five Elements.

Variation 2—Group task Three players wait backstage. They choose a simple task, for example, carrying a box, pushing something across the stage, arranging chairs, sweeping, etc. They enter, carry out the task as they cross the stage, then exit. The first time they cross they never look out. They exit and enter again, always looking out at the same time performing their task. They exit and enter again, this time choosing one moment to look out *as a group*. For the final round, the trio chooses a combination with the eyes as explained in Variation 1.

Note: *The entrance, cross and exit should be short, the task, simple. Let the rounds of enter-cross-exit, with the variations on looking, help develop the relationship, the activity, and the play with the audience. The players mustn't force anything to happen but let the scene and their relationship grow out of the progression of how the eyes are used over the three scenes.*

Variation 3—The observer One player sits on a stool or chair placed center stage. Three players wait backstage, each with a prop. They use the Five Elements for this exercise. The first player enters holding his prop in any way he likes with whatever energy he chooses to play with – he's angry, sad, feeling romantic, confused, etc. He decides how he will use his eyes in relation to the audience—never looking, always looking, choosing the moment (this stays the same throughout the cross), but he never looks at the Observer. The Observer keeps her eyes on the player the whole time until he exits. She then looks out at the audience.

As the Observer watches the player cross, she can ask herself one or all of these questions: Who? What? Why? Throughout the scene, a questioning, curious look plays across her face as she observes the player. She follows him with her eyes until he exits, then turns to the audience and shares her response with them. For example, she starts laughing, cries, smiles, or curses, calls him an idiot. She might keep her face expressionless, do a series of takes to different people in the audience, or look around the playing area in a mightily confused way. Her reaction can alter our perception of a player no matter what they're doing in the cross. It can create a story that is shared between Observer and audience.

The next player waits five counts after the preceding player exits, then repeats the sequence. Each player makes three crosses using the eyes in a distinct way each time. The players can enter then exit to a different place or exit the same way they entered.

Variation 4—Group task with observer Same as Variation 1, but with an Observer. She watches a trio cross and shares her reaction with the audience after they exit. The trio enters twice more, using their eyes in a different way each time.

Note: *Nothing needs to be added by anyone in the beginning—the players don't try to be clever or funny or make it a scene. Just enter, cross and exit, with the Observer taking it all in and sharing her response with the audience. This is an exercise in understanding how a repeating pattern can help to establish a setting, a rhythm. When the pattern is then altered, we see potential: the players start to express something about themselves by how they look or react, relationships are suggested, a story starts to develop. Patterns draw the audience in, create a structure they can tune into (like the melody in a song). The simplicity of this exercise encourages them to use their imaginations, to participate in the development of the scene and the trio's relationship. It's important that the players understand and experience the value of simplicity and how to build a scene slowly, leaving space for the audience to join in and fill in details.*

Variation 5—Player and observer Two players wait backstage; each one has a prop. The Observer sits onstage in a chair. The first player enters with their prop looking to the audience only, the Observer looks at him as he enters. At some point, the player with the prop turns to the Observer, they see each other. They both take it to the audience, then back to one another. The player keeps his eyes on the Observer as he crosses to her with his prop. He can move towards her any way he wants, threatening, seductive, joyful, confused, afraid, weird, passive, etc. As the player crosses to her, the Observer looks at the audience: she keeps her eyes on them as the player comes closer. The Observer then chooses her moment to look at the player. When she does, he freezes, looks out at the audience, then crosses to the exit without looking at the Observer who keeps her eyes on him. Just before he steps offstage, he looks back at her. She looks at the audience. The player exits. Another player enters with his prop and repeats the sequence. When he exits, the first player comes out again. They repeat this a few times, playing with different ways of reacting to the looks and seeing what develops in terms of relationships and story, but never forcing anything, just using the Five Elements, their movements, and the looks.

Note: *The adviser can call out the sequence to help the players remember it.*

Advice

- "Develop the comic and dramatic possibilities of a scene simply by how you use your eyes to share moments with your partners and the audience."
- "As an audience member, note your reactions to each use of the eyes: how do they connect you to the trio? How do they make you feel about them as a group and individually?"
- "As players onstage, how do you feel your relationship with the audience changes with each use of the eyes? How does it affect the Five Elements or the task?"
- "This starts as technical work, focusing on the looks and the Five Elements without trying to create a scene. As you repeat it, relationships and ideas will come to you. Trust the simplicity and pattern building of the set up and its variations to suggest more imaginative play."

Summary

This section introduced two important concepts: Using the body in a sculptural way to express emotions and finding eccentric ways of posing and moving, as well as recognizing the physical space as a living partner in the clown's play, finding ways to move through it more effectively and using it to introduce the clown to the audience. This is furthered explored in Sections 5–10 where it is combined with solo, duo, trio, and ensemble devising.

Imagining the space as a living partner is now carried forward into doing the same with props. The focus is narrowed down to something that can be held in the hand, more easily manipulated by a clown because of its size and proximity. The players continue to utilize the Five Elements in the next section, adding the interaction with the prop to how they use the space. The addition of a prop gives the players the opportunity to expand and elaborate on the visual play they discovered in the previous section, searching for ways to increase the emotional and visual impressions of a scene.

Figure 4.1 Windy Wynazz: Prop play. *Photo credit: Eric Gillet/Shoot That Klown.*

4

Prop Play

The Prop Whisperer

As part of the physical theater duo nakupelle, I helped create the show *La Boutique*. We set the play in a store selling expensive clothes. This allowed us to explore both the playful and oppressive aspects of the fashion industry.

Figure 4.2 Michael Hayes meets the singing chicken.
Photo credit: Eric Gillet/Shoot That Klown.

We wanted to challenge ourselves as actors: the two of us would play eight characters and bring to life a dog puppet. There would be lightning-fast changes of masks and costumes, dance numbers, slapstick comedy, and barrier illusions. Multiple entrances and exits—into and out of dressing rooms, up and down elevators, through mirrors—meant we had to tightly choreograph scenes to give us time to change from one character to another, and help the audience make sense of a story which included ghosts, shapeshifting, elements of the supernatural, and of course, clothes shopping.

Because we were wearing full face masks throughout the performance, neither of us would speak. Nor would we add a voiceover to help the audience follow the story. We were determined to tell a complex tale *visually*. The play we discovered with the props had elements of juggling, object manipulation, clowning, partner dance, and puppetry. We treated the props—clothes racks, hangers, costumes, mannequin parts, feather dusters, clothes and coats—as text, each object adding "words" to the story depending on how we handled them.

Because they're primarily visual performers, clowns have always had a special relationship with props. Through their inventive play, every object has the potential to be transformed into a collaborator, adversary, or friend, to help tell stories, and reveal more about the clown. And in transforming the prop, the clown is also transformed, physically and visually, as well as mentally and emotionally.

Think of Charlie Chaplin's cane, Avner the Eccentric's napkin which becomes a mask which becomes a meal, George Carl with his microphone, coat and harmonica, Jacques Tati and the props and machinery of the modern world, Bill Irwin sucked under the stage curtain, Buster Keaton with everything he came into contact with! This is the clown playing with the visible, physical world, reimagined as comic, fantastic, surreal, and absurd.

Players working in clown and physical comedy, need to know how to transform inanimate objects and make them come alive. Proper technique and a spirited imagination are crucial. The exercises below will help students develop the tools and the mindset that allows them to make use of props to develop comic moments, tell a story and create a world where everything is alive and at play. Because props are so essential to clowns, these are some of the most important exercises in this book. The players should be encouraged to practice and work with props constantly, seeing them as living collaborators in their play. The exercises will help the players understand the possibilities in the transformation and manipulation of props, bringing them to life as a partner, a puppet, or a mask.

PROP AROUND

> I've worked with actors who get nervous at the mere mention of props and for good reason: a malfunctioning prop, or one that is handled badly, can completely undermine even the most riveting performance. Carlo Mazzone-Clementi, founder of Dell'Arte International in California, once said, "Master your props or they will eat you!" The variations below get the players used to handling, manipulating and sharing prop play with each other, before moving on to more involved and imaginative interactions in the exercises that follow.

Props: Balls (tennis balls, beanbags or balled up newspaper wrapped with masking tape), objects of different weights and sizes (not so large they can't be held in one hand), two or more hula hoops, two durable hats (felt juggling hats work well).

Variation 1—Ball pass The players stand in a circle. Each holds a ball in their right hand. The adviser calls, "Go"! The players pass the balls from their right hand to their left, then to the right hand of the person next to them. They start slow, then speed up. The adviser says "Reverse." The players pass balls the opposite way. After a few rounds, the players switch places, so they pass to new partners.

Note: *If the group is large, break them into smaller groups of seven to ten.*

Variation 2—Mix up Same as above but use a mix of objects: balls, hats, sticks, stuffed toys, a small towel, etc. They need to be small enough or easy to grip and be passed with one hand.

Advice

- "Focus on timing: pass objects hand-to-hand and then to your partners in perfect sync."
- "Focus on rhythm: use your movements—the hands passing, flexing in the knees in time with the passes—to keep the objects in play."
- "Use rhythmic sound: clap the hand and ball together when you pass the ball between your own hands (if a ball is dropped, clap hands to

keep the timing until someone gets the ball back in play). Also try vocalizing a beat."
- "If an object is dropped, maintain the rhythm of movement and sound, pick up the drop and put it back in play. Don't just stop! Play with the disruption caused by the drop, keep the rhythm going, and work together to get the object back into the circle."
- "What's the best way to hold and pass the objects? Have everyone try with their receiving hand open, keeping their eyes on the hand of the person they're passing to so they can focus on handing off the object cleanly. This way the players shouldn't have to look at their own receiving hand."

Variation 3—Pass the hoop Groups of seven to ten players join hands and form a circle. Two players release their hands and the adviser places a hula hoop over the arm of one player. They rejoin hands. The players pass the hoop along arms and over bodies, stepping through it as they pass the hoop around the circle four times, and back to its starting point, without letting go of their hands.

Variation 4—Hoop and hat pass Same as above, with a hat placed on the floor in front of one player where the hoop starts. After the hoop goes around four times, the players set it down, and the player nearest to the hat puts it on his head. The player to his left reaches over with her right hand and puts the hat on her own head. The player to her left reaches over with his right hand and puts the hat on his own head. This pattern continues until the hat goes around the circle and back to where it started, four times.

Note: *The next player always takes the hat with their right hand when it's being passed in a clockwise direction, never the left. Maintaining the integrity of this movement is crucial when the variations get more complicated.*

Variation 5—Hoop and hat competition Groups of seven to ten players join hands, form a circle and are given a hoop to pass. The adviser calls "Go!" The first team to get the hoop around the circle four times and back to its starting point, wins.

A variation can be added as follows:

- The first team that gets both the hoop then the hat around the circle four times and back to its starting point, wins.

Variation 6—Alternate object The adviser assembles different props. For example, a hat, a large ball, a broom, a thick rope tied to form a hoop to go around the neck, a small cardboard box. The players form groups of five or more. One player starts with all the objects: hat on head, broom lying on the floor, rope hoop around their neck, box on the floor in front of them. Each object must be passed in a different way. For example, the hat is passed in a clockwise direction by having each player take it off the head of player to his right with his right hand then put it on his head with the same hand. The ball is passed to the right using both hands. The broom is taken with the right hand (when all objects are traveling clockwise), passed to the left hand, then passed to the next player's right hand. The rope is lifted off the neck by the player wearing it and placed over the neck of the player to his right. The box is scooted left to the next player by pushing it with the *outside* of their left foot. Run this a few times until the players get the hang of it.

A variation can be added as follows:

- Make it a competition: on a cue from the adviser, teams pass the objects around the circle four times. The first group to get all the props back to where they started, arranged on the starting player in the same way as when they began, wins.

Note: *This kind of object play could be used in a scene to pass props down a line of clowns standing shoulder to shoulder or exchanging objects in what appear to be random ways but are actually choreographed group movements.*

Advice

- "The method of passing should stay the same! This forces you to focus on different parts of your body from the head to the feet, while staying connected to your partners, the exchanging of the objects, and the timing of each pass. Don't cheat! It's a group juggling act with odd-shaped objects that must be passed in a certain way and in sync."

PROP IMPROV

This game is an opportunity for the players to experiment with how an object is used, transform it into something else, and generate

> ideas that can then be developed into acts or used in larger scenes. The variations allow everyone to get involved in creating material for solo or ensemble scenes. They can generate an extensive list of ideas for each prop that can then be used when devising new work or enhancing existing material. It's a good introduction to the more focused prop work explored in Sections 6–10.

When working with props I imagine them in eight ways (some props may require modification):

- **Prop used for what it is:** A broom is used to sweep the floor.
- **Prop used wrong:** The small end of a broom handle—or the side of it—is used to push wads of paper into a dustpan.
- **Prop malfunction:** The head falls off the broom, the handle keeps bending while sweeping, the bristles keep falling out until there's only one left.
- **Prop acts unexpectedly:** Sweeping in one direction sends wads of paper flying off in the other. A glass filled with water is upended and a lemon falls out. A silk handkerchief is stuffed in a pocket and when pulled out, it's a sock.
- **Prop wrongly made:** The bristles of the broom are made of crepe paper. A wine glass is made of paper so when wine is poured in, it falls apart. A chair is made of cardboard so thin it won't hold any weight.
- **Prop to show off a skill:** Balancing, juggling, prop manipulation, an aid to an acrobatic trick, body contortion, a show of strength, etc.
- **Prop transformed:** A broom becomes a golf club, a plunger becomes a stethoscope, a chair becomes a moose's antlers, a cardboard box becomes a car, etc.
- **Prop as friend or foe:** The prop is treated as an animate, lively being, a friend, foe, conspirator, or collaborator. It's brought to life so it appears to have eyes, ears, it can talk back, sing, throw a tantrum, be danced with, etc. (this one requires training in puppetry techniques).

Notes on prop play: *A player will spend time with a human partner in order to know how they think, respond, what their physical abilities are, etc. Through this interaction, the players learn to trust each other and find out what's possible when they play together. It's the same with a prop: the players must get to know it with all their senses, explore its texture, shape, the sounds it can make, how it handles when lifting it, throwing it to a partner, all the skillful* things that can be done with it, what can go wrong when playing with it. The more time a player spends with their props, the more it will suggest to them, and the more imaginative the play with the object will be.

Working with props requires the same disciplined practice as learning a skill. And skills training such as juggling, sleight-of-hand magic, puppetry or acrobatics, can enhance prop play: juggling helps a player learn to focus on many things at once; magic teaches misdirection, useful in prop play as well as physical comedy; puppetry helps the player bring a prop to life; acrobatics lends itself well to slapstick with props, or a skills display featuring object manipulation.

Prop jam session Tables are set upstage with enough room between them so the players can move around them on all sides. Center stage is kept clear. Props of all shapes, sizes, and functions are set on tables, but nothing fragile, with sharp edges, complex machinery, or anything valuable; they must be able to take some abuse. Three players stand next to the tables. The first one chooses a prop, steps forward and does something with it according to any of the eight ways mentioned above. The action is brief—a visual idea, a quick display with the prop, etc.—then the player steps back to let others have a go. They keep offering these solo ideas with props until the adviser calls time. A new trio has a go.

A variation can be added as follows:

- When a player presents their solo idea with the prop, the other two can join in with their objects to create a short duo or trio scene.

Note: *The players should bring in props they're working with to see what sort of ideas others come up: this is like a writers' jam session but explored through action, with everyone coming up with proposals, searching for what can be done with the objects.*

Advice

- "Let the props be catalysts for developing play, creating new possibilities, telling stories."
- "Certain props have more resonance or value to an audience. Treat a violin roughly, and you might turn people off. Brandish a machete and the audience might feel uncomfortable. That's not to say you shouldn't treat a violin roughly or brandish a machete, just be aware of a prop's significance to your audience and how you might toy with their associations."

- "Don't be afraid to go with the obvious: it may act as a stepping-stone towards more inventive play, and it keeps ideas flowing."
- "Notice the difference between you transforming the object (forcing it to conform to what you want it to do), and the object transforming you (as you explore the object, it suggests a way it would like to be used). This is an important difference: the second approach opens you up to the moment, encourages you to relate not only with the object but with the audience. You learn to take risks, and it increases your powers of observation: you search the *object* for inspiration rather than the inside of your head."
- "It's an exploration so allow yourselves time for invention. Don't let the pressure to come up with something clever or funny, stifle you. In the pauses, breathe, stay relaxed, use the time to focus your mind and the audience's attention on what you're exploring."
- "Take notes while watching others, develop a list of what can be done with a certain prop; it will come in handy in an improv and when devising. If someone does something you like, try it yourself, expand on the idea."

PROP ME

Giving focus to props with any part of the body is one of the simplest ways of showing its value and its relationship to a player. It's an introduction, "Say hello to this thing. Meet my friend. Take a look at what I have in my hand." It can also say, "I hate this thing. It scares me! What is this?!"

Giving a prop this moment of introduction or drawing attention to it at any moment in an act or scene, helps establish a relationship between player and prop, and brings it to life. These moments give the prop value, encouraging the audience to do the same; they see the object as a character in and of itself and begin to wonder how this mysterious being will respond as the scene plays out. Good prop play adds invention and intrigue to any scene.

In this exercise, the players explore the way the prop is held in relation to the body, the energy they express while holding it, and what that says to the audience about their feelings for the prop.

Props: Miscellaneous props set on a table, music, and player, wall-length mirrors.

Variation 1—Prop vogue The players choose a prop and gather in front of the mirrors or have them partner up, present for each other, and give feedback as they explore ways of presenting the prop to an audience. For example, they keep their eyes on the prop as if hypnotized by it, or they gesture to it with their free hand. They explore ways of holding the prop, so it's framed by their stomach or chest, an arm or both legs. They could frame it between two different body parts such as their hand and their head, the crook of their elbow and the side of their hip. Or they can use their clothes, pulling open their coat and holding it against the material or cradling it in their shirt.

The players should present the prop with an energy : pride, seduction, deviousness, silliness, arrogance, worship, etc. The way they hold it says something about the prop and the player's relationship to it such as, *This thing is so cool* ... Or it says something about the player, *I look cool when I hold it this way.* Or it says something about the player's relationship to the prop, *I hate this thing and the way I have to hold it so you can see it.*

The players explore as many presents as possible—and look at what others are doing for inspiration—then choose five they will show. The class watches each player go through their five poses. If there's time, give feedback: What did the audience like, laugh at? What made them curious about the prop or performer, and her relationship to the object?

Advice

- "Present the prop as if you're offering it to the audience for their perusal. Give it to them as a reward. Frame it with your arms or legs. Hold it up against your hip or clenched in your fist. Lay on your back, lift your legs and set it on the soles of your feet and gesture at it with your hands. Balance it on your head as you move about. Find as many variations as possible! Contort your body, be inventive, weird, exotic, sexy, cheesy, ridiculous!"

Variation 2—Hold it The players choose a prop and decide on a way of holding it: in their hand, tucked into the crook of the elbow or knee, under the chin, clenched in their teeth, etc. Once they have a secure grip, they strike a series of dynamic poses as they move about the room showing off the prop. After a few poses, they switch the object to a new grip. This can be done by simply taking it with the hand and shifting it, or in a more eccentric manner. For example, if a stick is held in the crook of the knee, a player might do a forward roll and grab it with his hand as he comes out of the roll, shifting it to the crook of his elbow. He might bend over and take the stick from the crook of his knee with his teeth or lift the knee up and snatch it away with his hand with a dramatic flourish. The player strikes a series of poses—expressing different energies—with this new grip, then shifts the prop again.

Advice

- "How many ways can you hold the prop with different parts of your body?"
- "How many different poses can you strike while holding the prop in eccentric ways? What sort of advantages do different grips allow? How inventive can you be physically when holding the prop in an awkward grip?"
- "How dynamic or energetic can you be in your movement while holding the prop in eccentric ways?"
- "Can you make smooth transitions between different ways of holding the prop? Can you incorporate grip changes into your movement as you walk around the room?"
- "Turn your explorations into a movement or clown piece that generates interest in the prop and in your relationship to it. What are the comic and dramatic possibilities of how you hold a prop?"

Note: *Many students I've worked with forget to value the prop by showing the audience that they value it—if they don't care about it why should the crowd? If it's treated in an offhand or pedestrian way, it has no life, can tell no story, will not serve either the players or the scene. As the object work becomes more involved—especially when using skill props such as juggling clubs—the players should still present and use their props in a way that shows how they feel about them.*

PROPS AND STATUS

A prop can add visual status instantly to a player: entering with a briefcase is different than entering with a bucket. The players can go

> with the status expectations a prop endows or undermine them: the briefcase carries cleaning tools; the bucket is used to carry stacks of money.
>
> In these variations, the players explore how to use props as visual aids to express status, and how to wield them to develop, raise or lower their position in a group.

Props: A collection of various props, a table to put them on.

Variation 1—Prop it up Three or more players stand next to a table set with props on it, placed stage left or right. The first player moves from the table to the playing area with a prop, and begins an activity playing high or low status. The second player sees what the first player is doing, grabs a prop, chooses a status—higher or lower—and adds to the scene. The third player does the same. They play a short scene and go again with a new set of props. Vocal noises and sounds are allowed but no intelligible words.

An example: The first player enters with a stick and starts marching, playing a soldier on duty. A second player grabs a helmet and enters as a general, who starts ordering the soldier around. The third player enters with a chair, stands on it, places his hands together in prayer and plays a military chaplain. The trio have a brief interaction showing the hierarchy, then end the scene. Any member of the trio grabs a new prop and starts a new scene.

The scenes are short and simple. The players don't have to play for laughs. The scenes can be serious, melodramatic, scary, absurd, etc. This is about exploring the many ways status can be portrayed when using props.

A variation can be added as follows:

- Add absurdity: the players start the scene straight. For example, the first player enters with a stick and plays a soldier with a rifle. The second player is a general with a helmet, scowling at the soldier. The third player stands on chair to pray with the others as their Chaplain. After establishing the status, they introduce absurdity with the props: the soldier grabs a bucket from the table, steps inside it and uses his rifle as an oar, propelling him around the room. The general grabs a rubber duck from table and plays it as his secretary. The chaplain fashions wings out of newspaper and becomes an angel standing on a chair.

Note: *The players should keep in mind not only the potential of their chosen prop to develop the visual story, but how it imbues—or robs—them of status. A* general's helmet grants an automatic status so entering with a rubber duck risks making him look ridiculous and losing status. Then he reveals it's a hand grenade . . . .

Variation 2—Give me that Same as above but the players can trade or take away another's prop at any point. Taking the prop also takes the status so make sure the hierarchy is clear. The exchanges can be overt—the players grab what they want—or they explore tactics for getting another player to offer, lay down or drop their prop so it can be taken, along with the status. When a prop is traded or taken, the players change status to match what their partners were portraying.

For example, if the lowly soldier is marching with a stick rifle and obeying the general and his rubber duck secretary, and the chaplain comes along and takes the rifle, that player takes on the role of the soldier and treats the stick as a rifle; he doesn't change what the prop is or the role already established. The general could force the new chaplain to take his helmet, become the general and treat his rubber duck as a secretary, as the general takes the wings and becomes an angel chaplain.

In this variation, we want to see how similar ideas, props and status play change each player physically, and how they take on their partner's ideas and status and find variations with the props.

Variation 3—Give me that, change status Same as Variation 2, but when player trades or takes a prop, she can choose any status, even change her role. For example, chaplain can take the stick and turn it into a golf club, play caddy to the now higher-status soldier who decides to lord it over all as the feted golf pro. The general can offer his duck as the ball and play the greenskeeper. They play the scene with the change (or changes) of status and props, then make an exit.

Advice

- "Use your body, your gestures, your facial expressions—as well as the props you choose and how you handle them—to communicate status."
- "You are responsible for presenting a clear status choice. Your partners are responsible for reacting to it to help reveal and elaborate on your status."
- "Observe what your partners' choices are in the moment and react to them to support their choices. Try not to force your ideas on each

other but let the scene grow out of how you listen and exchange ideas and how you use the props to create ensemble play."

Summary

This section started the exploration with props that will be developed in the solo, duo, trio, and devising sections of this book, which all involve the use of objects. Learning to use props and be comfortable onstage interacting with them, has enormous value to clowns, comedians, actors, and improvisers. They can walk into any room and create material because they see the huge potential for play in the inanimate world. The work in this section aimed to help the players realize that objects will resist and antagonize them, as well as make suggestions and join in with the games a player introduces. This sense that props have a life of their own and can offer endless possibilities, can inspire, and expand a player's curiosity (and that of the audience). They'll actively search the space around them for playmates hiding in objects, and search for ways to interact with them. The next section explores this curiosity in relation to the performing space: the players look for ways to use it actively. This builds on the work done in Section 3: The Talking Body.

Figure 5.1 Mary Hicks: Curiosity. *Photo credit: Eric Gillet/Shoot That Klown.*

5
Curiosity

Odd Fellows

The building that houses Dell'Arte International in California—a place to study Physical Theater, Mask Performance, Melodrama, Clown and Commedia dell'arte—is unique. The school is in—appropriately enough—an old Oddfellows hall, the structure is made mostly of redwood and is plain looking on the outside. Despite the renovations over the years, it retains

Figure 5.2 Wayward showgirl clown Sophia Knox-Miller. *Photo credit: Eric Gillet/Shoot That Klown.*

much of its rustic, spooky charm; it's a building that feels both haunted and full of lively spirits.

As a member of the core faculty, I led a five-week study of clowning for a class of twenty-four students, which culminated in three public performances. The theater itself had been newly renovated including a huge trap door in the middle of the stage. I discovered—much to my delight—that the pit beneath the doors would accommodate all twenty-four students.

The show opened with all the clowns save one, standing in the pit, the upper half of their bodies sticking out. We covered them with a white parachute so the audience could see movement underneath the cloth but not faces or bodies. The cruel boss clown—Big Daddy—entered from backstage and pulled away the parachute revealing the students wearing masks they'd made that represented their phobias, fixations and obsessions. After antagonizing his prisoners, Big Daddy left and the clowns slowly, cautiously, climbed out of the pit and closed its doors. With Eric Satie's *Gymnopedie No. 3* playing over the speakers, they began to remove their masks, revealing the clowns underneath. They danced and played, delighted to be out of the masks and the pit. But then a slamming door was heard, and the clowns scrambled to escape: Big Daddy was back!

High up on the backstage wall was a loft space for storing lighting equipment. Working together, the clowns scaled the wall, hoisting each other up, building human pyramids to reach the high space. All twenty-three clowns stuffed themselves into the loft and pulled the doors closed. Big Daddy returned to an empty room. As he thrashed the walls and tried to climb them in his rage, he heard a noise overhead. All went silent.

Above the theater is a large classroom: its floor is the roof of the theater below. This is a small black box theater that holds about a hundred-plus people on raked seating, so the top rows are pretty close to the roof. The clowns were hiding in the classroom above the theater and Big Daddy was on the rampage. So, the clowns ran. First two, then five, then all twenty-three clowns began to run around upstairs, stomping and stamping on the wooden floor of the classroom. The audience was jolted out of their seats! They looked up: the space above their heads was alive! The crowd laughed with recognition and delight as they tried to follow the clowns escape via the sounds of their feet across the floor/roof. Meanwhile, Big Daddy had found their escape route and had gone up after them.

The clowns stampeded as one across the floor one more time, then down the wooden staircase in the hall at the back of the theater. The audience turned in their seats as clowns burst through the back entrance of the theater at the top of the raked seating, scrambled through the lighting booth, stormed down the vom, climbed over the audience's laps, and scooted between the seats, as they made their way back to the stage to hide under the parachute. Big Daddy got lost in the building as he searched for the clowns, the sounds of his seeking and his rage slowly fading. Little by little, echoing the beginning, the clowns crept out from under the huge white cloth and began to play with the crowd.

For the next hour, the clowns snuck in their routines and vignettes, entertaining the audience, while avoiding Big Daddy. Until they couldn't. He caught up with them, corralled them together, threatened to beat them and return them to the pit. Suddenly the big doors to the loading dock at the side of the stage opened and a car drove in. A real car. The clowns scrambled to escape, stuffing themselves in like the classic clown car gag, but into a vehicle that had not been modified to fit all twenty-three of them. While this mad scramble was going on—clown legs sticking out of windows and the trunk of the car—the double doors of the loading dock stayed open and people walking by on the street outside peered in, wondering what the hell was going on. The audience laughed and waved at them, some of the clowns begged them to help them escape, Big Daddy threatened them with his club. The whole building—even the street outside—became the clowns' theater because of the way we made use of the entire space and everything in it.

I love that building, the otherworldly feeling of its Oddfellow's rooms and offices. After attending the school as a student, and later teaching there for eight years, I wanted to share what I knew about it with the audience. I wanted them to feel how alive it was for me. I did that through this show, and who better to lead the audience through the building than clowns! They had the audience looking at the stage in front of them, the roof above, had them turning around in their seats to catch the clowns storming in through the back of the theater, got them peering over railings to see the clowns running down the corridors, watched them climb under the stage, drive a car into the theater. The clowns transformed the building, brought it to vivid life by recognizing and celebrating its potential as a partner in their play and making the audience feel, in the words of the Bard, "all the world's a stage."

This section begins with thoroughly taking in the space, seeking ideas and opportunities within it. It moves on to truly seeing things in the space and learning to express a relationship to what is seen. The players then connect to the public's space, invited into it by the audience themselves. The final exercises encourage the players to bring to life the space backstage.

All the work in this section seeks to blur the lines between worlds, getting the players outside the space in their own heads, revealing secret places in the shared space around them, and making visible those things in the performance space hiding in plain sight. The exercises emphasize how clowns relate to the physical world and how they make it a living partner in their play. They utilize elements of neutral mask work, physical theater, cabaret, and street performance.

SPACE ODYSSEY

> Any time I enter a space—whether for class, rehearsals or performing—I do a thorough check, studying the space in detail. This isn't just for safety reasons: in clown and physical comedy, the space and all the elements in it—from furniture and props to the very walls, ceiling and floor—should be considered partners. Every space can give a player material to work with and help connect them to their audience—especially if it's a space that's familiar to the crowd such as a school assembly room, a popular meeting place or a street in town.
>
> These variations teach the players to get to know the space, treat it in a respectful, observant way. This can help a player introduce the space to the audience in a way that is intriguing, exciting, and startling. I encourage the players to study their workspace on a daily basis: no space is static, there are always slight changes being made to it. It's alive . . .

The players study the floor, its surface, its texture, how light affects it. They take note of dents, marks, bumps, discoloration, etc. What the floor is made of, its texture: is it smooth or rough, is there a pattern in its surface, where is it uneven, etc. They open their field of vision to study more of the floor as they walk. The adviser calls an end to the exercise; the group forms a circle. Each player mentions three things they observed. "There's a dead fly caught in a web in that corner. I noticed a splash of red paint on the floor by the door. There's a scuff mark on the third step." When everyone has named three things (the players can repeat what others noticed) the exercise continues.

The players study the walls exploring them as they did the floor, first looking at details, then increasing their field of vision. The adviser calls an end to the exercise, the players form a circle, each mentions three things they observed.

The players study the ceiling lying on their backs at first. They study all they can see from one vantage point, then move to another, lie down, and study the section above. After a few changes, the adviser asks them to study the ceiling as they roam, exploring it as they did the floor and walls. The adviser calls an end to the exercise, the players form a circle, each mentions three things they observed.

The players close their eyes and visualize the whole room in their head, recalling all the details they've observed. Then they open their eyes and take in the whole room as they continue to recall the details mentioned by all players. The adviser calls an end to the exercise and asks the group the following questions:

- "When you look at the room now, do you feel more, or less comfortable?"
- "Do you feel a connection to the room or is it still just a space to work in?"
- "Did the study give you ideas about how you might use the space during class work or in performance? Name some ways you could use your discoveries."

LOOK, SEE, REACT

In physical comedy terms, a "take" is more than just a look at something: it's a game you play with how you see an object, a person, an action or a moment in a scene, and how you respond. The response not only says something about a player, but also about what they see and their relationship to it. The take is an invitation, tempting the audience to enter the player's world through something they both see and share; the object becomes a doorway and the player's reaction draws them further into their world.

A physical take is a good way to enhance any moment of discovery, so it's an important technique to learn and embody in clown and physical theater. It's a simple yet effective way of drawing an audience into a story, giving them time to join in, to make discoveries and respond to changes along with the clown, and get more deeply involved with what's happening onstage.

> Thinking of the take as a game means using the playful mind of the clown: a player physically looks at something and, in that moment, makes a deliberate choice to draw the audience's attention to it. They now have something in common: both player and audience see the object and establish a connection to it. Once the player has inspired their curiosity and has the audience wondering how she will respond, she can toy with them. She can do multiple takes, play with the amount of time between each take, vary her reactions with each take. This anticipation, this building up of curiosity as the player invites and teases with various takes, becomes part of the game between audience and player.

Props: Two stage flats or curtains to create wings with a six-meter gap between them, miscellaneous props.

Variation 1—Head takes Three players wait backstage. The adviser sets two stage flats or curtains upstage to create a left and right-side exit, then sets an object on the floor downstage. The first player enters, does a take to the object—sees it with their eyes, turns their head towards it—then exits. For this first round it's just a simple head take, the reaction is subtle. The players can cross to the opposite wing to exit or go back the way they came. The second player enters as soon as the first exits, does a take to the object, then exits. When he exits, the third player enters and does the same sequence. They continue this sequence, and with each take, develop their reaction to seeing the object, expressing different emotions, playing with how they move their head, react with their body, keeping the play subtle. This first variation is simply an introduction to this technique.

Variation 2—Directed takes Same as above, but the adviser talks the players through the variations below. She calls one out, each player tries it on three or more passes, then the adviser calls out the next one. The same trio can try all of them, or switch trios after a few variations. At the end of each take, the players exit any way they like. Keep the scenes short: it's not an act. It's a chance to practice *physically* seeing something for an audience and reacting to it.

Note: *For all variations below, the players can vocalize, preferably sounds or gibberish, not words.*

1. The eyes see it first *pulling* the head around, which then turns the rest of the body till you face the object, feet fully turned to it as well. Do it as a series of isolated moves: eyes, head, chest, full torso, arms, hips, legs, and feet. Don't rush it.
2. Do a double take: see it once, turn away, look again. Vary the timing between the takes and the reaction to seeing the object each time.
3. Do three or more takes in succession. Play with the timing between each one and the reaction.
4. You want to take but you only pause, never fully turning to look at the object. Toy with the audience: will you turn, will you see it and acknowledge that you see it? Or will you resist the desire to fully turn to the object and look at it?
5. The eyes see it, the head turns to the object but the rest of the body refuses to turn and there is a short tussle between the eye's and head's desire to investigate, and the body's desire to leave! Your body pulls you offstage, but the eyes stay focused on the object until you're completely off.
6. The take and the reaction are broad: the eyes see it and there is an exaggerated response—the whole body gets involved! Seeing the object leads to a jump, an acrobatic move, a dance, a flurry of gestures!
7. When you see the object, shrink, visibly contract inwards. You can walk off in this shrunken state, or contract so much that you must crawl off or curl up into a ball and roll off.
8. When you see the object, swell up, visibly expand, inflate like a balloon, raising your arms, spreading your legs wide, inhaling deeply. You walk, float, or stride off the stage.
9. After you take to the object, vocalize your reaction upon seeing it. The sound can be short or continued until you exit. Let the sound express how you feel about seeing the object.
10. Do a series of takes to the object that express a different emotion with each take. For example, you see it and get angry, look away, see it again and get confused, see it again and smile broadly. You can change the emotion when you turn back to the object or wait till you look away to change it.
11. Three players backstage decide on three variations of the takes. For example, each player does a cross with a simple, single take on their solo pass and then exits. On the second pass, they all do a double take. On the third pass, they contract when they see it. The trio establishes

a pattern with their first three solo crosses then breaks it for the second and third set of solo crosses.

12 Some part of the body other than the eyes "sees" the object first. For example, the index finger sees it, points, then pulls the rest of the body around to face object. Or, after the finger points, the eyes look at the finger, then the object and then the body turns. For each pass, let a different part of the body see the object—the chest, the elbow, the groin, the palms, the spine, etc. The body part is moved or pushed out towards the object first, then the rest of the body turns.

13 When the eyes see the object, isolate a single part of the body and respond with that (keeping the rest of the body still). For example, the eyes see it and the hands flutter, or the legs tremble. The choice of the body part—and the way you move it—can give us clues as to how you feel about seeing the object.

14 Do the take as soon as you enter, or wait till you walk past the object, then look. Enter quickly then slow down for the take or vice-versa. Toy with the audience's expectations by how you play with timing and rhythm in the look and the reaction.

Note: For variations 1-2, as soon as one player exits, the next one comes on. Part of the pleasure in watching this exercise is the transition between the players, how they leave the scene after seeing the object and how the next player enters on top of that energy. A series of solo scenes starts to look like a trio's act.

Variation 3—Duo and trio takes Two or three players enter together. As they cross the stage they take to the object (separately or all at once), react, then exit. The group makes three or more crosses. Play with any of the variations above. Duos or trios can improvise in the moment, choose three before they start, or the adviser calls out the takes before they enter.

Variation 4—Scene takes The players form trios, scatter about the space, and explore the variations above on their own. They choose a prop, decide on a short sequence of passes, takes, reactions and exits, rehearse it, then present it to the class. This is a chance to explore the use of takes only: the players don't handle the prop or try to make it into a longer scene. The objective is to create a short, engaging scene with just a series of crosses, takes and reactions, and to see how much can be expressed about the players, their relationship to the object, the audience and each other.

Advice

- "Enjoy the physical play—entrance, reaction, exit—without laboring it. Keep it simple and see what develops."
- "Is your reaction honest and believable, or is it just a movement of the head? Do you truly *see* the object and react in a convincing way?"
- "How does seeing the object make you feel and how can you show that in your body and face?"

IN AND OUT

> This exercise focuses on what I think is one of the most important aspects not just of clown and physical comedy, but all theater: entering the performing space. As I stated in the Introduction, curiosity is one of the defining traits of a clown. It's the same with a clown's introduction to the audience: they want to make the crowd curious about who they are, why they're coming onstage, and what they're going to do. One of the best ways to induce that curiosity is by how the clown enters the space. The adviser should emphasize the importance of a strong entrance (and exit) to the point where they become second nature. In these variations, the players make a series of entrances and exits giving them plenty of chances to explore the possibilities. The adviser should ensure that the preceding player is completely offstage—no part of them is visible, not even a coat tail—before a new player enters. Be a stickler for this! It keeps the players focused on one another rather than just obsessing about their own moment onstage.

Props: Curtains for entering from and exiting behind, or two stage flats that are moveable.

Variation 1—Body parts Three players wait backstage. The first player makes an entrance with just a part of her body. For example, she sticks her hand out from behind the flat, slaps the front of it, then pulls it back in quickly. As soon as her body part exits, the second player's body part enters. They might stick their leg out, stomp the floor repeatedly as if trying to squash a bug, then slide their foot offstage. The third player might stick his butt out from behind the flat, turn it out as if it's looking at the audience, then bump the flat as his butt hurries offstage. This continues—body parts entering and exiting—only one player at a time—until the adviser tells them to stop. Three more players give it a go.

Note: *This should be treated as an idea "jam session" with all the players offering possibilities that are open to anyone to borrow and expand on. Even if a player were to do the same bit—such as the sequence above with the hand— it would read differently. The trio could all choose to do a hand entrance three times in a row—or experiment with nothing but hand entrances—giving the audience a chance to observe the variety of options available with a single body part presented by different bodies (and different imaginations). This is a great way to build curiosity in the audience, make them wonder who is going to enter and what the rest of them looks like.*

Variation 2—Flatcurtain Three players wait backstage. The first player makes an entrance, this time stepping out with their entire body, but they must use the flat or curtain to frame their body in some way. For example, they step out and embrace the flat, pressing their body against it. They might stand with their back against its edge and try to straighten their spine, so it matches the line of the flat. They could drape the curtain across their body, wear it around their head like a shawl, or over their shoulders like a cape. They might hop onstage, then in front of the flat, so it acts as a background to frame their body, or just lean in towards the flat so it frames just their head. They could slink along the curtain or flat, pressed up against it as they sneak to the exit, etc.

They have a moment to show this image—their body in relation to the flat or curtain—then exit. The next player enters and uses the flat or curtain to frame their body. As soon as they exit, the third player goes. The trio continue this play—making multiple ins and outs, using the flat or curtain in imaginative ways, keeping each moment brief—until the adviser tells them to stop.

Note: *Anything big enough to fully hide behind—tables, blankets or sheets hung on a line, large pieces of furniture, stacked suitcases, gym mats, etc.—can be used for this exercise. Scatter them around the performance space and have the players use them for entrances and exits.*

The adviser should draw the players' attention to the actual object used for ins and outs: what can be done with the curtain, the flat, the door and its frame, a big lounge chair, a table stood on end, etc. Can a player come in under it, over it, get tangled in it, push it away to reveal themselves, fall over holding onto it, carry it to another part of the stage and then step out, rotate it until they're revealed, etc.

Advice

- "Make us curious about who's getting ready to come onstage and what you're going to do!"
- "As you watch others, take note of how the flat or curtain frames their body. Does it create a stronger image, draw more attention to them? Does it make you more curious about the clown than if they just walked immediately center stage?"
- "Interacting with the flat, curtain or scenic element in these ways draws our attention to it, animates it and turns it into a partner in your act, offering more possibilities for play with the space."
- "Use your body in inventive ways. Don't just walk in, *leap* onstage! Come in walking backwards or fall out from behind the flat. Hurl the curtain aside as if you're the king of the world! Crawl onstage, exit sliding on your back. Drag yourself on, then run off full of energy! Enter in a rage! Exit mightily confused . . . Enter pointing at everything onstage, exit as if an invisible monster is chasing you. Imagine someone has thrown you onstage! Slouch off nearly weeping. Enter as if you just discovered the secret of life! Exit as if you forgot what it was. Exhaust the possibilities."

LISTEN

Clowns are always seeking a connection to the audience. It has been said that for clowns and comedians, the audience is their ultimate collaborator: they are writer, director, and main partner in the creation of material. For the clown, the fourth wall either doesn't exist, or is easily pushed aside, so they can play the game of acting from within their own world onstage, while always ready to break out of it into the audience's world. These exercises help the players to be more aware of the crowd, to listen more acutely, to interact with them in a more direct way while at the same time, focusing on what they're doing onstage.

Props: Two stage flats or curtains for entrances and exit, miscellaneous props, cards with activities written on them (see Variation 2).

Variation 1—Big ears The players find a prop and decide on a simple task: cleaning with a feather duster, flipping a juggling club, putting on a coat and hat, folding a bedsheet, etc. They form groups of four and find space in the room to work separate from the other groups. One player performs their actions or tasks while the others observe. As they watch, observers make sounds—loud, soft and everything in between. These can be vocal—whispers, shouts, whistling, gibberish—or percussive—hitting the floor, clapping the hands, striking a box, etc. The player doing the task reacts. Observers should be cautioned not to overdo it: play with silence as well so the player has to wait, involving themselves in the task, before being interrupted by the sound.

While the player carries out their task, they keep their ears open and respond to whatever they hear.

The noises might make them fearful, confused, happy, irritable, curious, surprised, etc. This is expressed in the way they take to the sound, the expression on their face, how it changes their body, and how it changes their handling of, and their actions with, the props; the player may only pause, react and look towards the sound, then continue, or be completely thrown off, forget what they were doing, start doing something completely different with their prop. The response is brief—the player doesn't get too involved with the one who made the sound or make a scene out of the interruption; they must get back to what they're doing. The potential to be interrupted—and the rule that the player must react—keeps them attentive to the crowd and the "in-between space" between audience and player.

Variation 2—Big ears onstage Three players wait backstage, each with a prop. All others are observers. The trio enter and perform tasks with their props, all the while listening and responding to whatever they hear outside the world onstage. The players' reactions to the sounds may cause the audience to add more, or repeat ones that the players react to, encouraging them to repeat their reactions. The adviser sets a time limit of one minute then cues the trio to exit.

The difference in this variation is seeing three players reacting together and how it alters each of them separately and as a trio. They can also take to each other after responding to the sound or not look out but turn to their partners onstage as if one of them made a sound. Everything is brought into the play: the tasks, the play with the props, the play with the audience, and the relationship amongst the players onstage.

Note: The players shouldn't always react directly to the audience but instead, make everyone aware of the liminal space between the reality onstage and the audience's space. In other words, the players may look directly at the person making the noise, but other times their reactions have a curious or suspicious quality; they react but don't know the source of the sound (like hearing a noise outside of a room but not opening the door to investigate).

Variation 3—Go! No! Three players choose a task. For example, they're all cleaning the stage. They gather the props they need—brooms, dustpans, rags, etc.—and go backstage. The adviser has a series of activities written on cards. For example, playing tennis, baseball, making a pizza, musicians playing rock-n-roll or classical music, cowboys rounding up cattle, chefs cooking, etc. He shows one of these to the audience. The trio enters and begins the task of cleaning the stage. Once they establish this, they start to guess what the activity is by how they use the props. For example, the activity is playing tennis: if a player starts to use the dustpan like she's chopping wood, the audience says, "No." They continue to say "No" for as long as the trio fail to act out the activity once they start to guess at it. If a player starts to swing the dustpan in a way that suggests hitting a tennis ball, the audience say "Go." If other players join in with similar play, the audience says "Go!" louder and more often, encouraging the trio to keep guessing until they are into a full-on tennis match with the props, playing the game vigorously as the crowd shouts, "Go! Go! Go!" They can finish the scene on their own when they feel it has peaked and make an exit, or the adviser cues them to finish and leave.

This can be done with any set up such as a trio entering and sitting in three chairs each with a newspaper, entering with coats, hats, and scarves, folding bedsheets, setting up objects for a circus act, etc. Any props, scenic elements or costume bits will do as long as they can be used in an imaginative way to act out the activities written on the cards.

BACKSTAGE BUTTING IN

> In clown and physical comedy, there's no such thing as a neutral backstage. Any space in view or within hearing distance of the audience is a potential performing space. This exercise helps the players explore this, find comic play in how they use any space, and expand the potential for any venue whether it's a theater, a living room, or the street.

Props: Stage flats or curtains for entrances and exits, miscellaneous props.

Variation 1—Backstage forget Each player needs a prop and a hat or other costume piece that is easy to put on. These are set backstage. The player enters, ready to perform her act. Soon afterwards she realizes she's forgotten her prop. She reacts to this; for example, she gets angry at herself, scared of the crowd's reaction, paranoid that someone is messing with her, laughs and has a "Duh! I'm an idiot!" moment, etc. She exits, and returns with the prop. At some point she realizes she's forgotten her hat (or other costume piece). Whatever emotion she revealed the first time increases. For example, she gets angrier. She exits to retrieve the hat. While backstage, she leaves the prop, returns with the hat, realizes she's forgotten the prop, reacts, goes back to get the prop, but exits the wrong side. She leaves her hat on this side, enters and crosses to the side where her prop is, enters again, comes downstage to perform her trick, realizes she's forgotten her hat, exits to the wrong side to get it, crosses to the right side, gets hat, enters, makes sure she has hat and prop, then comes downstage.

There are a number of options now: she recovers from her reaction to the forgetting and does the trick; the forgetting can carry on a few more times, building in energy to see where it leads and how the props get mixed up; she realizes she's forgotten another costume piece or other props or loses her shoe backstage; she sees she's got the wrong prop and/or costume for the act she wanted to do and goes looking for it; she's ready to do her trick but realizes she's forgotten what it is; her partner comes out and takes the prop and hat and tells her to go get *her* prop and hat, "These are mine!"

This is an exploration in playing with props, entrances and exits, developing a series of predictable and unpredictable actions, and the minimum-to-MAXIMUM of a series of actions and emotional reactions, all of which can be used to develop an act.

Note: This can be done as an improv for the class, or the players are allowed to rehearse, decide on the props that will serve their ideas, and develop a short scene before showing it. The players can vocalize at any time, onstage or off.

A variation can be added as follows:

- As a lead-in to a scene: After exploring this with the class, the players can be assigned to use this exercise as an introduction: The Forget is the lead-in to whatever type of act, task or scene they will play (devised by the players or using a scripted scene). This encourages the players to explore multiple entrances and exits and make the backstage—and the actions that occur out of sight of the audience—a part of their scene.

Variation 2—Backstage news Three players wait backstage. Each player chooses a simple, short trick or task. It can be a juggling or acrobatic trick, carrying a box across the stage, coming out and sweeping, pouring water into a paper cup, etc. Each player decides what is their "backstage news" (this is not revealed to the audience). For example, just before he enters to perform a cartwheel, the player is told his house has burnt down and everything he owns is gone. He enters in complete despair, but he must come onstage and do his cartwheel, then make an exit. Whatever energy he brings onstage, he must maintain and express it throughout the act (he can keep repeating silently to himself, "My house has burnt down, I've lost everything"). The backstage energy affects his entrance, how he comes into the space, how he does his cartwheel, how he moves out of the space, and how he exits. The players are given a few rounds with the same trick or task in order to explore a variety of emotions: how does each energy affect the same action: a sad cartwheel or an angry one, sweeping while paranoid or full of pride, carrying a box across the stage while mightily confused or madly joyful.

Variation 3—Backstage onstage Three players wait backstage. They decide on a scenario that will create noise. For example, they are having a raucous party; having an argument about who didn't flush the toilet; weeping over one person's hamster being eaten by another person's dog; terrified that there's a killer hiding somewhere looking to take them out. They develop the soundscape of this scenario, making noise backstage, banging things around, laughing, shouting, weeping, screaming, etc. The language should be mostly gibberish or unintelligible with a few recognizable words thrown in now and then. The noise level builds and when it's near its peak, one player—the Entertainer—enters the stage to do an act, bringing with him the energy from backstage—he enters laughing, raging, weeping, etc. Upon entering, he tries to calm himself in order to present and connect with the crowd. He moves downstage to do his act—it's short and simple such as flipping a stick, bouncing a ball high and catching it, or standing on a chair. While this is happening, the scene backstage continues—it's noisy, props or costume bits are thrown onstage, a player might step out emoting, then exit again. While this is going on, the Entertainer does his act, playing it for the crowd, torn between responding to what's going on backstage and delighting his audience. The Entertainer finishes the act and exits.

The players backstage can choose to randomly interrupt the Entertainer the whole time he's onstage, but never come out and stay, or they can build up the level of noise and interruption until they completely undermine what the Entertainer is doing and carry the scene from backstage, onstage, with the Entertainer completely giving up. The players find an ending together, and exit.

This is repeated with a different player from the trio acting as the Entertainer (use the same backstage scenario but a different Entertainer's act), or let another group have a go.

Note: *This can be done as an improv for the class, or the players are allowed to rehearse and develop the scene before showing it.*

Advice

- "Carry the energy you build offstage, onstage. Don't drop it when you enter!"
- "When playing the Entertainer, keep the tension between the various problems and the two worlds. Show us how you feel about what's going on by how you react to it and how you try to keep the crowd's attention on your act."

Summary

At a basic level there are three elements in any theater piece: player, audience, and space. An audience—and novice players—may not be consciously aware of the effect the space has on them, but it has a profound impact. This section encouraged the players to become familiar with the performing space wherever and whatever it may be. To shape it to serve their needs, as well as find out what it wants, what it suggests, how the space itself wishes to play. The exercises urged the players to transform the space by how they entered it, moved through it, played in it, to find ways to draw the audience into their world and the space they *all* inhabit; there are no rigid borders, no hard dividing lines between any space or reality. The players were also invited into the audience's space by listening to them and responding directly, as well as bringing areas alive that are not visible to the crowd to broaden the potential for playing with the space.

The objective of all the previous sections was to prepare the players for solo, duo, trio, and ensemble devising. In the following sections, the players begin to create short acts and scenes, telling a story using their bodies, the space, and their interaction with props, all animated by imaginative, inventive, and energetic play.

Figure 6.1 Ariel Speedwagon: Clown solos. *Photo credit: Eric Gillet/Shoot That Klown.*

6

Clown Solos

Catching a Salad on Your Face

Solo clowning is always a humbling experience. No matter how brilliant you think your ideas are, how you want to claim that your routine is your own unique creation, the reality of a live performance will change your notions that you are the sole creator of your act. I've devised a number of solo shows

Figure 6.2 Joe Dieffenbacher at Fiestas del Pilar, Zaragoza, Spain performing *Bon Appetit! Photo credit: Matilda Dieffenbacher.*

over the years, directed other artist's routines, and developed solo turns within many ensemble productions. Below are a few episodes from my own work that convinced me that a solo show is always a team effort.

When someone from the audience throws a head of lettuce and I catch it in the face, I have a visceral experience of "audience participation."

When part of my solo show involves slicking down my hair after licking my hand, then doing the same to members of the public, and when at a ten-day festival in Segovia, Spain—where a good part of the town has seen my show by day nine—and I walk into a bank and the bank employee behind the counter beckons me closer, licks his hand and slicks down my hair, I have to laugh at the notion that I'm alone onstage.

When an actor at Shakespeare's Globe, London, who I've been helping to find moments in *Taming of the Shrew* to play with the crowd, suddenly turns to an audience member standing in the pit area at the foot of the stage and asks for her water bottle to wake up her master Lucentio who has fainted, and a hush comes over the crowd as she not only breaks free from the world onstage, but literally steps out of the show as she reaches for the bottle, pours it on her master and tosses it back, and you hear the crowd go from hushed disbelief at being addressed so directly, to bursting into laughter and applause at the nerve and playfulness of the actor, I witness the power of the solo artist when they choose to make their audience an active partner in their play.

When I offer "shnicky-shnacks" (small cookies) to my audience throughout my street show, presenting them as a bribe and a thank you for their help, and I do this so often that a child—who looks like she's just learned to walk—wobbles through the crowd and onto my performing space, and I see this kid out of the corner of my eye while doing an acrobatic headspring off a table—a little girl who looks like a cherub with her light blonde hair and white dress—and she reaches out her hand as she continues towards me, oblivious to the crowd, their laughter and my crazy clown's antics, and I know I have to interrupt the show to give her a shnicky-shnack...I realize this show doesn't belong to me and will forever be a collaboration between me and the crowd.

Devising work as a solo artist can feel like one of the loneliest things you'll ever do. No one to trade ideas with, play off of, share the joys and frustrations of the creative process. Your first showing of new material feels like holding up pieces of thin paper with your ideas written on them as a strong wind blows them about and the audience struggles to comprehend what you've come to share with them. Or to paraphrase English author Samuel Butler, "Clowning is like playing the violin in public and learning the instrument while people stare at you"...

But when a solo player truly connects with the crowd, they experience something essential about clowns: they're eager to share their thoughts, emotions and imagination intimately with their audience. When they have those moments of complicity, a player gains in self-confidence and courage, and realizes, they're never alone onstage; they learn to constantly reach out and connect with others by engaging directly with the crowd.

Because performing solo is tough, exercises that challenge and provoke the players are important. The adviser—acting as an enlightened heckler—engages with them in such a way as to push them beyond their comfort zone and get them to explore other possibilities. These challenges will build a solo player's confidence, preparing them for performing for an audience that is at best indifferent, at worst, resistant. The adviser's side-coaching also pushes the players to stay connected with their audience, making them aware that their performance is meant to be a conversation, that they're always in dialog with the crowd.

The exercises also motivate the players to mess about with adversity rather than be shut down by it. Improv games often advocate the use of "Yes, and …" to evoke a positive atmosphere and stimulate creativity. This is important, but I found that sometimes saying "No … so now what?" can encourage the players to go deeper, search for a greater inner strength, a more imaginative response, let their instincts lead them. The adviser makes vocal the audience's opinion and judgement, but also their curiosity and delight. It's brought out into the open so the solo clown can play with it, use it to generate material and develop new ways of engaging with the crowd.

The following exercises contain techniques that can help structure a solo routine or scene and give it a greater coherence, as well as offer ways to develop performance material.

PASS IT AROUND

> The first three variations have the players moving and vocalizing in a big, broad way, while the latter three get them focusing on their partner's physicality and sharing transition moments with each other and the audience. These variations usually produce some joyful, crazy play, at the same time teaching clarity, specificity and good comic timing.

Variation 1—Silly sound The players stand in a circle. They do a vocal warm up together, rising up and down in pitch, making sounds that are soft and loud, slow and fast. The starting player steps into the center, looks at her audience in the circle in a formal way as if she is about to perform high art. She takes a deep breath . . . and makes a silly sound and a movement to go with it. She repeats this a few times, takes a bow, all formal and serious, steps back to her place in the circle, raises her hands like a conductor preparing the orchestra, brings her hands down and the group repeats the silly sound and movement, together. The group bow to each other, impressed with themselves. The starting player gestures formally to player to her left. He steps into the circle and repeats the sequence. Continue around the circle.

Advice

- "Show a clear difference in physical attitude, facial expressions and energy, between the formality at the start, the silly sound and movement, then back to the formal bow. Enjoy playing the contrast."

Variation 2—Big gesture, big sound The players stand in a circle. They do a vocal warm up. The starting player steps into the circle and makes eye contact with everyone, giving the impression he's about to perform something amazing. He takes a deep breath, assumes a big, expressive pose and lets loose with a loud, bellowing sound. When he's finished, the group applaud and cheer for him. The player receives his applause, quite pleased with himself, steps back into the circle and gestures formally to the player to his left. She steps into the circle and repeats the sequence. Continue around the circle.

Variation 3—Silly walk The players stand in a circle. The starting player hops in the air and lands inside the circle. As soon as they land, they break out into a silly walk (player can vocalize if they wish). They move inside the circle making eye contact with everyone as they show their walk to all. As soon as they step back into the circle, the player points to anyone in the circle. He hops in the air, lands inside the circle and does his silly walk, moving in all directions within the circle, making eye contact with everyone, showing off his walk. As soon as he steps backs into the circle, he points to another player and she repeats the sequence. Continue around the circle.

Advice

- "The hop in the air at the start is like being jolted with electricity! Always be ready to hop into the circle with energy, ready to silly walk at any moment. Don't fret about what you'll do when you're suddenly pointed at: work it out when you land from the hop into the circle and start silly walking."

Variation 4—Mirror me The players stand in a circle. The starting player makes a face and assumes a strong pose using his entire body to express an emotion. He shows this to the group then turns and shows the face and pose to the player to his left. She mirrors face and pose exactly, shows the reflection to the group, turns and shows the same face and pose to the next player, who mirrors it, shows it to the group and turns to the next player. Continue around the circle. When face and pose gets back to the player who started it, is it the same? The player to the left of the first player starts a new face and pose.

A variation can be added as follows:

- When a player turns ready to be mirrored, the adviser counts to six: the next player in the circle has to mirror the pose in the allotted time. After the count is through, the Mirror turns and shows the audience, then turns to the next player who has six seconds to mirror the pose. How fast can players mirror the pose, show it to the audience, pass it on and still be accurate?

Advice

- "When observing a player to mirror them, do a full scan of their body: check the position of their feet, their legs, how they're holding their hips, the curve of their spine, the shape of their arms, hands, and fingers, not just the expression on their face but the emotion they're expressing. Be thorough and mirror *all* parts of your partner's body."

Variation 5—Reaction Same as above but the player who is turned to, *reacts* to the pose and face instead of mirroring it, shows their reaction to the group, turns and shows reaction to the next player who reacts to her pose and face. He shows his reaction to the group, turns, and shows his reaction to the next player. This sequence continues around the circle. When it gets back to the starting player, the next person in the circle starts a new pose and face, turns, and the sequence is repeated around the circle.

Variation 6—Change Same as above, but the player who is turned to reacts to the pose and face, shows his reaction to the group, *changes his pose and face for the group,* then shows his new pose and face to the next person, who reacts, shows his reaction to the group, changes his pose and face for the group, shows his new pose and face to the next person. This sequence continues around the circle. When it gets back to the starting player, the next person in the circle starts a new pose and face, turns, and the sequence is repeated around the circle.

Note: *Variations 4–6 can be done in smaller groups of five to seven players.*

Advice

- "Be sure the change is shown to the group *before turning* to the next person in the circle. Don't rush the transition moments: you want your audience to see what's being offered *before* offering it."
- "Fully engage with your partners and the audience in every part of the sequence."
- "These simple exchanges can be very funny to do and observe. Part of the enjoyment is the moment of transition and the anticipation it sets up as to what will happen next. How can you use that simplicity in performance?"
- "Give your partners your undivided attention so you can fully and clearly receive what they give you, show this to the audience, and pass it on. Think of it as a gift you unwrap, discover what's inside, react to it and share it."
- "Make no apologies for the faces, sounds or movements that you make! Be goofy, odd, beautiful, melodramatic, absurd etc. Work with sounds and movements that surprise you. Go outside your physical and vocal comfort zone and provoke others to do the same."

THE REAL THING

Clowns often play in worlds that are absurd, fantastic, surreal. This may bewilder an audience as they try to catch up to, or comprehend, the strange new world that a clown's act or scene is introducing them to. Students of clown will often jump right to overplaying an action, trying to "clown it." They think the clown must exaggerate an activity, present it in a cartoon-like manner. My belief is a clown must expand an action, make it larger or more extensive, give a fuller, deeper version of it, always connecting the actions and reactions to real thoughts and emotions.

This exercise starts with an unremarkable action or task to ground a routine or scene in the real. It then explores ways to embellish the action. The variations toy with the actions required by the task, finding comic play by reducing, then expanding the amount of time a player has to accomplish it. And then embellishing the actions, turning even the most mundane task into a dance peppered with absurd, fantastic, and surreal play.

Props: Stage flats or curtains for entrances and exits, props and costumes for scenes.

Prep: The players decide on a simple task they can present: setting a chair and sitting in it; putting on a pair of shoes and tying them; sweeping the stage; stuffing a pile of clothes into a suitcase; hanging a bedsheet on a line, etc. The players rehearse the task, so they know the basic actions required to perform it so it's easy to repeat a number of times. While the task is important, the main focus will be on the Five Elements. The players gather the props they need for the task and a costume (or the beginnings of one).

Variation 1—The basics The players take a simple action such as sitting in a chair and do it the normal way, paying attention to the mechanics of it—bending at the knees, leaning forward, sticking the butt back, lowering it to the chair. The players work on their own to edit the action down to the essential moves and practice doing it in a normal, unadorned way.

Variation 2—Presenting the basics The players show their action as a short scene. It shouldn't last more than a minute. The objective is to show each of the Five Elements:

1. **Enter:** A player first appears from backstage.
2. **Move into the space:** The player moves towards the spot on the stage where she will present.
3. **Present:** The player presents her action.

4 **Leave the space:** The player moves towards the exit.

5 **Exit:** The player presents a final picture of herself just before she exits.

For this variation, the players don't embellish anything, just keep it economical, specific.

Variations can be added as follows:

- At the end of each element, the player holds a pose as if a photo is being taken.
- The end of each element is marked with a sound, either vocal (e.g. the player says "Oh"), physical (e.g. a single clap or stomping the foot) or made with the prop (e.g. knocking on the chair with the knuckles).
- The end of each element is punctuated with a movement of the body or the prop such as a high kick or turning the chair.

Variation 3—Speed tasking Three players wait backstage ready to run through their action. Their presentation should be no more than a minute long. As soon as a player exits, the next one enters and does their task. After everyone has shown their one-minute scene, they return for a second go: in this round they must do the action in thirty seconds. They must do everything they did in the first round, not cutting anything out. For the third round, the players run the scene in fifteen seconds, for the fourth round, ten seconds. (In these last two versions, the players can edit, cutting the actions down to the most economical way of completing the action.)

The players are encouraged to move faster, choose bigger, longer movements. For example, they could leap onto the stage rather than enter walking, take long loping strides as they move into and out of the space, find a flow from one movement to the next in the most economical way possible, etc. They should also try using the punctuation when speeding up—brief still poses, sounds, or movements – to see how that adds to the play.

Variation 4—Expanding the task The players take what they've learned from Speed Tasking—shortening the scene and finding a way to flow from one moment to the next—and stretch this streamlined version to two to three minutes. They use the extra time to expand certain moments, to reveal more about what the clown is thinking and feeling, as well as develop the entrance and movement into the space to build curiosity, tension, drama, as well as the comic potential of the entire presentation.

Now they can embellish, find variations on the movements required to perform the task (sweeping gets turned into a dance, tying the shoe becomes an acrobatic-contortion act, etc.). The players experiment with takes, multiple ins and outs, they play with patterns of success and failure (accomplishing the task easily and repeatedly, and then screwing it up or something falls apart). They look for moments to let the audience in and reveal more about the clown. The first two variations were about clarifying the basic actions needed for a task and playing with time, pace and movement. Now they explore how to embellish on what they've learned, all the while grounding it in the actions necessary to complete a real task.

The adviser can let a few acts try to improvise and expand their actions in front of the audience to see how it affects their play, or let the players work their pieces in a rehearsal before presenting. When embellishing, they should play with speed (go faster in some places, slower in others), genre (play the action like a horror movie one moment, a RomCom the next), add absurd elements (a suitcase comes alive and tries to eat a player as she puts clothes inside it), etc. Using the simple action as the foundation, find variations and ways to expand on it to create a stronger relationship between the clown and the audience.

Note: *This sequence of variations can also be done with duos and trios performing a task.*

Advice

- "First learn the basic actions to accomplish a task and then how to present them using the Five Elements. Then you can build, embellish and enrich."
- "When *Speed Tasking*, find a flow between each moment. Cut out extraneous movements, gestures, steps. Could you skip or cartwheel to the spot where you will present rather than walk? Could you run on doing the action, pose, then run out of the space still doing it, with a final pose before you exit? Can you enter with your props ready to go right into the action so you don't lose time fumbling with them?"
- "Learn how to effectively edit a scene as well as creatively embellish it."
- "Put an emphasis on an action: stick one leg out straight and hold it there while bending the other and lowering the body to the seat. Stand on one side of the chair in profile to the audience and sit, eyes on audience the whole time. Stand on the chair then drop, legs falling to either side before sitting down."

- "Do the action the wrong way, for example, do a headstand on the chair, lie across it, lie with the back on the seat, the legs draped over the back of the chair, etc."
- "Add a flourish: do a pirouette before sitting. Do a back roll into the chair, do a cartwheel. Throw some confetti in the air and then sit. Move the arms about, posing and tutting before sitting."
- "Try any of the above adding an energy: How would an angry person approach the chair and sit, a paranoid one, an exuberant one? How does the energy affect the movement towards the chair, the normal action of sitting, what sort of flourish might an angry person add?"

THE PARTICIPATING AUDIENCE

There are many ways to begin devising a new act or scene (more on this in Section 14: Devising for Clown and Physical Comedy). Below are some of the ones I've tried both for my own performances and when collaborating with others creating new work. These exercises utilize provocation, variation, group improvisation, patterns of success and failure, and the Five Elements to develop, clarify and expand an act.

Props: Stage flats or curtains for entrances and exits, props and costumes for acts.

Prep: The players develop a solo routine that involves a simple trick. The whole sequence uses the Five Elements and should take no more than a minute from entrance to exit. The trick can involve a skill such as juggling or acrobatics, or it can be as simple as running in place at breakneck speed, throwing a stick in the air for a double spin and catching it, popping a balloon by squeezing it, etc. The players rehearse the trick, so they know the basic actions required to perform it. While the task is important, the main focus will be on how the adviser and audience affect the presentation of the trick, and the trick itself.

Variation 1—Reactions The adviser has a series of cards with single words on them (the words are in bold below). She shows the words to the group and explains the actions for each word.

Whisper: After a player does their trick and bows, the audience begins whispering comments—good or bad—to each other about what they've just seen. They comment on the trick, the player, the way they look, their presentation, etc. The player onstage reacts, then exits.

Bravo: After the player does their trick and bows, the audience leaps to their feet and cheers wildly, shouting, "BRAVO! AMAZING! INCREDIBLE!" and other superlatives. The player reacts and exits.

Backs: After the player does his trick and bows, the audience stands up and turn their backs on him, sometimes glancing over their shoulder to see if the player is still there, sighing and harrumphing because he still is. The player reacts and exits.

Salute: After the player does their trick and bows, the audience stands formally and salutes the player, and stays this way, stiff-backed, chests thrust out, hand by head, as the player reacts and exits.

Seduce: After the player does their trick and bows, the audience looks at him seductively. They can vocalize, stay seated, kneel, or stand, pose however they like. The player reacts and exits.

Hide: After the player does their trick and bows, the audience scrambles to hide from her. They can whisper, shout or scream as they curl into a ball or hide under their coats, if there is furniture in the room they scurry under or behind it, etc. The player onstage reacts and exits.

Boo: After the player does their trick and bows, the audience starts to boo. They can stay seated or stand, as they holler at him to get off the stage, "Boo! BOO! Go away!" The player reacts and exits.

Once the cards are explained, three players go backstage with the props they need for their trick. The adviser shows a card. First player enters and performs, takes a bow. The audience reacts. The player's response to the crowd is short, they don't draw it out or milk it. If they want to protest a response or seek more of it, they can do so as they move out of the space towards the exit. Once they're gone, the adviser shows a new card and cues the next player. They enter and perform. Once all three have had a turn, a new trio go backstage.

Note: *This can be developed into a group scene to perform, with some of the players in the audience ready to react to the player onstage. He could exit and reenter a few times, get a different response each time. Players in the audience can even encourage the crowd to join in! The group can develop this simple set up into a scene that brings all of them onto the stage including those players planted in the audience.*

Variation 2—Substitute The player enters and presents her act. At any point, anyone in the audience can call "Sub!" The player onstage freezes, while the person who called out assumes the pose of the one onstage (and takes their prop if there is one). The player onstage steps into the audience and says "Go!" The sub can back up a few beats to show a new way of playing the previous moment or continue on from the place it was stopped. Sub continues until someone else calls "Sub!" or they finish the act and exit.

Subs should come in with a strong idea, commit to it and play it until someone—including the one whose act it is—calls "Sub!" This can be called out to replay any of the Five Elements. For example, if someone thinks of a better entrance, they can call "Sub!" as soon as a player steps onstage; Sub offers a different way for a player to enter. Or after watching the act and a player's exit, Sub can offer another way of leaving the stage that she thinks better suits the act.

Variation 3—Love–Hate One player waits backstage. He enters to present his act. When he's finished and receives his applause, the adviser—playing the part of the Interrupting Critic—praises the player. "We love your act. You're so talented. How did you get so good? Can you show us that one part again? Amazing." The player shows the "one part" again (the Critic doesn't say which part, the player has to guess). The adviser abruptly changes the critique. "Actually, you know what? That was terrible. Do that one part again. That was awful! I can't believe you thought this was good." The back-and-forth between love and hate from the Critic continues as the player responds, however he feels in the moment. The player can exit at any time or the Critic sends him off.

The player should react honestly to whatever is said—grow sad, irritated, apologetic, pleased, joyful, defiant, etc. He should look at ways to use his reaction to gain sympathy and create an alliance with the audience. The objective is not to turn the Critic into a villain, but to use what she says to connect with the audience and show various sides of the clown by how the player reacts to the comments, the love, and the hate.

Advice

- "Use the critique to push you to develop new ideas, willing to carry on no matter what is thrown at you. Turn the negative into an advantage. Use it, play with it."

Variation 4—The fail The players are given rehearsal time to create a moment in their presentation when something goes wrong (e.g. they drop a juggling ball, a player trips as he goes into a cartwheel, bumps the flat or gets tangled in the curtain on her entrance, their prop breaks just as they start the trick).

When the fail happens, the player reacts to it honestly. For this variation, they don't try to make it comic, but show how they really feel when something goes wrong. The adviser tells the players to think back to times when they had failed and asks how that felt. Can they recreate that same depth of feeling in this moment? The player decides on the fail and explores their reaction.

They can also recall their responses to earlier exercises like *Reactions, Speed Tasking, Love/Hate*—any variations that caused problems during their presentation—and see if these will help them find a believable fail. They then rehearse it into the act: they enter full of poise and confidence, ready to entertain their audience! The fail happens and reveals an opening, a crack in the mask of the strong, confident performer. The player explores the moment of failure and their reaction to it, then makes an exit.

The adviser sets a one minute time limit for the presentation and the fail.

Advice

- "What is the most dramatic, surprising, upsetting way for your trick to go wrong? Drop one ball or all three? A slight trip and stumble or crash into a wall? Have the leg on the chair break, or put a foot right through the seat? Create surprise, tension, sympathy, etc., in the way you craft the fail."
- "Rehearse with all the elements—costume, space, props—so the fail is believable. Practice the fail, make us believe it's really a problem. Don't create a "clowny" problem, one that the audience will never believe is a real obstacle for you. Create drama alongside the comedy."
- "When you enter, make us believe all will be grand—you're a *master!*—before you fail. Create a strong contrast between who you appear to be when you enter and prepare, and who is revealed after the fail."

- "Create a moment of failure that is real, that affects you and us. Then—and this may sound like a contradiction—rehearse it so you can repeat it, make it real for you and for us, every time. It requires you to show vulnerability in the moment, each time you do it."
- "When watching each other fail, make notes about how you feel about the player's reaction, your reaction to them, and how it changes your relationship with the player onstage. Use this information in your own explorations."
- "Use the Five Elements wisely: Where do you enter from, how do you move from the entrance to the place where you'll prepare? How do you then move to where you'll present? How will you exit after the fail? The objective is to not only to present an act but reveal something about yourself using the Five Elements."

Variation 5—The bounce Once the adviser feels the players have found a strong presentation and trick and have learned to work the fail so it's believable and the reaction opens the player up, he asks them to find the bounce: the moment after the fail when they recover. The player takes the energy of the fail—which is usually one of defeat, disappointment, irritation, frustration, etc.—and moves from this "negative" energy towards insight, a new direction, an opening up into play. Once the audience witnesses the player's response to failure, they see the fail transformed.

For example, her reaction to the fail is stomping on the balls after dropping them, only to discover that she can kick them up from the ground with her feet into a three-ball juggle. Or, pulling himself up from a fall, he trips again and again, recovering suddenly by throwing himself into a cartwheel, transforming the trick into something more playful—the accidental execution of the trick surprises both player and audience. The prop that has broken during the act gives player a new idea and she creates a whole new game on the spot, invents a brand-new trick with the broken prop.

The players should allow themselves to sink into the fail, play with its negative energy, and see if that leads to a new possibility. Their act then flows from the self-assured, graceful, larger-than-life energy of the confident, performer, into the negative, revealing energy of the fail, to the transformative, playful spirit of the bounce. The fail has the potential to build tension, add drama, deepen the act to reveal more about the clown. It can give a presentation more dimension and create a much richer comic and dramatic experience.

Advice on all variations

- "The provocations that are part of all these variations, are there to help you accumulate ideas and comic business that you can use to develop your clown, your act and your way of playing. Take notes, create lists of ideas, things that worked and didn't work, things you could do differently."
- "Ask yourself, what did the audience respond to? Did I feel focused in what I was doing, or lost? How did the audience respond in those moments of strength or what felt like weakness (the fail)? Did I feel connected to the audience and to what I was doing even while I was being interrupted? The players observing should share feedback, help each other understand what the audience responds to, wants from a player, likes or is not so crazy about. Help each other gain insights."
- "Find the fail and the recovery through your play with the actions and props; don't simply map it out in your head. If you carry out the actions and rehearse them - no matter how committed you are to getting them right - something will naturally go wrong. Explore all the real ways your action can go wrong, then expand and embellish the fail. The same with your reaction: what is your genuine response to things not going according to your well thought out plan? Open this up to the audience, give them time to witness your vulnerability. This will help you find a bounce that is honest, surprising and inspiring."

Summary

Even if a player wants to work only in groups, they must develop their ability to hold their own as a solo performer. In every ensemble there will be times when one player is called upon to do a comic turn, display a skill or take the lead in a scene. It's a chance for a player to show more of who they are, develop their relationship to the audience and their onstage partners. This section offered exercises that challenged the solo player to think for themselves and act on their feet, in the moment. The exercises helped develop the players' imaginations and their instincts, making them stronger as a solo performer, and able to offer more when working with an ensemble. The challenges presented by the adviser via the exercises aimed to "toughen up" the players, encouraging them to explore a number of different ways of responding to provocation. They learned to work with different emotions, energies, and attitudes. This emphasis on failure and variety when devising gives them a greater range of tools to help build confidence in playing openly with an audience.

In the next section, we take these stronger solo players and pair them up: the ideas, energies and physical play developed in Clown Solo are expanded upon as two players interact, applying the lessons learned from the adviser acting as Boss Clown and using them in their duo play; the players take on this role of provocateur, challenging each other as they explore and develop their solo work in conjunction with a partner.

Figure 7.1 Amica Hunter and David Cantor: Clown duos. *Photo credit: Eric Gillet/Shoot That Klown.*

7

Clown Duos

The Wet Towel Intervention

During a five-week study of clown I had a student—I'll call him Mark—who was really struggling. Mark would overthink his play to such a degree he became dumbed down, growing bewildered as he tried to systematically figure out how to be funny. This led to him always being a few beats behind the action, struggling to catch up with what others were doing in a scene. This is a hilarious quality for a clown if they know how to use it, but he lacked the support of the others; they just thought he was slow and not able to contribute fast enough when they would trade ideas. By week two he was so lost the other students were avoiding him, afraid that he would only make

Figure 7.2 A little bit off—David Cantor and Amica Hunter in *Bella Culpa*.
Photo credit: Steven L. Price.

them look bad when playing together onstage. I had to find a way to make them see that his natural absent-mindedness could be transformed into clown play if properly framed.

Enter The Washerwomen. This is a well-known clown gag where two or more male players in drag enter with buckets and clothes to wash. One bucket is for soaping the clothes, one for rinsing, the other, wringing out. In the course of washing, the clowns end up hitting each other with the sopping clothes, dumping buckets of water on each other's heads and creating a soaking, soapy mess. I rarely used this gag in teaching—it lacked any nuance and the playing of it kept students from exploring clowning in deeper ways. But I needed something extreme that would get Mark out of his head.

I paired Mark up with two other students, I'll call them Bill and Peter. Peter was one of the stronger, more experienced, and mature players in the class that year. I explained what he had to do: Peter was to play the scene as Mark's clown partner but when developing and rehearsing the piece, approach it as his teacher, patiently helping him understand the specific sequence of washing, rinsing, and wringing out. This way of working was the antithesis of the exaggeration and knockabout usually associated with the gag. Peter played the boss as a slightly exasperated father-type, accepting Mark's slow-wittedness as his lot in life: "See the cross I must bear? I love him, even though he drives me crazy." And in time he did: As the scene evolved and Mark's slow-wittedness began to undermine the specific sequence of wash-rinse-wring out, Peter grew angrier, his (genuine) exasperation expressing itself in the slapstick of the slinging and hitting with the wet clothes, throwing water, slipping and sliding on the soapy floor. But the build from the necessary, very specific, tasks to the bedlam—with everything ending up in disarray, wet clothes and water everywhere—including a few wet rags tossed into the audience to be thrown back—came out of the slow development and reveal of the bond between Boss and Fool.

It was a valuable lesson for everyone: they saw clearly how dynamic, rambunctious play must grow out of a true relationship between two clowns. If they can establish this and express it in their actions, the audience will go with them almost anywhere, trusting and delighting in the duo's play.

And Mark had a massive breakthrough: suddenly his slowness—the thing that had so vexed him and led others to avoid him—was seen as a great advantage when consciously utilized in his clowning. Rather than being trapped inside his frustration, he was able to step outside of it and use his slowness with intent; he learned to control it rather than it controlling him. Mark was better able to contribute ideas because he understood his apparent weakness as a strength in regard to clowning. Thrilled by the laughs he was getting, he became much stronger onstage, and delighted in the fact that now everyone wanted to work with him.

One of my favorite explorations in the classroom is to mix and match partners and let them experience what different people draw out of them. The right partner can bring out qualities a player didn't know they had, and for this reason, duo work has an enormous effect on the development of a player's understanding of clowning.

When partnering, all elements should be taken into account: the natural energy of each player—match fast and pushy with slow and thoughtful, match eager with eager, angry with overly helpful, etc. Consider their physical differences: small with large, brawny with gawky, sour-looking with kind-faced. How the partners look when simply standing next to one another is one way to find compatible comedy comrades; some duos can walk onstage and get a response simply because of the visual contrast or underlying harmony (or disharmony) between their look and their perceived energy.

The play between two clowns can take many forms. They can be two fools, or the smart Master and her dumb Servant. The relationship can be mean-spirited or teasing, romantic or testy. Their union can be based on the pleasure they experience in playing off one another, or they can turn their antagonism towards one another into comic play onstage, always a bit acrimonious and hectic.

The relationship between two clowns should never be forced: the games and exercises that follow allow partners to discover a natural, honest and spirited way of interacting, which can then be expanded upon, embellished, and channeled into clown routines.

REMEMBER ME

> This section begins with a simple game of remembering; partners are given time to get to know each other visually. This is important for developing familiarity and complicity, as well as increasing the players' powers of observation. This is a good game to start partner work because it puts an emphasis on really seeing others. Taking in physical details, being able to recall as well as copy them, is a good first step towards getting to know a partner and playing with them.

Variation 1—Study The players find a partner and decide who is A and who is B. They face one another about two meters apart. The adviser sets a time limit of thirty seconds. Player A studies his partner's appearance—hair and eye color, clothes (color and style), any distinguishing marks, facial features, posture, etc. The adviser calls "Time!" Player A turns his back on player B and tries to describe her, giving as many details as he can recall in thirty seconds. The players switch roles. Try again with new partners.

Variation 2—Change The players find a partner and face one another. They study each other's appearance briefly—the adviser counts off fifteen seconds—then turn their backs on each other. They each change one thing about their appearance (hair style, clothes, posture, etc.). When they have each done so they say "Ready!" and turn to face one another. They each try to discover what their partner has changed (the change must be visible). Repeat a few times, then try it again with new partners.

Variation 3—Handshake The players find a partner. They stand in lines facing each other with about three meters between them. On a cue from the adviser, they walk forward, meet in the middle and agree on an eccentric way to shake hands. For example, they make a sawing motion, or swing their arms side-to-side (make sure no two duos do the same action). Once each duo has established their eccentric handshake, all the players start to roam around the room with their eyes closed. The players reach out and shake the hand of anyone they come into contact with. As soon as contact is made, they try their eccentric handshake. If the person they find is not their partner, there will be confusion as both players try to do their moves, but it will only end up a mess. They keep searching until they find the person who is in sync with their handshake. Once this happens, the partners open their eyes, step aside and let the others continue until all have found their partners. Try again with new pairs.

PUSHERS

> Acrobats and dancers have a trust for each other that is based on physical interaction. Although some of the variations that follow are competitive, the players maintain a proximity to one another that forces them to listen and connect with their partner in a way that other types of competitive games don't encourage.

Props: Masking tape.

Variation 1—Hand-to-hand The players partner up, facing each other about half a meter apart. They bring their own feet together and press their palms against their partner's palms (this remains open and relaxed – they don't grip each other's hands or grab them if they lose their balance). The objective is for each player to make their partner lose their balance and shift their feet. No other body contact is allowed except the player's pushing each other palm-to-palm, gaining a point each time they force their partner to shift their feet. The players go for five rounds then try again with new partners.

A variation can be added as follows:

- Same as above but done in slow motion, no sudden moves allowed.

Variation 2—Back to back Partners sit back to back. Pushing with their feet, they press their backs together and try to stand up. When they have achieved this, they walk their feet out slightly and sit again, always maintaining back-to-back contact. The players can press their hands against their thighs to assist the up and down movement.

Now the players sit back-to-back and lock arms. A tape line is laid down at the feet of each player (at the toes). The objective is to push their partner back until the winner crosses over their partner's line with both their feet. The players should stay low, only slightly raised from a seated position. They go for best out of three, end by repeating the standing and sitting together as above, then try again with new partners.

Variation 3—Shoulder-to-shoulder Partners bend over and lock the top of one shoulder together (e.g. right shoulder on opponent's right shoulder), their necks pressed against each other's, heads to one side. They maintain this contact throughout. A tape line is laid down about half a meter back from the heels of each player. The only point of contact is shoulder-to-shoulder, no grabbing each other with the hands. On a signal from the adviser, the players push their partners from this shoulder to shoulder connection to get over their opponent's line with both feet.

Advice

- "Play with degrees of force but also consider tactics: sometimes strategy can overcome a stronger opponent."
- "Find ways of getting your opponent off balance rather than always trying to win by brute force."

Variation 4—Up and down Partners face each other and reach past their hands to wrap their fingers around each other's wrists. They bring their feet closer together, so their toes are nearly touching. One partner leans back and straightens their arms as the other bends at the knees and sits. So, one player is up, the other is down. The player standing then begins to squat as the other rises, counterbalancing each other so as not to falter or lose their footing. They continue the up and down seesawing until they can do it smoothly, at varying speeds, without moving their feet.

MIND LEADING THE BLIND

> I have found that some of the best exercises for clown and physical comedy involve working with the eyes closed or blindfolded. It forces players to use their other senses, as well as developing their kinesthetic awareness. They learn to listen, to focus and to concentrate more acutely. They are especially useful in duo work as they build trust and teach players to be both good leaders and good followers.

Props: Blindfolds, or eye masks (like the ones used for sleeping) enough for half the class with extras (they may get sweaty).

Variation 1—Blind finger The players partner up. One partner is the Follower, the other the Leader. Followers are blindfolded (or keep eyes closed). The Leader places a finger under the Follower's chin. Before they begin, the adviser shows a gesture that will signal that the Leaders should swap Followers at some point in the exercise.

Leaders guide their Followers around the room, controlling them with the touch of the finger under the chin. Pulling the finger forward—always maintaining contact—cues the Follower to walk forward. More pressure cues them to move faster, less pressure, slower. Removing the finger means stopping. Pressure towards the left or right under the chin, signifies a turn in that direction. The Leader focuses on using the finger and changes in pressure applied to direct the Follower. *Verbal directions are not allowed at any time.* Only finger pressure is used to lead the partner to stop and start, run, jump, speed up, slow down, lie down, go up on a table, sit in a chair, etc.

The Follower focuses on the pressure of the finger against their chin/neck and uses this to discover what the Leader wants them to do. The Leader must be careful to prevent the Follower from bumping into other Followers or allowing them to trip: the Leader must inspire trust. The Follower must stay sensitive to the finger under their chin and what the Leader is trying to communicate via this sole point of contact.

The adviser signals the Leaders to swap Followers: two Leaders make eye contact, move their Followers closer and take their fingers away signaling the Followers to stop. Leaders switch, placing their index finger under the chin of their new Follower and continue (try to do it so the Follower isn't aware of the change in Leader). The adviser can signal any number of switches. Finally, she calls an end to the exercise and the Followers remove their blindfolds. The players switch, and the Followers are now acting as Leaders. Try again with new partners.

Variation 2—Blind automobile The players partner up. The Driver (eyes open) stands behind the Automobile (blindfolded or eyes closed, hands held up by chest, palms out). The Drivers take their Automobiles for a drive: to move forward they press a finger against their back between the shoulder blades. Increased pressure means go faster; a light touch means go slow. To turn left, a Driver moves his finger to the left shoulder, to turn right he moves his finger to the right shoulder. To reverse, the Driver slides his finger up to the back of Automobile's neck. To stop, he takes his finger away (no contact). The Drivers must control their Automobiles with care so there are no collisions. The Automobiles should put all their attention on their Drivers' point of contact behind them rather than worry about what they can't see in front of them. They start slowly, getting used to the commands, then get more creative. After an allotted time, the adviser tells the players to switch roles; they then try again with new partners.

Variation 3—Blind doorways Half of the class partner up. Partners stand randomly around the room and join hands overhead creating a series of doorways. Each doorway must devise three different sounds: a soothing, musical sound that lures the players towards their doorway, a warning sound that tells players they're about to collide with someone, and a victory sound that tells players they've passed through their doorway successfully. (the Doorways don't all have to make the same sounds.) The other half of the class now close their eyes; they are the Seekers. The Doorways make their soothing sounds to lure the Seekers towards them. If they see a risk of collision with a Doorway or another Seeker, the Doorway makes a warning sound and the Seekers stop or move cautiously. If a Seeker manages to get through, the Doorway makes the victory sound. The Seeker keeps track of these: when she has passed through five Doorways, she can open her eyes. She then steps aside until everyone has passed through five Doorways. The players then switch roles, with the Seekers creating Doorways and the Doorways becoming the Seekers.

Variation 4—Blind voice The adviser sets up an obstacle course using mats, tables, chairs, wooden boxes etc. All pieces should be sturdy enough to climb or step on and should have no sharp edges. The players partner up. One is blindfolded (or closes their eyes). They are the Explorer. Their partner is the Director (whose eyes are open). The Director leads their blindfolded Explorer around the room, giving them verbal instructions on where to move to avoid bumping into things and other players, directs them to walk forward or backward, turn left or right, sit, climb, step over, crawl under, roll over, etc., the obstacles scattered about the room. The Director walks close enough to her partner so she can be heard but will not confuse other blindfolded Explorers. The Director avoids any physical contact with her Explorer unless this is absolutely necessary to prevent their partner from getting hurt. The Explorer keeps their hands up to protect themselves, but should try not to grope about too much and instead, trust the Director to lead them. After an allotted time, the adviser tells the players to switch roles, then try again with new partners.

FOLLOWED

One clown following another in sync is an effective way to visually connect players; right away the audience sees them relate and play. Shadowing someone like this inspires curiosity and builds suspense: the audience waits for a break in the shadowing to see how the duo will interact. It's a good way for players to start a partnership: without too much discussion or debating over ideas, they make a connection and can develop material from this simple interaction.

Variation 1—My companion The players partner up. One is the Companion, the other the Leader. The Leader begins to move with his partner shadowing him, imitating what he does while walking in sync behind him. The Leader walks, runs, stops, slows down her movement, looks about, gesticulates etc, thus giving his Companion lots of things to copy and play with.

Though following, the Companion has a mind of her own. For example, the Leader gestures to something. Her Companion moves to it and stops following the Leader. But the Leader was only pointing at it. He grabs his Companion and pulls her back to stand behind him. Or the Leader may ask his Companion to fetch something by gesturing to it, but his Companion just copies the gesture. The Leader gets irritated and bullies his Companion. His Companion bullies back. They start to wrestle . . . .

It begins as a simple exercise of walking behind a partner and imitating them, which then leads to a development and expansion of the clowns' relationship. Partners roam about the room exploring leading and following. After an allotted time, the adviser tells them to switch roles, then try again with new partners.

Variation 2—My companion in and out The players partner up. They decide who will lead first. They go backstage. The Leader enters with his Companion following. The Leader can decide on a task, for example, he's going to set up some chairs. Or they create an environment: they've come to the big city to take a look around. Or it can be simply a movement exploration. Play the shadowing as in Variation 1, with the addition of entrances and exits and actions played for an audience.

Variation 3—Following fool This variation starts with the Companion following and imitating, maintaining a low status. Once this is established, the Companion finds moments to caricature the Leader and make fun of her. Every now and then, the Leader looks back or turns completely around trying to catch him. Her Companion must not get caught out: when the Leader turns, her Companion pretends to be doing nothing, simply following as he's supposed to or scratching his head, combing his hair, etc. The Leader plays the game of trying to catch her Companion who plays the game of trying not to get caught (while taking every chance he can to make fun of the Leader).

The Leader should do things that beg to be caricatured: strut around like she's queen of the ball, fix and admire her hair, do a task in a self-important way. She can also do something that would be difficult for her Companion to imitate, such as an elaborate dance sequence. After an allotted time, the adviser tells the players to switch roles.

A variation can be added as follows:

- Players are given time to create a short shadowing scene, rehearse it and present it to the class.

Advice

- "Find variety: The Companion is supposed to follow the Leader but sometimes steps out on his own. The Leader instigates everything but may also allow the Companion to go off on his own and then play the game of reminding him that *he* is following *her*. The Leader may also follow her Companion for a few moments to see how they'll react. Make it a game as well as a scene."
- "The Leader can use a variety of movements to challenge the Companion, then get annoyed when they can't keep up or gets things wrong. The Companion can stop following and simply observe the Leader, wonder what he's doing. The Companion could even try to sneak off and quit following."
- "Explore not only how the physical play expresses your relationship, but how to find variety in your roles as a leader and a follower. Status does not always have to be shown in an overt way."

Variation 4—Energies All players find a partner. The adviser lays out a series of props. Each player mentally chooses two energies: an energy is an emotional state that animates and drives the clown. Some examples are joy, anger, frustration, curiosity, greed, confusion, paranoia, etc. These energies should be strong enough that they encourage dynamic play; don't choose tiredness, for example, or boredom. Once they have two energies, the players choose a prop through which to reveal them. They step backstage with the prop. The adviser calls out the following sequence:

1. Player A enters expressing his first energy in how he enters, uses the prop and moves about the stage.
2. Player B enters expressing her first energy in how she enters, uses the prop and moves about the stage.
3. A sees B and changes his energy to match hers.
4. B notices the change and switches to her second energy.
5. A notices the change and switches to his second energy.
6. B changes to match him.
7. The players find an ending and exit.

Here's an example: Player A chooses a rope and joy as his first energy. Everything he does—the way he enters, moves through the space, plays with the rope—expresses joy. For example, he jumps rope, swings it over his head, laughing and leaping about. B chooses a cardboard box and shyness as her first energy. She enters gradually, tries to hide in the box. A sees this and finds the moment when he takes on her energy—shyness—and expresses it in how he uses the rope: he may try to hide in the rope, wrap it around himself. They play this change for a few moments, then B switches to her second energy, anger, suddenly thumping A with the box. She could try to strangle the box, tear off a flap ... Player A reacts to this (with shyness) trying desperately to hide behind his rope. He finds his moment to switch to his second energy, lust. He gets flirty with the rope, stroking it, dancing with it in a seductive way, which only makes B angrier! She finds her moment to match his energy. Now they are both lusty, expressing it through how they play with the box and the rope. They improvise an ending and exit.

It's important that the players stay with the energies they choose throughout the scene. Due to nervousness or inexperience, they will sometimes switch to a completely different emotion as they react to their partner. Forcing them to stick to the energies they've chosen encourages them to explore *the degrees of these emotions.* For example, to express anger as it increases towards rage, or lust as it softens towards being coy. This enables the players to learn how degrees of an energy affect them emotionally, mentally, and, most of all, how they express it physically and share it with the audience. Too often, players will shy away from expressing a higher level of an emotion and veer off into something less challenging or try to be clever in an attempt to get an easy laugh. This exercise is an opportunity to develop the expressiveness and expansiveness that is crucial to clowning.

Note: *The adviser can let the players explore on their own to get a feel for how to use the props to express an energy, before doing the exercise for the class. The adviser can call out the sequence of switches if necessary.*

Advice

- "Explore as many possible uses for the prop to express the energies you choose."
- "Stay connected with your partner so the exchange of emotions has a flow. Don't try to be clever or force a transition. Let ideas come out of the play between you both."

- "Find degrees in the emotional state: play it subtle, play it big, and everything in between."
- "Make dynamic choices so your partner has something to play off of, and the audience can clearly see what's driving the clown."

Variation 5—Juxtapose In this variation, the players use the solo pieces they developed in Section 6: Clown Solos. Two routines that involve a simple trick are played side-by-side (the adviser can decide which pieces might go well together because of their similarities or because they might create interesting juxtapositions).

The players enter, stand side-by-side with a two-meter gap between them, and present their two solos at the same time. They don't change what they've rehearsed, nor do they interact with the player next to them. The pieces are presented as is, with no deliberate attempt to connect them (like a two-ring circus). The audience looks for moments of synchronicity, strong contrasts, a convergence of ideas, etc., and gives feedback. After everyone has gone, the partners are given time to rehearse the pieces and incorporate the feedback, finding ways of interacting and creating more of a relationship and a scene as a duo while still presenting their solo acts.

Advice

- "Play with your reactions to each other as you explore each of the Five Elements. Are you surprised by each other when you enter? Are you confused but carry on, occasionally glancing at this person performing next to you? Do you stop and watch them perform, then do your act? You could choose to support one another, alternate who gives who full focus as you run through the Five Elements."
- "Explore how two distinct, separately created solos can be comingled to create a duo act."

MATCH MY MOOD

These exercises further explore the clown as energy. They help the players develop rhythm, timing and the ability to listen. Just as we exercise our bodies to build up strength and encourage new possibilities in movement, so we must work with our

> energies/emotions to increase their depth and range in order to develop and deepen the relationship between partners and the audience. These exchanges can be used any time the players are improvising or devising: by matching energies with a partner you immediately establish a connection, engaging with them emotionally and physically.

Props: Stage flats or curtains for entrances and exits.

Variation 1—Duo match Two players, A and B, are backstage. Player A enters in a relaxed state, displaying no particular energy or emotion. B enters with an energy and a physicality that expresses it. For example, joyful, angry, frightened, depressed, confused, etc. A matches B's energy, taking on the same level of intensity—neither higher nor lower. They play with the energy together, both expressing happiness for example, then A exits. B continues with the energy she entered with. Player A reenters with a new energy, B transitions to match it. They interact with each other for a few moments, then B exits. A continues with the energy he just entered with. B reenters with a new energy. A transitions to match it. They interact with each other for a few moments, then both players exit expressing the energy.

The players should be reminded of the work they did with the Five Elements and explore ways of entering and using the space to help express the energies they're working with. How can they use the flat or curtain, how do they move into the space, where do they move to, in order to better express the energy?

These are a series of mini scenes combining entrances and exits, observing, listening and responding to a partner, mirroring their energy (not just their physicality), and playing with the transitions between energies. Though the scenes are short, there's a lot going on.

Variation 2—Opposites Two players are backstage. Same sequence as above but player A changes to the *opposite energy* of B. For example, after A enters in a relaxed and neutral state, B enters full of energy, and is joyful. Player A transitions to being sluggish and surly. They play with these opposite energies, then A exits. B continues with the energy he entered with. A reenters with a new energy, B transitions to the opposite of it. They interact with each other for a few moments, then B exits. Player A continues with the energy he entered with. B reenters with a new energy. A transitions to the opposite of it. They interact with each other for a few moments, then both players exit.

Advice

- "Make strong clear choices so the energy you enter with is easy to read and understood by your partner and the audience."
- "Don't comment on or question the energy your partner enters with but validate and support it by participating in it. This creates an immediate connection and encourages complicity."
- "Share the changes with the audience, get them engaged with your play."
- "Don't try to force the play into a scene right away, just explore the energy between you."

THE BIG WIND UP

> When I worked in the Ringling Bros. and Barnum & Bailey circus, I noticed that many of the clown gags went from minimum to MAXIMUM: the energy and action built up until it exploded. Many times, there was an actual explosion, a bit of gunpowder in a small sheath of plastic film set off by an electric match. This "squib" was built into costumes and props: pants exploded, hats, boxes, furniture . . . In this exercise, the players build the energy and tension in a scene till there is a physical and emotional explosion.
>
> This is a good exercise for teaching the players the basics of minimum-to-MAXIMUM! Learning to master this kind of escalation gives the players an important tool to work with in any scene. The variations below can be worked on over a period of days so by the end, they will have created strong scenes as well as learned how to use the technique in an improv situation.

Props: Stage flats or curtains for entrances and exits, props for the scenes players create.

Variation 1—Count to ten Two players, one is the Jobber, the other, the Interrupter. The Jobber enters and starts an activity that requires him to be focused and concentrated. It can be as simple as sweeping the floor, setting a chair, or measuring the stage with a tape measure. The Interrupter enters and interrupts the Jobber deeply focused on his task. He sees her and silently counts to ten (he can go still, continue what he is doing as he counts, or find a variation on the action), as the Interrupter keeps trying to get his attention or distract him. The Jobber builds the intensity of his reaction with each count so that on ten he's ready to EXPLODE! On the count of ten, the Jobber chases the Interrupter off stage. The players take a breath and run the scene again, switching roles.

Note: *These are meant to be short scenes—thirty seconds or less—so the players can run them a few times. They don't spend time discussing what they'll do: they enter, run the scene, exit, switch roles, run it again. They sit and watch others have a go, then go again, using ideas they picked up from watching their classmates. Once they get the hang of a straightforward vertical escalation of energy, they explore ways to vary their reactions. For example, vary the timing, allowing more space for reactions between counting each number, in order to build suspense. For example, at nine, just before the explosion, the Jobber might go completely silent and relaxed ... then EXPLODE! At six, after getting angrier and angrier, the Jobber might smile, put an arm around the Interrupter, before throwing them offstage at ten, and exiting after her. Adding time between numbers gives both players the opportunity to interact and build the tension, always winding up the energy towards an explosion (see Jackie Gleason's slow build and bombastic responses to Art Carney in* The Honeymooners*).*

Variation 2—Interrupting in and out There are two players with the same roles as Variation 1. The Jobber enters and starts an activity that requires her to be focused and concentrated. The Interrupter enters and exits a number of times: the entrance can be just a look, a stumble onto the stage, a walk through, etc. The constant in and out interrupts the Jobber at her work, escalating the dramatic tension and comic play between them until it explodes (each entrance breaks the Jobber's concentration and increases her irritation). The Jobber chases the Interrupter offstage.

Note: *In either of these variations, the players can choose the energy they'll escalate: the most obvious is to get angry, but they can also choose to become romantic, sad, frighteningly happy, etc. The Interrupter is both the catalyst and the target for the energy that will be released. For example, the Interrupter's entrances scare the Jobber. The fear increases until the Jobber is terrified and runs off screaming (rather than chasing the Interrupter off stage). Or the entrances intrigue the Jobber and she tries to charm the Interrupter (both players must maintain the game of focusing on the task, the entering and exiting, and counting down, and not turn it into a drawn-out scene).*

Advice

- "As the Jobber, be intensely focused on what you're doing no matter how simple or absurd. The more concentrated you are, the more effective are the moments when you're disturbed by the Interrupter."
- "As the Interrupter, find the best moments to enter to build tension. Make the interruptions jarring, dramatic, subtle, comic. Use the entrances to build the energy in the scene. For example, wait until the tape measure is fully extended, then enter, distracting the Jobber and the entire tape snaps back into its case. The Jobber has to start all over again."
- "Both of you are responsible for escalating the energy in the scene, the tension between you—and the comic possibilities of that tension—by how you react to each other. Each interruption builds on the previous one, and though things may appear to return to normal—the Jobber goes back to his job—the energy underlying the scene should be building to an explosion. This must be evident to the audience; they should feel the build in energy and agitation."
- "Start small: set up the situation in a relaxed way. Take the time to establish the activity, draw the audience in, build a relationship with them via a familiar task. Control the escalation in order to bring the audience with you. The right moment to speed things up and find the explosion will come if the escalation is set up properly and not rushed."
- "The Interrupter can be both helpful and irritating. The Jobber can be polite and accepting, as well as frustrated and angry. If you get stuck on one way of playing, try its opposite. Vary the relational dynamic."

SURPRISE, SURPRISE

These variations utilize props to get partners to challenge and play off of each other. They're explorations, a way to generate ideas for different props that can then be used in most any scene. The players should both provoke each other and collaborate as they use the props in inventive ways.

Props: Objects to play with, preferably soft, like a towel, a ball, a foam bat, a plastic bottle, a newspaper, a hoodie, a pillow, a soft purse, etc. Nothing fragile or with sharp edges.

Variation 1—Object play There are two players, A and B. Each one chooses an object. B does something with his object—turns it into a mask, a hat, throws it high in the air, drops it on the floor and stomps on it, hits himself with it, etc. A reacts then does something with her object to get a reaction from B. They continue this back-and-forth with their chosen props. They can also threaten each other, entertain each other, try and shock, disgust, confuse, or scare each other, with how they handle the prop. They can try seduction, intrigue, repetition, nonsense. They take a breather when they feel they've run out of ideas, then try to work out a sequence in a more deliberate way: what props and actions should start the sequence, how do they move things along, escalate the energy, what moments are engaging, what don't seem to achieve a desired effect? From these choices, the players construct a minimum-to-MAXIMUM sequence, building the prop ideas and reactions so they top out, building up the energy between them and then making an exit. They rehearse the sequence, then show their scenes to the class.

Variation 2—Same object Same as above, but each player uses the same object, trying to find as many different ways to get a response from their partner with only a single prop to play with.

Variation 3—Box o'objects Same as Variation 1, but each player has a box full of objects and they choose which ones they'll use to surprise and play with, with their partner.

Variation 4—Script it Same as Variation 3, but as the players develop the scene with one object, they deliberately script in other props and choreograph the scene. "A hammer would escalate this—let's get a hammer!" They rehearse the sequence then show their scenes to the class.

Note: *These don't have to be finished scenes; they are explorations, a chance to develop a list of ideas, actions and exchanges that utilize props. These can be included in more advanced scenes as moments of duo play, or improvisations where two players confront one another and start grabbing props to intimidate, charm, argue with, or express love for their partner.*

EMBRACE

> This is a simple and at times, beautiful exercise, which gives the players a chance to experience an emotional build, an explosion and a release that is nonverbal, physical and playful.

Divide the class in half. They form two lines at opposite corners (use the diagonal corners so there is more space between the players). The first player in each line turns so they face away from each other. They take a few deep breaths to get into a relaxed state. At some point, they sense their partner is near. They turn and face them from across the room. The partners see each other: there is a feeling of relief and joy at seeing them, they are filled with gratitude and love. The emotions increase. As it builds, it animates and agitates the two players, the strong emotions and the desire to connect, affecting their bodies, their faces, the sounds they make; they don't want to stand apart, they want to close this gap between them. They let the energy build to the point where they suddenly launch themselves from their spot and meet in the center of the room and embrace! The embrace has its moment; the players experience the connection and let it play out without trying to force a scene; they just enjoy the connection. The players step away and sit to watch the others embrace.

Advice

- "Build to the moment of connection, play out the anticipation until it EXPLODES! and is released into the movement towards one another and the embrace."
- "Keep it honest and real. Truly connect with your partner and build the moment together."

Summary

Building a relationship between two players takes time. Some of the exercises in this section allowed the players to progress their connection slowly and with subtlety, using observation and simple physical contact to develop an awareness of their partner and their reaction to provocation. These exchanges continued the process of building trust in the ensemble, but now it's focused on only one person. The players learned to follow, lead, and to give themselves over to their partner in a responsible way. Other exercises encouraged a more vigorous interaction, with the players challenging one another in ways that were both earnest and ludicrous. Connecting with a partner emotionally was emphasized: this increased and deepened the players' ability to connect to the world around them and manifest this awareness in how they played with their partner.

This section also carried over the solo work, encouraging the players to use their explorations from the previous section and see how working with a partner altered and enhanced their ideas and solo acts. Status play between the Boss and the Fool was introduced. This will be explored further in the next section.

Figure 8.1 Devin Shacket, Ariel Speedwagon, and Windy Wynazz: Clown trios. *Photo credit: Eric Gillet/Shoot That Klown.*

8

Clown Trios

Boss, Negotiator, Fool

I've had a number of experiences with clown trios over the years both as a performer and teacher. The first trio I worked with was the Abbotts of Unreason. We met at the Ringling Bros. and Barnum & Bailey Clown College and had a good rapport while there. After declining an offer to tour another year with the circus, I joined Mark Renfrow and Bob Schiele in Michigan, and together we began the slow process of discovering how to play as a trio. The most obvious approach was to combine our solo talents into duo and trio routines. We all had some skill at juggling and acrobatics, so we evolved these into ball-and-club passing routines interspersed with acrobatic

Figure 8.2 Clown trio Rebecca Hammond, Katrina Kroetch, and Paul Philion. *Photo credit: Eric Gillet/Shoot That Klown.*

slapstick comedy. As our relationship evolved through our explorations in the studio, various routines we created, and time spent hanging out together, our natural tendencies were transformed into status play onstage.

The personalities of my partners were quite different. Status play with Bob was gentler than it was with Mark: he and I battled for the crowd's attention more often. In time, we learned to honor each other's contributions to the group and not always fight for laughs or applause. The skill routines helped that process: we had to learn to cooperate when passing juggling clubs or throwing each other for a backflip. This is one of the great things we discovered about shared skills: they can help partners build a deeper trust and a way of cooperating that goes beyond ego and competition.

As we got to know one another, we let our offstage relationship feed into our clown play: we tried not to predetermine too much and let the hierarchy evolve according to how we interacted naturally. We also discovered that the trio play helped us develop our individual clowns, which then fed into how we played with group status. Our show became a combination of trio, duo, and solo turns that expressed and expanded on the connections we'd made as creators and as friends. By exploring the natural interplay between us, in combination with the skills we chose to feature, we began to develop our trio and our status play *organically*, rather than impose roles on each other and set a strict hierarchy from the start.

This also happened with the second group I worked with, Los Payasos Mendigos (the Beggar Clowns). We were all strong solo performers so, when we got together, we fought for the crowd's attention. But the respect we had for each other's solo work is what brought us together, and that soon altered how we played onstage: we learned to step back and let each other take the lead, trust and give support to solo moments, keeping the status play fluid. No one was stuck always being the Boss, Negotiator or Fool and some of the best clowning came when one of us broke away from our usual role within the group and shattered any notion of a set ranking, sometimes all of us fighting to be number one, or all playing the fool.

In both groups, we maintained a healthy balance between collaboration and competition, respect and irreverence, hierarchy and anarchy. It was a constant balancing act, but it added a giddy tension to our play.

My work with these trios taught me the value of honoring a student's natural tendencies, expanding on them to develop their way of clowning, and letting these tendencies feed into their partner work. It's not a process of memorization, imitation, or imposing roles. It's a personal search and a development of all facets of a personality. This process increases a player's powers of observation, requiring them to tune into what is actually going on within themselves, in the room, and in their relationships with others. This training in observing and listening not only helps the players in their explorations into clowning, it's vital to how they play with the audience; the key to good clowning is the ability to constantly tune in and respond to the crowd while staying aware of a partner's needs onstage.

The play between the Boss, Negotiator, and Fool creates the perfect set up to explore variations in status. It is vital for the players to understand status and its possibilities for comic interaction and creating dramatic tension. People come up against authority figures every day of their lives—their boss, the police, the implacable authority of bureaucracy, the rigidity of a physical object, the complexity of a computer—so how a clown deals with authority will captivate everyone. It presents a gold mine of potentially hilarious and compelling moments if the players have a strong understanding of how to toy with the tension created by authority and hierarchy, by rules and by status. The trio is the perfect playground for this: like the proverbial third wheel, the third player knocks everything off balance and keeps the players on their toes by offering them opportunities to find multiple variations in their relationship: the Boss can team up with the Negotiator and antagonize the Fool; the Fool and the Boss can laugh at the Negotiator's attempts to make peace; the Fool and the Negotiator can make fun of the Boss. They can play as three solos trying to win over the audience. They can play together with a gentle harmony.

In some of the scenes suggested below, each player is jockeying for position and attention from each other and the audience. This should give the scenes a sense of urgency and dynamic play. Actions in the scene are presented as challenges, the players provoking each other as they toy with their status within the group and search for comic play as they interact.

Notes on Playing the Boss

Students will often play the Boss as a dictator, rigid and mean, shutting down the play by constantly saying no and stopping what the others are doing. This approach only works if all the players understand the role: the Boss' job is to make the rules. Those rules can be straightforward or absurd. The Boss simply says, "*This* is how it's done!!" even if how it's done looks completely mad (see the Monty Python sketch, *Self Defense against a Person Armed with a Banana*). His job is to create rules and set up structures so the others can question and toy with them and, in time, undermine them. His attempts to maintain discipline, his strict adherence to the rules, his demanding nature, may all appear to shut down the play, but the Boss's perceived severity should be played as a provocation, encouraging others to bend and break his rules, toy with his structure, make fun of him as they turn rigid routine into spirited play. Part of the pleasure and the comedy comes from watching the Boss attempt to control the situation, to see it break down and his rigidity fracture until he loses it and/or joins in the play.

Another way to perform the Boss is parental rather than authoritarian, suffering these fools he's partnered with gladly, guiding them, trying to teach them in a patient and persistent way.

The Boss also acts as a director within the scene: she has to keep her antennae up at all times, feeding the others, supporting them, keeping the scene moving, knowing when to allow tangents and when to rein them in, all the while listening to how it's playing for the audience. Though she may appear to be a fun-killer, the Boss often provides the foundation on which the fun is built: they provide structure and coherence amidst the hurly-burly and potential chaos inherent in most clown play.

Notes on Playing the Negotiator and the Fool

The Negotiator and the Fool must find the balance between maintaining the hierarchy by heeding, sometimes fearing the Boss, versus provoking her, bending her rules and destroying all pretense of a hierarchy. Too often, students will become self-indulgent when playing subordinate roles, rebelling and creating chaos too soon, losing the dynamic tension that draws an audience into a scene and creates empathy for the players. It helps to establish rules and roles at the outset, creating expectations that can then be challenged and undermined, as well as adhered to, to create variations in the trio's play.

Once the trio sets the scene, the Negotiator and the Fool can test the Boss to see what they can get away with. It's a tease as well as a challenge, a game as well as an outright provocation. They might anger the Boss who retaliates mercilessly; they must show that they fear this possibility. But their curiosity and play might also offer new insights, loosen up the Boss, make her laugh, get her to join with them in breaking the rules. This is when status play can become a game that all find delight in, even the authoritarian Boss. But the players mustn't make it easy: the fear of reprimand, retaliation and punishment are what helps create drama, builds suspense, ratchets up the tension, and makes the final release that much more enjoyable.

Like the explorations in the last section, trio work starts with games of collaboration, encouraging observation, and listening. We then move onto both overt and subtle expressions of hierarchy and tampering with status relationships.

GET RHYTHM

> This exercise use sounds and beats made with the body—in combination with movement—to connect the players in a trio. They learn to listen and play as well as create short vocal and movement-oriented scenes. The players must adjust to each other's strengths and weaknesses, picking up information by concentrating on their partners via sight and sound. I've used this exercise to create short interludes in scenes or trio routines: audiences always enjoy it when a group of clowns move as a chorus; the added sounds made with the body and voice, create another level of enjoyment.

Variation 1—Rhythm trios The players form trios and decide who will use their hands (clapping) to create a beat, who will use their body (slapping their hands on any part of their body), and who will use their voice (à la beatboxing). So, each trio has a player called Hands, Body, and Voice. All the players spread out around the room making sure to be as far as possible from their partners. The players create a beat with their chosen method, keeping the volume low and concentrating on their own beat. If theirs is similar to someone else's, that's OK, but they shouldn't do it deliberately.

Once everyone has a beat, the adviser calls out, "Trios!" The sound each player is making increases in volume: they stay true to their own beat as they seek out that of their partners. As they get closer to one another and hear their beats, they work to get in sync as a trio. They don't change the method of creating the beat—they stay Hands, Body, Voice—they just match the rhythm so they are all on the same beat but using different methods of creating it. After a minute or so of group play, the adviser calls out, "Split!"

and the trios separate, scatter about the room, and transition to a new solo beat. The adviser calls out "Trios!" and the players move towards their partners to sync up again with their new beats. They can repeat the exercise in the same trios playing with different beats or create new trios.

Note: *When trios come together, they improvise and elaborate on the sounds they've created as solos, turning it into a three-person jam session. They should take note of the contrast between what they play alone, the more complex music they create as a trio, and the return to something simpler when they split apart.*

Variation 2—Rhythm and movement Same as above, but this time the players add movement to the beat they create on their own; they get physical and dance to the beat they're making with their hands, body or voice. When the adviser calls "Trios!" they sync their beats and dance, so the trio is moving in a similar way to the same beat. Elaborate and embellish as above. The adviser calls out "Split!" and trios separate, scatter about the room, and transition to a new solo beat and movement. The adviser calls out, "Trios!" and the players move towards their partners to sync up again. They can repeat the exercise in the same trios playing with different beats or create new trios.

Advice

- "It will be difficult to maintain your beat, find your partners, and get in sync while all the other trios are doing the same all around you. Take it as a challenge, pushing you to listen more acutely, focus more intensely on your partners, and learn to tune out the other sounds in the room."
- "Try not to over think it. Keep it simple and let the rhythm, sound, and movement guide you."
- "Try to make the transitions smooth. Stay with your solo rhythm dance until you understand what your partners are offering and make a smooth change so you're in sync. Stay with your beat until you find it – try not to drop out or change abruptly."

Variation 3—Rhythm conversation The players form trios, each takes a letter, A, B, and C. They create a small circle. Player A thinks of something to say, turns to B and expresses it as a rhythm dance, utilizing clapping, slapping his body, stomping on the floor, making sounds with his mouth, etc. It's a beat/movement conversation, not a mime exercise or charades. No words are involved, only sound.

The players should be sincere in trying to translate their thoughts and communicate using sounds made with the body, voice, and movement. Player B watches and listens. When A finishes, B answers him in a similar way, then turns to her right and expresses her thoughts to C using rhythmic sound and movement. C watches and listens then gives his answer. C turns to A and the pattern continues. The players can also send it back: player A answers C as if to say, "Tell B what I just said," rather than turning and "speaking" to B directly. The adviser ends the exercise after an allotted time, the players create new trios and try again.

Advice

- "Explore and indulge in trying to express yourself with rhythm, movement and sound, not words."
- "Don't rely on charade-like gestures. Let it be abstract, playful. Find movements that express not just words but emotions, energies. Find a way of communicating that is rhythm, movement, and sound, not dumbshow (illustrative mime gestures that spell out an idea or emotion)."
- "Enjoy the absurd play of it! Imagine it as a language—like gibberish—that may sound incomprehensible to others, but you and your partners understand it completely."

PAPER AND BALLOONS

> This game encourages interactive physical play, encourages the players to develop strategies as a trio, and is a good ensemble building game (it can be done with more than three people). Here the trios must work together to keep the papers or balloons from falling and help each other to stay balanced. I have used this to develop clown acts and scenes, with trios and larger groups having to hold paper, balloons, as well as other objects between them while carrying out a task in front of an audience.

Props: Sheets of paper of different sizes—office paper, postcards, sheets of newspaper, etc.—at least twelve or more sheets per trio, chairs to set paper on (one chair per group), balloons of different sizes and shapes, large boxes to hold inflated balloons (one box for each group).

Variation 1—Paper play The players form trios, each group is given twelve sheets of paper to start with, set on a chair close by. The objective is for the players to hold all the sheets of paper between different parts of their bodies. For example, one player places a piece of paper against his shoulder, a second player leans his shoulder against this trapping the paper between them. The third player sets a piece of paper against her hip and pushes it against one of her partners to trap the paper in a new place (this can be hip to hip, or hip to thigh—it doesn't have to be the same body part). The players continue to pick up sheets of paper and trap them between their body parts—fingers, foreheads, backs, butts, etc.—never repeating the same holding spot (one player should keep a hand free until the end to pick up papers). If twelve sheets are easy, then try more.

Variations can be added as follows:

- Competition: Once a maximum number of paper sheets is decided upon, then have the trios compete: first group to hold all their sheets of paper, without dropping them or falling over, wins.
- Time: The adviser sets a time limit of one minute (or less). The trio who can hold the most papers before the time is up, wins.
- Sculpture: Trios must create an elaborate three-person sculpture while holding the papers. They explore ways to support each other, for example, one person places a paper under their thigh, then lifts it up to be held in their partner's hand, forcing them to stay balanced on one leg until the full sculpture is created. This encourages the groups to get more creative in how they position themselves while holding the papers.

Variation 2—Balloon play Same as above, but the players must trap balloons of different sizes and shapes between their bodies. Balloons are lighter, softer, may pop or roll about, making them more difficult to trap. Add Competition, Time, and Sculpture as above.

Note: *Once the trio have six or more sheets or balloons held between them, picking up more papers or balloons may prove difficult. Have them work out* *the best way to do this—make it part of the play—or work in groups of four with one player handing off and helping to set the paper or balloons.*

THUMBS

> This exercise gets the members of a trio improvising together as they solve problems, all the while having to listen for the audience's help in guessing solutions. It's a good way to develop the players' ability to focus on a number of partners while carrying out an action.

Props: A sturdy table and a chair (both should be strong enough to be stood on), a blanket or sheet.

Table, chair (with seat facing the table) and a blanket are set in a line with a two- to three-meter gap between each.

Three players leave the room and the adviser shows audience how the trio must travel past the three props. For example, they must crawl on all fours over the table, sit on the chair then lift it, holding it against their butt, and turn body and chair towards the blanket, then crawl under the blanket to the other side. When everything is set, the trio returns and lines up by the table. The first player shows a way of getting around the table, for example, he walks around it. The audience gives him a thumbs down. He returns to the trio. Another player has a go. If she fails and gets a thumbs down, the third one tries. They keep trying until one of them gets it and the audience gives them a thumbs up. The others imitate what she does, and they try to guess the way around the chair, then the blanket.

The attempts should go quickly, with the players rushing forwards to try things and watching the audience's thumbs. If a player's attempt is close—for example, they walk across the table rather than crawl—the audience gives them a thumb up, thumb down gesture, rotating their wrist between the two. This tells trio that they are close and should look for variations on what they're doing. The audience can also vocalize sounds of disapproval, approval, and something in-between when the players are getting close. They can nod, waggle, and shake their heads as well.

This can be done in smaller groups with one trio deciding on the props and the journey and giving a thumbs up to a second trio. Once the first trio makes it through, they switch roles; the first trio then decide how the second trio crosses.

Note: *Any props can be used as long as they inspire creative ways to get over, under or around them.*

Advice

- "This exercise demands you figure things out *physically* while creating a direct relationship to the audience. You must constantly offer suggestions and seek answers in the form of actions."
- "The guessing game with the audience will be frustrating at times—enjoy it! Allow yourself to be bewildered, to be at their mercy and still keep playing with them."

FOLLOW YOUR LEADER

> This exercise helps partners develop physical harmony and ensemble play, as well as making their connection visible to the audience. It encourages members of a trio to keep focused on each other as they develop their relationship and explore status play.

Props: Stage flats or curtains for entrances and exits.

Three players wait backstage. They're going to make a journey across the stage from one wing to the other. They decide who is the Boss, the Negotiator, and the Fool. They enter with the Boss leading the way, the Negotiator and Fool right behind her, *keeping their eyes on her at all times* so they can follow everything she does; they look where she looks, move and stop whenever she does, etc. They aim to be so attentive to the Boss that the movement across the stage—and the energies and attitudes expressed—looks synchronized. The Negotiator and/or the Fool may step away from the trio and do something, but only after checking if that's OK with the Boss. The players can use vocal sounds but not words. They may pause as they move across the stage but only briefly: the objective is to travel from one side to the other and exit, following the Boss's lead. The trio can reenter after switching roles and go again, or a new trio goes.

Note: The adviser can let the players improvise in front of the rest of the class or give them time to play with Follow Your Leader on their own before presenting.

Advice

- "As the Boss, give the others time to see your reactions and make sure they are with you – keeping their eyes on you – each step of the journey."
- "Play with time and speed: the Boss can suddenly run then stop abruptly, move in slow motion with long strides or creep along with short steps. The Negotiator and Fool can move slow when the Boss speeds up, or rush past her when she stops abruptly. Make it a game, a dance, a scene."
- "Play with building up drama and comedy by the use of stops, pauses, and starts. Explore head takes, big moves and small, move upstage and down, walk in diagonals and straight lines, double back, crawl, sneak about, walk tall, stomp, slide yourself along the curtain or wall. Let the journey across the stage be filled with movement and physical play!"

STATUS SNAPSHOTS

For physical comedy, it's important that a player knows how to show status with their body and be able to snap from high to middle to low, instantly, using poses, gestures, and facial expressions to express status. The players must also know how to flow from one status to another so their position in the group—and the changes in status as the scene progresses—are not always obvious to the audience; they're given time to discover the hierarchy on their own, and enjoy the slow realization that things are not what they appear to be.

In this exercise, a trio creates strong tableaux that reveal status. The adviser gives the groups time to "sculpt" their tableaux using mirrors. This will help them understand how to use their bodies to show status and learn some of the visual triggers that say this person is high or low. For example, high status might try chest and chin up, fists on hips, looking down their nose at everyone, while low status might cower, shoulders hunched, eyes downcast. The trios create a series of tableaux, then show them to the class.

Props: Stage flats or curtains to make entrances and exits, large wall mirrors so groups can observe themselves as they create tableaux. Or let groups observe each other and give feedback.

Variation 1—Tableaux: Body and space Working in different areas of the room, the trios create tableaux, arranging themselves in still poses representing their status relationship. They wear the clothes they would normally wear in class; for this variation we're looking at how their body—unadorned—expresses status. For the first tableau, they show the hierarchy in an obvious way using physical attitude, their location on the stage, how they would use the light (standing in the brightest light or in the shadows).

For the second tableau, the trio changes who has high, middle and low status and shows the hierarchy in a more subtle way.

For the third, the trio creates a tableau where all have equal status.

They rehearse these three tableaux separately, then put them together, physically shifting to present each tableau in a sequence.

Variation 2—Shifts Once the players rehearse three tableaux, they present them to the class. The trio enter together and strike their first tableau (it's obvious who has what status). They then shift to the second tableau, changing status gradually as they move to a new position (showing their status in a more subtle way). They move again, the status shifting to a tableau where all have equal status. Is this possible or do the players' body types naturally suggest a hierarchy? The adviser can discuss this question with the audience and give feedback to the players to see if they can achieve equal status visually.

When changing to a more subtle display of status, the players should consider even the smallest change in how they position or hold their body; any single part could be used to express status. They should also think about where they are onstage and use where they are in the space, in relation to their partners to show status. Does the high-status person come downstage closest to the audience or stand center stage? Does the lowest status player hide upstage in the corner out of the main light, or cower downstage, close to the safety of the audience? The players explore different variations and get feedback from the audience.

Variations can be added as follows:

- Add costume elements: The trios add costume pieces and explore how they might make simple changes in what they're wearing—tilt their hat, drape their coat upside down over one shoulder, have a shoe untied, etc.—to show their status and how it has changed.

- Add props: Props and any scenic elements such as a table, blanket, chair, etc., can be used to show status. The players keep the choices simple and explore how different statuses can be revealed through their physical relationship to a prop (proximity, how it is held, used, sat on, etc.). Using these accessories, they show a status tableau in an obvious way, then more subtle, then all are equal in status.

Note: *It's important that the players understand the power of stillness and creating strong visuals: these tableaux can be used as held "snapshots" to begin or end a scene; at any point in a performance; or a busy scene can slowly coalesce into a strong tableau that is held or simply slows down the action—the tableau is more of a pause rather than a completely still moment. When the players use tableaux effectively, they encourage the audience to see the world onstage in new ways. The audience will appreciate the time put into the visual play, how it adds to the performance, and brings the physical / visual world into greater relief, opening up more dynamic possibilities for connections between the audience, the players, and the world around them.*

Advice

- "Take an inventory: How are you holding your chest? What is the shape of your spine? How are your feet planted—do you feel grounded, balanced or unbalanced—and how does that affect your status? What are you doing with your arms? Is your face involved in expressing your status? Stay aware of every detail!"
- "Learn how to shape your body willfully and know what it's expressing so you can show status without having to use a mirror. Find the energy or emotion that will also support the physicalization."
- "Use the breath to fill the poses with energy as well as express status – long deep breaths, short, panting ones, long inhales then hold the breath, loud exhales through gritted teeth, etc.
- "This is a *group* exercise: How do individuals fit into the total picture? Show your status but be aware of how your physicality affects and enhances the poses of others, shows various relationships and creates an intriguing group picture."
- "Are you able to display equal status? Or does your physicality express high or low even when you're trying not to? What makes a person appear high or low even if they try to be neutral or equal to everyone else?"

GET UP

> This is based on the old clown gag of clowns fighting over who gets to sit in a chair. It can be a mental chess game exploring tactics for getting the chair, as well as getting more physical—even acrobatic—as the players contend for the chair and play with taking and giving status.

Props: Stage flats or curtains for making entrances and exits, gym mats, a sturdy chair (check that it is solid, no loose screws or sharp edges).

Variation 1—One chair The adviser sets a chair onstage. Mats are set around the chair (this can be set on the mats as long as it doesn't damage them). Three players are backstage. They have one objective: all want to sit in the chair. Player A enters and sits. B and C can enter together or one at a time.

This is a game of tactics and, sometimes, brute force: the players can physically remove each other from the chair by pushing, pulling or dumping their partners. Or they beg, tease, charm, form alliances (two gang up on one), remove an article of clothing—such as a hat—from the person in the chair and force them to come and get it, try to befriend, scare, or threaten them, offer them a gift, encourage them to come to another part of the stage to see something, etc.

The player in the chair can resist the others' tactics, encouraging them to be more inventive, as well as playing along, giving up the chair to see what happens if they fall for a tactic. They may even offer the chair because they want to see if they can then convince their partner to give it back to them.

Advice

- "Make the actions and tactics believable! Get up because your partner does something that truly makes you curious. If they try to lift you out of the seat and can't manage it, don't *pretend* he's strong enough. Or make it obvious you're pretending as a tactic."
- "Don't just turn it into a never-ending wrestling match: pause, give the audience moments to experience what you're feeling, thinking, planning. Show the relationships between you and your partners, give us time to see and experience your reactions to each other's efforts."

- "Work as three solos, at other times, form alliances, two against one. Form alliances then switch them, double cross each other: B might do all the work to remove A only to have C get to the chair first. Or B might get A out of the chair only to offer the chair to C. Or player A might create a rift in the alliance between B and C by offering the chair to one of them while blocking the other."

Variation 2—Two chairs Same as above but use two chairs. The players enter and explore as many variations as possible for claiming the chairs using solo tactics, duo and trio strategies. For example, one gets lifted out of the chair only to have the third player lay across both of them.

Advice

- "Stay aware of how you can use status even while you're playing in an actively physical way."
- "You can choose to give in to a partner and obey them, play low status; another player may take pity on you and give or win the chair for you. You can make allegiances, then switch them because you see an opportunity for yourself to get the chair, or because you feel your current partner has insulted you. Or hang onto an allegiance even if your partner treats you with disdain. Make it a scene as well as a game."

TOP THAT

> How a player handles a prop is important: attitude is everything in this exercise! The player must give off the sense that what he has done easily tops what the others do, even if to the audience's eye it's not all that impressive. This is the art of chutzpah, exuding self-confidence or audacity despite appearances to the contrary. What you do can be fairly ridiculous but you commit to it with the attitude of, "Oh yeah? Top that!!" The way each player presents themselves in the scenes is meant to be a parody of an overconfident person.

Props: A long table to put props on, set backstage or off to one side. The props should be ones that aren't easily broken, with no sharp bits. Things that can be treated roughly, torn or crushed such as cardboard boxes, newspapers, sheets or pillows, paper cups or plates, etc. are good choices.

Variation 1—Swagger There are three players, A, B, and C. They choose a simple task for the trio to enact. For example, setting a chair onstage, placing a cloth over a table, putting on a hat, etc. The trio enter with the prop and begin the scene. The first player does something impressive with the prop. The next player tries to top that: what she does with the prop is even more impressive. The third player does the same.

An example: A and B enter and give focus to the entrance of C. They come out holding the chair at chest height, swing it outwards with one hand and set it down. B grabs the chair and exits as C joins A to watch. B enters with the chair overhead and drops it from this height, catching it just before it bangs the floor. A grabs the chair and exits as B joins C to watch. A comes out with the chair in one hand and swings it around her body, switching hands as it travels around her. She ends by swinging it right to the floor downstage of everyone. C grabs the chair, exits, and they have another round. Each attempt does not have to involve an entrance and exit, but the in and out can be used to help show status; they each try to top the others' entrance as well as the play with the chair.

The players explore both obvious and subtle examples of one-upmanship, actions that are clearly meant to say, "I'm the best at doing this!!" as well as actions that make everyone wonder what the player's intention is; the actions don't always have to be bigger or broader. Sometimes being calm and quiet can achieve a higher status.

The adviser sets a time limit from one to two minutes. The players exit when time is called.

Variation 2—Alliances Same as above, but the players gang up on each other by switching allegiances throughout the play. For example, player A establishes his high status by slamming down the chair. B reinforces A's status by slamming it down exactly as A did, then sidles up to A. C puts a finger against the chair and topples it. A or B can then try to top that or do something that shows one of them is switching sides and joining C (B applauds C's action and stands beside him).

The action for the change of allegiance can be with the prop: B slams down the chair too. Or without: B congratulates A on his slamming down of the chair, stands next to him and waits to see what C will do.

The adviser sets a time limit from one to two minutes. The players exit when time is called.

Note: The advisor can allow the players to explore both variations on their own, make discoveries and set some things before presenting to the rest of the class.

Advice

- "Attitude is as important as action! Think of roosters strutting, or the display of animals challenging each other. You can perform an action with a prop that suggests nothing in itself in terms of status. But *the way* you perform the action says everything about who you aim to be!"
- "Your attempts to top each other can be obvious or subtle, straightforward, oblique or absurd. Try not to judge yourself or your action but play it with confidence."
- "It's a competition, the stakes are high. Each action lays down a challenge, throws down a gauntlet. Don't just play it for laughs, try to build drama and suspense into the scene as well."
- "It's also a game: keep the play in the exchange, enjoy the pretense, the near ludicrous, over-confident attitude, especially when doing something absurd, aggressive or not so impressive."

DOWN THE LINE

> These variations explore a progression of ideas and energies, and how each of the three statuses—the Boss, Negotiator, and Fool—react to each other as they play with props. For the players, these variations are a good way to explore status using objects. For the adviser, it's a way to find out which players would make good trios and who naturally gravitates towards a particular status.

Props: Stage flats or curtains for entrances and exits, a long table, set with miscellaneous props on one end, and a hat, a book, and a cane.

Variation 1—The little things Three players wait backstage. One wears a hat, the other holds a book, the other a cane. Each player should wear or hold the object in a particular way. For example, the hat is set so the brim sits straight, the cane is held by the top end with both hands, the book is held closed, against the chest.

They enter and face the audience, standing shoulder to shoulder. They greet the audience in small ways, smile, nod, etc., but continue to wear or hold the prop the same way as how they entered with it. At some point, any one of them does something with their prop that alters the way it was when they came in. For example, the one with the book opens it and looks at the pages. Her partners look at her and react, the various expressions on their faces reprimanding her for altering the position of the book. She returns the book to its "proper" position against her chest. This play continues with each player adjusting their prop—tilting the hat brim, throwing it in the air, tapping the cane against the floor or their palm, etc. Each time someone does something, the others shoot them surprised, disapproving, scolding looks. The player reacts and goes back to the way they were, with their prop held the "proper way."

Only one player at a time changes: the others watch to see what she will do, react, and then chide her for the change. Vocal noises are OK, but no words are allowed.

The players explore these exchanges and see what develops: they could build it until one of them loses it and does a series of adjustments, not caring about the "proper way," or their partners' reprimands. Or they can keep the interactions subtle, enjoy the focused play, and make an exit on their own or on a cue from the adviser.

A variation can be added as follows:

- The players vary their reactions so they aren't always reprimanding their partners but encouraging them to develop more variations on how they wear, hold or handle the props. This version is more playful and can be developed from the first variation, or the trio start right in with the play.

Advice

- "Don't force anything! This is one of those explorations where you honor the small exchanges—prop play, looks, reactions. Be patient and see how things develop. This can then be expanded into more vigorous play."

Variation 2—The right way Three players wait backstage. They decide who has high status, middle and low. The adviser sets a table center stage with props all at one end of the table. The trio enters and stands behind the table facing the audience. The player closest to the props is the Boss, the middle player is the Negotiator, the last player, the Fool. The Boss takes a prop from the table and uses it as it is supposed to be used. The actions should be short, straightforward, and easily repeatable. For example, she picks up a towel, dries her hands in "the right way," (remember, this can be a normal use of the object, or absurd to the audience's eyes), and passes the towel to the Negotiator. He dries his hands in the right way and adds a variation by neatly folding the towel. He hands it to the Fool. She makes an attempt at drying her hands, but begins to rub the towel over her body instead, tries to balance it on her nose, or turns it into a hand puppet, etc. The fool's play can be an absurd variation on what the Boss has displayed or have no relation to it at all. The Fool sets the prop down; the Boss picks up a second prop and repeats the sequence.

Each trio passes five props down the line, then exits. A new trio gives it a go. If there is enough time, the trios can go again and switch roles.

Advice

- "Keep it simple. The exploration with the prop for each player is short and sweet (though the Fool may go off on a tangent until either of the other two—or both—stop her)."
- "What the Fool does may or may not be hilarious in and of itself: often the comedy comes from the reactions of the others. This is important: it's your job to support each other's play and not leave your partner solely responsible for making her moment work. Give them focus, react and decide how you will respond, look for both comic and dramatic possibilities in your interactions."
- "Don't drop out once you hand over the prop: focus the audience's attention to where you think it should go and encourage their response by how you focus and respond to your partners. But don't overdo it. The objective is to support your partner's moment, not steal it."
- "As the Boss, find a balance between keeping things moving, and allowing the Negotiator or the Fool to build on an idea and their play with the prop. Listen closely to how your partner's play affects the audience and how you might expand on it and increase the crowd's response or end it and move on."

- "As the Fool, don't get indulgent. Play and improvise but listen to the audience: do they want more, or should you hand the moment over to your partners? You don't always need to do things wrong or try to get laughs—you could repeat your partner's actions to the letter now and then to build a pattern, an expectation that you or your partners can disrupt."

Variation 3—The right way with tasks Three players wait backstage. They decide who is the Boss, Negotiator, and Fool. The Boss comes up with a simple task that has a very specific way of being done. For example, a folding chair is held *exactly like this*, opened in *just this way*, and set in this spot *and only this spot*. The Boss demonstrates the right way to the others and lets them have a go. He can let one of them do it wrong and then correct him; he can interrupt his partners if they don't follow the instructions to the letter; he can let both players do it wrong—even watch them enjoy screwing it up or inventing variations—before stopping them and reminding them of the right way. The more nit-picky and authoritarian the Boss is about how the task is done, the more it provokes the other players to screw it up, either deliberately, out of misunderstanding, from a desire to play, or plain stupidity. The mistakes build the tension between the players as the Boss tries to assert his status by getting the others to follow his instructions to the letter. His partners continue to provoke him and expand on the possibilities with the prop, the rules, and their relationship, by how they interpret the task. The adviser sets the time limit for the pieces from one to two minutes. The players exit when time is called.

Variation 4—Changing status Same as Variation 3, but the players can switch status at any point. This is usually revealed by the reaction of others to what someone does. For example, the Boss reacts to the action of one of his inferiors as if he has handled the prop in a clearly novel way! The Boss bows down to him (literally and/or figuratively), and that player takes on the attitude that he's in charge; the others try to imitate the new set of rules (the way the prop is handled by the new Boss). The players can switch status again or exit with the new hierarchy.

The adviser sets the time limit for the pieces from one to two minutes. The players exit when time is called.

Note: *In all the variations above, the adviser can allow the players to explore variations on their own, make discoveries and set some things before presenting to the rest of the class.*

Advice

- "Keep the task short, simple and precise so the demonstration on how it's done is easy to repeat."
- "Don't fret over being funny or brilliant. Stay open to simply exploring, getting to know one another and how each of you plays with status revealed by the prop or task."
- "As the Boss, play the authoritarian in such a way that outwardly, it appears to stifle the play, but in inwardly, supports and encourages it. The Boss shouldn't stop the action every time the others do it wrong. Instead, let the partners play, and let the audience see how a player's actions affect each person in the trio."
- "Keep the balance and tension between following orders (and fearing the consequences of getting it wrong) and provoking the Boss by screwing things up. Your reactions to each other's actions are key to helping the audience understand the group's hierarchy and how it might change."
- "Can you play a believable simpleton? Can you portray someone who really doesn't understand how to do a simple task and make the audience believe that you are truly a fool? Think *child-like* not childish. Play with a curiosity and sense of wonder so intense it makes you appear dumbfounded, foolish."
- "Explore status shifts, low to high and high to low. Anyone can change status at any point in the scene—even as you make your exit."

Summary

The focus on this section was on status and exploring the comic and dramatic possibilities of creating a hierarchical relationship within a trio, setting up expectations for the audience, and then toying with both the hierarchy and the expectations that that ranking creates. Some of the exercises created a competitive environment for trios to work in, while others had them collaborating, finding comic interplay in a less contentious way. They encouraged the players to actively listen to one another and the audience, to find pleasure in following authority unreservedly, as well as toying with status, developing comic play through lively confrontation.

Active listening and observing is one of the most important skills a performer can have, gathering information with their eyes and ears that they can utilize at any moment. Trio work teaches this in a way that is both informative and motivating, because you have more partners and possibilities to play with but not so many that it gets overwhelming. Trio explorations feed into all clown work whether solo, duo or ensemble, and inspires play that can be used in any venue, from a theater to a circus ring, a hospital room to a refugee camp.

This section expanded on the solo and duo work, widening the scope of the clowns' relationships not just to others but to themselves, teaching them more about their individual strengths and weaknesses which are brought into higher relief when working in a group that is more provocative; there is the possibility for greater disruption in a trio and thus greater comic play.

The discoveries of the trios will be developed in the next section as the players expand their powers of observation and listening to take in more people, finding moments to express themselves from within a large ensemble, while supporting others' solo, duo and trio moments.

Figure 9.1 Clown ensembles: (left-to-right) Amica Hunter, Carasue McClendon, Sophia Knox-Miller, Kate Brehm, Sydney Schwindt, Christian Schneider, Windy Wynazz, Barbara Gonzalez, Tommy Toxic, Devin Shacket, Andrew Pulkrabek, Rebecca Hammond, Paul Philion, Ariel Speedwagon, Katrina Kroetch, Lars Adams, and David Cantor. *Photo credit: Eric Gillet/Shoot That Klown.*

9

Clown Ensembles

Fractious Fun

While working with Los Payasos Mendigos, I discovered the comic power of choral movement (even silly choral movement). Whether it was running around the stage in improvised patterns while slapping our thighs, doing a group hand jive that ended in a clapping, slapping salute to the heavens while shouting in unison, "Believe it!" or performing percussive patterns with sticks, this unified movement visually established that this was an ensemble, that these guys were in tune with one another, working together with tight synchronicity. We then proceeded to dismantle that assumption through slapstick, status play, making fun of machismo, and grown men behaving like children.

I use this friction in my teaching, this tension between everyone getting along in wonderful harmony, versus the disruptions caused by factions,

Figure 9.2 Los Payasos Mendigos (the beggar clowns): Joe Dieffenbacher (Yahoo), Rudi Galindo (Lupita), Cosmo Kuzmick (El Excremente), and Dave Ferney (Guapo). *Photo credit: Matilda Dieffenbacher.*

cliques, and individuals wanting to be seen and applauded on their own. Anyone who has worked in a group situation has experienced this: individuals must cooperate and work as a team, all the while wanting their own voices to be heard. There is the feeling—sometimes subtle, other times overt—that it all could blow up at any moment, and with so many people potentially at odds, there will be a bigger mess to clean up. Rather than create anxiety, the clown's playful mind embraces this tension and sees it as an opportunity: they know that these discrepancies can create a varied and headier mix based on the true dynamics of a group.

When we look at clown groups at odds with one another we wonder why they stick together. The strange, awkward juxtapositions of energy and emotion, and the physical differences between the players, would make us think they ought to find more compatible companions. But it's the very tension this question creates in the audience's mind that intrigues them and they take delight in watching how the group negotiates the various arguments, alliances, and affections, wondering when it will descend into competition, conflict, and slapstick. Then they consider how and if the clowns will reunite, find group harmony and playfulness once more.

Ensembles also create the kind of variety that everyone can engage with: an audience member may love the brainy clown but not the acrobatic one, they find the pun-telling clown humorous but the one who keeps entering at the wrong moments, hilarious. The mosaic of personalities, faces, costumes, movements and the possibilities of physical play is so much richer in a large ensemble and will always pique the crowd's curiosity.

The games and exercises in this section encourage stronger ensemble play, offer ensemble movement ideas, help groups generate comic moments, explore how individuals influence the group energy, how the players can work as a chorus to support each other's solo, duo and trio moments, and promote the acceptance of accident and absurdity in ensemble play.

ALL TOGETHER NOW

These variations go from simply standing up together to vigorously chasing one another. They're good to use as an ensemble warm up, team building, and exploring how to work together to find balance and group stability in physical ways.

Props: A sturdy chair.

Variation 1—Stand up The players partner up. They sit on the floor back-to-back, knees bent, their arms reaching back behind them to link together with their partner's, crossed at the elbows. Using their feet, they push against each other's backs and stand. Now they try with three people back to back (or shoulder to shoulder), their arms linked as above. This continues until the whole class links arms and all stand together.

Variation 2—Chair chain One player sits on the edge of a chair; another sits on his knees. The player on the chair grabs the second player's waist. Another player sits on the second player's knees; the second player grabs his waist. This pattern continues until all are seated on each other's knees. The players lean forward slightly to keep the line from tipping backwards (the adviser can remove the chair or leave it in place), they count together and, on three, stand up by leaning forward still holding each other's waists. Then, on the count of three, all sit back onto each other's knees. Repeat a few times until the group can do it cleanly.

Variation 3—Circle up Sitting in the line, the players chant together, "Left, right, left, right" … leaning side-to-side, lifting their feet in time. When they're in sync, the player at the front walks the group into a circle so she can bring her knees under the butt of the last player (as they come around, the chair is removed). Once the first player's knees are supporting the last player, they all let go of each other's waists; the circle is self-supporting. Once in the circle, the adviser counts off: on three, the group all stand at the same time. The adviser counts to three again, the players all sit on each other's knees.

If walking into the circle proves too difficult, have the group start by standing in a circle all facing the same direction, grab the waist of the person in front of them, then, on the count of three, slowly sit back on the knees of the person behind them. Then try the stand and sit again.

Note: *Play with proximity—how close do you need to be to sit on each other's knees—and remember to lean forward and slightly inwards to keep from tipping over.*

Variation 4—Tail of the dragon This is be played with five to seven players for each dragon. The players line up holding the waist of the person in front of them (ties, belts, or scarves tied around waists may help the players hold on once the dragon starts moving). The player on the end of the line has a sock tail tucked into his back waistband. The player at the front of the line must try to grab it by curling back along the line (the dragon is chasing its own tail). Do those in the middle help the head or the tail? When the head grabs the sock tail, a new head and tail are chosen, and the group starts a new game.

A variation can be added as follows:

- If the room is big enough (or played outdoors), a number of dragons made up of five to seven players can play at the same time. The head of each dragon tries to grab the sock tail of the other dragons. If they do, that dragon sits out or those players join the remaining dragons till there is only one left.

FOLLOW ALONG

These variations have fairly simple set ups, so they allow the players to focus on one another more acutely to develop physical harmony and ensemble play.

Props: Stage flats or curtains for entrances and exits.

Variation 1—Floating hands The players sit close together on the floor, or in chairs in a circle. They place their left hand over the right hand of the person to their left (thus everyone has their left hand *over* a hand and their right hand *under* a hand). Everyone closes their eyes. Every player moves their right hand up, down, forward, back, in circles, etc., lifting the left hand of the person sitting to their right side. Thus, all the right hands are initiating the movement of all the left hands, all the left hands are relaxed and being moved by all the right hands. The adviser lets this continue for a period of time and then tells the players to switch: the left hands now go *under* the right hands, so while the left hand initiates the movement, the right hand is relaxed and allowing itself to be led. This exercise creates an interesting split in the body as the players learn to relax one hand/one side of the body and let it be led, while leading the action with the other hand/other side of the body.

Variation 2—Mirror mix The players form groups of six. They face each other, three to a side, arm's-length apart. One side are Mirrors, the other side are Leaders. The Leaders begin to move, and the Mirrors imitate exactly what's shown by their partner directly across from them, adding nothing. The players explore movement only; they don't act out a scene. The adviser reminds the Mirrors to pay attention to everything: facial expressions, the position of the feet, the shape of the spine, how the hands are held, etc.

Once both Leaders and Mirrors are in sync, any Mirror can choose to follow any Leader. They don't move from where they are, they just use their eyes to observe and follow someone else. If the Leader loses their Mirror, they stay in the game: another Mirror may decide to follow them. If so, they give them their attention and play with them (but stay where they are). This continues, with the Mirrors switching Leaders as they please and the Leaders keeping an eye out to see if they're being followed. The adviser calls an end to the exercise. The players switch roles and go again.

A variation can be added as follows:

- A Leader who is not being followed, can choose to become a Mirror and follow the person directly across from them (they follow only their Mirror, not someone else). So, they might find themselves mirroring a Leader next to them or at the other end of the line. This could lead to everyone mirroring one Leader. The adviser calls an end to the exercise. The players switch roles and go again.

Note: *No discussion or verbal direction is needed: communication is with the eyes and through movement only.*

Variation 3—Mirror line Divide the class in half. The players line up in two rows holding hands. The lines face each other about two meters apart. One row is designated as the Mirror. The players from the other row—the Leaders—start moving slowly, still holding hands. The Mirror row reflects all movements of the Leader row. They focus on and copy the Leader directly across from them all the while holding hands with each other (the Leaders can move as they like, they don't have to sync their movements with the other Leaders). After an allotted time, the players switch roles.

Variation 4—Elevator Five or more players are backstage, all others observe. The first player enters as if stepping onto an elevator. He does a simple action: for example, putting his hands in his pockets. The adviser says

"Ding!" Another player enters the elevator and does an action; for example, crossing her arms. The first player sees this and does the same (this can be right away or after a few beats). The adviser says, "Ding!" Another player enters, does a new action such as vigorously scratching themselves, or swatting at a fly. The first two players join in at some point. This pattern continues (the adviser cueing each entrance with "Ding!"). The elevator gets more crowded (the floor can be marked out with tape or rope to keep the players cramped together or surround them with flats on three sides if they're available), all the players doing variations on the same action.

Once all are on and doing the action of the final player to enter, anyone can go back to the action they entered with to see if others join in. Duos, trios or the whole group can switch between the actions introduced, but they don't invent new ones. They improvise until the adviser says "Ding!" The elevator doors open and all exit.

Advice

- "When a new action is introduced, you don't have to take it on right away. Let the new arrival act it out, establish it, you react to it, then find the best moment to join in to increase the comic play, as well as build up tension and anticipation. You can also choose to imitate the action as soon as you see it. In other words, play with the timing."

FOLLOW ME

> These are good games for partner work and can be incorporated into a staged routine. The Follower (the Fool), learns to focus on the Boss to such a degree that he can appear hypnotized. The Boss enjoys her power but should keep her wits about her: the Fool can take over and hypnotize the Boss!

Room prep: If chairs, strong wood boxes, mattresses and gym mats are available, spread them around the space to create levels to play with.

Variation 1—Follow the hand The players partner up. One partner is the Follower, the other is the Leader. The Leader holds his open palm about twenty centimeters from the Follower's face. They maintain this distance the entire time as the Leader begins to move his hand up and down, side to side and all around. The Follower locks her eyes on the hand and never looks at anything else. The Leaders get the Followers to stop and start, run, jump, speed up, slow down, lie down, go up on a table, sit in a chair, etc., all by how they move their hand. They should enjoy their power but not abuse it: take care of the Follower and don't create any distrust; they'll be leading next.

At any point, the Leader can pull his hand away. The Follower snaps out of being mesmerized by the hand and is free. But as soon as the Leader brings his hand up again, the Follower locks her gaze on it and the game continues. The Leader can make a game of this by playing with the duration: release the Follower for five seconds, let them think they're free, then snap the hand back in front of their face, grabbing their attention again. Or pull away and snap it right back. After an allotted time, the adviser tells the players to switch roles.

Variation 2—Switch Same as above, but when the Leader pulls hand away, the Follower can choose to bring her hand up and take over, becoming the new Leader. This switching continues, each player making a game out of who will grab the other's attention and become the Leader. They can make the switches quickly or tease one another as to who will take over first (or one can refuse to take over—they love being the Follower).

Variation 3—One leader two hands Same as above, but the players form groups of three. The Leader holds both hands up and has a Follower on each hand. They play the game of pulling the hand away and any member of the trio taking over as in Variation 2.

Variation 4—One leader, hands and feet Same as above but the players form groups of five. The Leader lies on his back and holds up his hands and feet with a Follower for each one. They keep their faces about twenty centimeters away from the hands or feet of Leader as he moves them. He can move how he likes but must keep the palms and the soles of his feet exposed so the Followers can follow (avoid standing or placing hands down on floor). The Leader should take care not to move too abruptly and the Followers should keep a safe distance from the hand or foot to avoid being hit if the Leader makes an abrupt movement.

Variation 5—Random parts Five players form a circle. One player steps into the middle and becomes the Leader. Those around them choose a part of the Leader's body they will follow—wrist, chin, feet, chest, right knee, etc. The Leader begins to move. One player from the circle moves closer and begins to follow the body part she's chosen. Others come forward and do the same (the distance between the Leader and others will vary; they do not all have to be the same distance away and can change as they play).

The Leader can move everything in the same direction, for example, turning clockwise while moving his body up or down, or he can move in a random way so the chest might move left while the chin moves right and the arms flap up and down, with the players following their chosen body part. They play for an allotted time, then switch who is the Leader.

Variation 6—Leader, follower, leader, follower This can be done in groups of five to seven or the entire class. One player steps forward to follow a body part of the Leader, a second player steps forward and follows a body part on the first player. A third player follows a part of second player's body and so on. The players must stay aware of those around them and avoid sudden movements all the while keeping their eyes locked on the body part they're following; this exercise will improve their kinesthetic awareness. The group plays for an allotted time, then starts again with a new Leader.

Note: *These games of following can be used in any group scene and are easy ways to begin the creation of ensemble movement. They can be used to show status or as a way to grab another's attention; in a scene, a rule is agreed that any time a player raises their index finger, all the others must lock eyes on it and follow its movement.*

SUPPORT STAFF

This exercise connects the group physically as they lift, carry, and support a single player. The ensemble is focused on one person but must also stay aware of how others are moving in the room. It's great for developing physical trust and getting players to give their complete attention to their partners, supporting their needs and requests.

Props: Music is optional. If you use it, find pieces that aren't dominating; it's there for ambience and inspiration.

Room prep: Gym mats are good to use if available, covering as much floor space as possible. Ensure there is nothing in the room that might be a potential hazard. Keep the Leader away from raised levels, hard edges, corners, etc.

Physical prep: Do a good physical warm up, paying close attention to backs, legs and shoulders. The players will be lifting and supporting each other so have them take each other's weight as part of the warm-up. They should be reminded to lift with their knees not their back. All players should acknowledge their limits and shouldn't try to do things they're not strong enough to do.

Variation 1—Supported One player is the Newbie, five or more are the Support Staff. The Newbie makes offers; the Support Staff respond. For example, she offers her foot by lifting it. A member of the Support Staff takes her foot in hand, or someone goes down on all fours so the Newbie can place her foot on their back. The Newbie offers another hand, someone takes it. Another supports her arm so she can stand on the backs of the Support Staff members down on all fours. The Support Staff can lift the Newbie up and carry her around the room. Or they let her move as she likes until she signals for support. She can make eye contact with a Staff member and jump into their arms, climb on their back, embrace them. She can allow herself to be dragged, spun, pulled, pushed, etc.

The Newbie is the leader: she calls for support in the form of a physical offer. If she communicates that she wants to be put down or allowed to run unhindered, the Support Staff give her room, always ready to help if she signals for support.

Advice

- "When offering help try not to tense up; move in a focused and relaxed way."
- "If you're supporting, stand in a wide, low stance like you're sitting on a horse, ready to move in any direction."
- "Lift and support with the legs, not the back."
- "As you focus on the one needing support, stay aware of everything around you: other players, objects in the room, what's on the floor, changes in levels, etc. Train yourself to observe the space and register how it may be useful in the play or hinder it and be avoided."

- "The Support Staff must be attentive to suggestions made by the Newbie. Offer support, then wait to see how they accept or reject it."
- "Know your limitations: if you have a bad back, don't try to lift the Newbie on your own. Bring in others or transfer the Newbie's offer to someone else."
- "The Newbie should take risks but not be irresponsible. Make it known what you want from the Support Staff but without words: communicate through how you use your body, your gestures, your eyes. Sounds are allowed but the focus should be on *physical communication*."

Variation 2—Faint

Physical prep: The players should practice faints first: let the faint be a slow, spiraling move so they go gently to their knees then roll out along their thigh to their hip and lay out on their side, using their hands to lower the torso to the floor. Avoid dropping straight to the knees. The players should practice these controlled faints in case no one gets there in time to catch them.

The players count off. They walk randomly but keep close to one another, about arm's-length apart. The adviser calls a number. That player faints: it should be telegraphed—an obvious physical wind up before the faint, a loud sigh before dropping—to give others time to find and catch him before he falls to the ground. He's lifted to his feet, quickly recovers. The players walk until a new number is called. The adviser can choose to call out more than one number.

Note: *For both variations, the players shouldn't wear clothing that's loose as it may get tangled in a hand or stuck under foot.*

Advice

- "Use all parts of your body to catch the player who is fainting: catch with your back, the soles of your feet, lock arms with another player and catch in this cradle, use your chest, etc."
- "If you're fainting and see a player setting up to catch you, adjust your faint. For example, lift an arm to let it fall over a player's neck, or turn and lay the front of your body over someone's back as they bend over."

CARETAKERS

> This is one of my favorite exercises for developing ensemble play and physical trust. I return to it often: the players find new possibilities in this exercise the more they do it. Caretakers requires strong concentration to really tune into your partners and pick up cues from their movements.

Props: Blindfolds or veils (have extras as they will get sweaty), music player, playlist of instrumental music; use compositions that are lyrical, such as classical or jazz. Don't use music with a strong, heavy beat: the music should encourage large, flowing movements. Mats, mattresses, exercise balls, blankets, and other soft objects can be scattered about the room for the Leader to crawl over, be laid onto, be led up and over, etc. Whatever is used always keep safety in mind.

Notes on blindfolds or veils: There are two possibilities: a veil to cover the face, sheer enough to see through but not so transparent that the Leader's face is easy to see. Or a blindfold. A veil will encourage the Leader to take more chances as she can see where she's going. A blindfold can give the Leader a more intense experience because she can't see at all and must trust both her own kinesthetic sense and the partners who are guiding her.

Room prep: Gym mats are good to use if available, covering as much floor space as possible. Walk around the space and ensure there is nothing that might be a potential hazard. Keep the Leader away from any areas that may be unsafe—raised levels, hard edges, corners, etc.

Physical prep: Do a good physical warm up with a few lifts, with groups of two or more lifting a single player (remind the players to lift with the knees not the back). Make sure everyone acknowledges their limits; the objective is to work as a team to support the Leader.

The Dance: Six players, all others observe. Five are the Caretakers, one is the Leader. She wears a veil or blindfold. The Caretakers surround the Leader, place a hand on her shoulders, and all breathe together. Music starts, the Leader begins to move, The Caretakers pull their hands away and step back. They give the Leader room to move while remaining close enough to help her should she make an offer. The Leader should start slow, get used to not having full use of her eyes. She leans into the Caretakers, lets them take her weight, see if they will lift her. As she feels more confident, she can move faster or make bolder offers always keeping everyone's safety in mind.

The offers can take many forms. For example, if the Leader leans back, the Caretakers must be ready to take her weight. If the Leader extends her hand, the Caretakers may take hold of it and guide her forward. The Leader may jump into the Caretakers' arms, climb on them, try to move away from them, allow herself to be lifted, etc.

The Caretakers make offers by placing a hand on the Leader, pushing or pulling her gently, lifting her, etc. But if the Leader resists or wishes to move on her own, the Caretakers let her go and give her space.

The Caretakers maintain a circle around the Leader at all times and stay aware of any gaps. If the Leader gets through a gap and gets ahead of the Caretakers, she risks stumbling or walking into a wall. The Caretakers must also keep focused on the group's movements all the while keeping an eye on the Leader (who is also responsible for her own safety and that of the others).

The Caretakers should keep a wide stance, ready to move in any direction to support the Leader, while not colliding with other Caretakers. Because of the blindfold, it's hard to read the Leader's intentions via her eyes, so the group must remain attentive at all times to how she shifts her weight or signals which direction she will move; they must constantly improvise to protect and serve the Leader.

At the end of each session (keep them to no more than four minutes), get feedback from both the Caretakers and the Leader. Let them share observations, especially tips on how to take care of the Leader and the best ways to follow them; sometimes the pelvis or feet will signal which way the Leader will go. The head will also "look" turning towards the direction the body will run even though the Leader cannot see with the blindfold on. Some Leaders will actually point and then move in that direction. The players take notes and are encouraged to use the information when it's their turn.

Advice

- "Caretakers, be ready for anything that the Leader offers or requests, but don't try to be a hero: if you can't lift someone on your own, get help or steer the Leader to someone else."

- "The Leader should take risks but stay aware of the Caretakers' capabilities (don't leap into someone's arms if they can't support you). Be a smart Leader."

EH? OH . . .

This exercise is a playful way to work with group sound and movement and can be used to develop scenes, improvise or create set choreography for an ensemble performance. It also works as a group voice warm up and builds up the energy of the entire ensemble.

Variation 1—Voice contortions The players stand randomly about the room. Each chooses a single vowel sound—A, E, I, O, or U—and begins singing/chanting it. They change their relationship to the floor: stand on one leg, go into a plank position, do a headstand, curl into a ball, lie on their stomach, their back, twist their bodies to one side, etc. With each change, they choose another vowel. The explore both volume, pitch, duration, and execution: how much effort is required to project their voice with the body in unusual positions?

Advice

- "Don't force the voice. Feel your way into what's possible in different positions. Take note of how you inhale and exhale when your body is curled up or holding its weight on hands and knees, balanced on one leg, bent over at the waist, etc."
- "Get into as many eccentric poses as possible and see how that affects the sounds you're making. Don't worry if the sounds get weird or ugly: as long as there is no strain on the voice, welcome all sounds!"
- "Use conscious breathing to strengthen your sounds, their volume, force, and pitch."
- "Borrow from others if you see someone doing a pose and sound you like."

Variation 2—Duo warm up The players partner up and stand about five meters apart. Player A chooses a single vowel sound, A, E, I, O, or U, and begins singing/chanting it, matching the volume to the distance between him and his partner, with closer being soft and further away being loud. Player B toys with the distance between them—moving closer, moving away—while A raises or lowers his volume accordingly. After a minute of play, switch roles with B using their voice and A playing with the distance.

Now reverse it: when player B gets closer, player A gets louder, then softer as B moves away.

Advice

- "Don't push the voice too hard nor create tension in the throat. Keep the whole body as relaxed as possible."
- "Treat it as a game, enjoying the tease and how it changes the sound, as you play with the distance and the response."

Variation 3—The stranger and the locals One player is chosen as the Stranger. She stands at one end of the room. The rest of the class are the Locals; they stand at the other end of the room, scattered apart (a meter or so between each other). The Locals check out the Stranger from a distance, repeating softly and in unison, "Oh . . . oh . . . oh?" They're curious about the Stranger as well as cautious, and this is reflected in how they repeat "Oh." The Stranger starts to move towards the Locals. As she does, the group moves closer together and repeats "Oh" a little louder as a suspicious tone creeps into the way the word is voiced. At some point it turns into "Eh? . . . eh . . . EH!?" (sounds like the "ay" in play). The tone has gone from curious and cautious to suspicious, fearful, and aggressively challenging. The closer the Stranger gets to the Locals, the louder they cry "EH?!" (as if saying, "Back up! Don't come so close!" etc.).

For both "Oh" and "Eh?!" the Locals can all say the word in unison, as well as individuals and smaller groups within the ensemble voicing the word with different attitudes, pitches and volumes. The game is about how the Stranger changes the sound, attitude and movement of the Locals by her distance from them. The Locals should play with changing their body shape (as in Variation 1), and with up-and-down movements, rising up high or cowering, like meerkats, as the Stranger toys with the distance. The Stranger should consider her reaction: is she enjoying this tease and her power over the group? Is she angry or sad that the Locals are responding this way? They play for a minute then a new Stranger is chosen.

ADD ON

In these variations, the players memorize the movements of others, adding to them to create a chorus of eccentric movements. These can be used to generate material for an ensemble scene or to tell an existing story through physical play and movement.

Variation 1—Circle add Groups of five to seven. Each group stands in a circle, arm's-length apart. The starting player does a single action. For example, he inhales. The next player repeats it and adds to it. For example, she inhales and starts to laugh. The next player might inhale, laugh, and go down on his knees. Continue around the circle, each player repeating what's gone before and adding an action to the sequence. The players can talk to help each other remember, then work towards remembering and adding moves without talking. The adviser can assign the number of passes around the circle with the players adding something each time their turn comes around, then stopping after they reach the assigned number, or let them keep going, building up as many actions as the group can remember until they find it impossible to go on. They then stop and start a new round.

Variation 2—Circle add chorus Groups of five. Each group stands in a circle, arm's-length apart. The first player does a single action. She looks at the player to her right and together they repeat her action. The second player adds to this, looking at the player to his right. The first three players repeat all three movements. This pattern continues around the circle once until everyone repeats the group moves. The group repeats the sequence four times, a little faster with each round. Repeat with a different player starting.

Variation 3—Circle add scene Same as Variation 1, but the players treat each movement as a line in a story. For example, the first player raises his hand. The second player raises her hand then mimes hailing a taxi. The third player repeats the first two moves then mimes getting hit by the taxi, etc. The last person must do all the moves to tell the story and add her move to end the scene. The players can talk to help each other remember.

RUN, STOP, RELAX

> The players explore the dramatic and comic possibilities of going from extreme activity to complete relaxation, playing with the tension generated by the activity (in both the players and audience), and the release into stillness and nonchalance.

Props: Drum and drumstick.

Variation 1—RUN! Five players wait backstage. They decide on a signal—it can be obvious or subtle—anything from laying a hand on the cheek, crossing the arms, stomping a foot, making a flapping fart sound with the lips, etc. This signal cues the group to start running about. The adviser cues the group to enter. One player signals the others and they enter with a manic burst of energy. They run madly around, arms flailing, legs kicking, shouting, yelling, clapping their hands, exiting and reentering, acting like a bunch of noisy, raving lunatics!

They continue this until one or more players stops moving. This can be abrupt or gradual, but when the players see it happening—the energy of the group stopping or slowing down—they gather close together facing the audience, all coming to a complete stop. The players go from crazed movement to face and body relaxed, the group just chilling, as if they haven't been doing anything out of the ordinary. They exchange glances, smile, look worried, annoyed or unhappy—whatever they feel in the moment. They continue this quiet exchange of looks until someone in the group signals. When this happens, they can pause a few seconds before running amok again, or all immediately take off running madly around the stage and continue until one or more players comes to an abrupt stop or a slow down to a stop. They gather close together center stage facing the audience, looking nonchalant.

The time between the mad running and the signal to start again can be a few seconds or a half minute. The group plays with each other and the audience; they know that at some point, the players are going to go physically crazy. They can choose when to make an exit and end the scene, or the adviser cues them to go.

Variation 2—Drum The players still signal but also, at any point, the adviser can hit a drum to cue the run.

Variation 3—Tease The players still signal, the adviser can hit a drum, but he can also tease them by saying, "You know you want to run but you can't. I can see that you really want to run. But you can't. Until I hit this drum . . . ." The players can wait and take the cue from the adviser, or interrupt him, cue the group themselves by their agreed signal and run.

Advice

- "Be mad with anticipation! It agitates your bodies with small movements, an impatient look in your eyes, etc. You want to run but you have to wait for the signal."
- "Center this powerful desire to run in your belly, let it radiate outwards, build it internally until the audience is also agitated, nearly screaming for you to RUN!"

Variation 4—Smile This can be added to any of the variations above. When the group stops, they form a line shoulder-to-shoulder, facing the audience. Slowly they all smile with big wide grins, absolutely delighted with themselves and the fun they've had as they stand still, at ease. It's a playful, mischievous grin. This is usually a good one to throw in just before the players exit.

Advice

- "Explore the contrast between extreme physicality and neutrality, the manic running about with the quietly playful grin."
- "The bigger, more frenzied the run, the more interesting or funny is the stop. The stop after the manic movement allows the audience to study the effect of all that action: it leaves traces of energy, animating the body in subtle ways. How do you control—and play with—that energy as the audience studies you as you stand still?"
- "As you wait for the signal, how does your body express anticipation, the powerful desire to run in a way that agitates you to such a degree that it affects the audience? Build up the energy from within (it doesn't

need to be physically obvious) so it can explode into movement when the signal comes."

REVEALING

These variations explore ensemble play within a simple set up, combining group movement with solo introductions. The group acts as a chorus, with the ensemble following one player's lead. The variations are good for improvising group play and developing this into set routines, and a good framework for creating group improvisation when performing outdoors or in large spaces.

Props: Stage flats or curtains for entrances and exits.

Variation 1—Reveal the lead Groups of seven or more wait backstage. They count off. The group enters in a clump, murmuring, mumbling, commenting, as they look out at the audience (see Note and Advice below). Number 1 whispers to the group how he would like to be revealed and then hidden again. For example, "Everyone run away from me/Everyone step back and style to me/We all run then I stop, and group keeps going/I step out of the group/Someone pushes me out of the group" … etc. When he's revealed, he has a moment with the audience. For example, he takes a quick bow, makes a face, does a trick, gestures, does a little dance, etc. Then he goes back to the group, or the group gathers around him. As the group begins to move again, always in a tight clump, number 2 tells the group how she would like to be revealed. This continues in numbered order till everyone has their moment, then they all exit in a clump.

Note: *The ensemble is both gleeful and timid, excited to be coming onstage to play with the public but nervous as to how they'll respond. For the one who steps out, they can play the moment however they like: showing off for the audience and their companions in the group, or they could grow nervous after stepping out and quickly rush back to the safety of the ensemble all massed together. They might offer a trick or tell a joke, expose their belly or show off their shoes. It's a tease and a test to see how the audience will respond to the individual and how the ensemble supports the solo moment.*

Variation 2—Take the lead Seven players wait backstage. They count off. The group enter as above, massed together, but they are following the lead of #1, mirroring and shadowing her, until she makes a signal for them to stop and watch her. She steps away from group, does something solo, they respond (applaud, imitate her, join in her sing-along, follow her dance steps, etc.). She steps back into the group and focuses her attention on #2 (or he signals he's taking over), and all follow #2 until he steps out, has a solo turn, then passes the lead to #3. This pattern continues with each player getting a chance to lead the group around the space however they like, then having a solo moment.

A variation can be added as follows:

- All members of the group have a prop and, when they're revealed, perform a short trick or task with it. The group reacts however they like—applaud, boo, act confused, frightened, etc.—then surround the player, or the player steps back into the group and passes the lead onto the next person in the count.

Advice

- "Work as a pack. Go with the choice of the person being revealed and do it with playfulness and gusto."
- "Imagine yourselves as a group of mischievous misfits vying for the audience's attention as a group, as well as individually in your solo moment."
- "Be playfully conspiratorial in your relationship with each other and with the audience."

MISFITS AND MASTER

This exercise is closer to bouffon play than clown, but it's useful for exploring a more extreme expression of hierarchy and the relationship between Master, and everyone below her. Working together, the players use the group energy to tease, tempt, insult, intimidate, create intrigue and play with both the Master and the audience.

Props: Stage flats or curtains for entrances and exits, chair, foam bat (pool noodle or thick-walled pipe insulation about seventy centimeters long), ragged clothes that makes the players look a bit worse for wear.

Six players wait backstage. One is chosen as the Master. The adviser informs the others that they are "Misfits, you don't belong. You've come here today to challenge the Master. But beware, she may punish you mercilessly if you go too far." The adviser sets a chair downstage left. The Master enters with the foam bat and sits in the chair.

After a few beats, the Misfits enter in a clump, eyes switching between the Master and the audience. There is a visible tension and fear in the group, as well as a feeling that it's time to challenge all relationships, to test the status quo. The clump moves closer to the Master: her reaction will determine how close the Misfits can get. One person steps forward, the others watch intensely, both eager and shocked by his audacity, secretly hoping he will do something surprising. The Misfit who has stepped out is a bit scared, also a bit confused (Misfits aren't too bright). He has decided to tease, taunt, insult or even threaten the Master. Misfits in the clump explore the struggle between their confusion, fear, and simple-mindedness, with their attempts to challenge the Master.

For example, a player might say to the Master, "I'm gonna pinch you. *Hard*. On all your body parts." Others in the group might encourage him to show them where he will pinch the Master (he starts pinching himself trying to find the place that will cause the most pain, hurting himself in the process), or other Misfits might step forward, pinch him, and start to enjoy this game of hurting the one who stepped out. The Misfits find the play between what sounds like a real threat or a nasty insult but this is tempered by the sad state of the group and their sorry attempts to be intimidating. Hovering over all these emotions is the real threat of retaliation.

With each attempt, the rest of the group are shocked by the actions of the one who is bold enough to step out, as well as being curious about the Master's reaction. Each Misfit toys with the Master until they have all had a go. They should work to make each taunt more challenging, more outlandish, more ludicrous.

The Master can sit calmly watching their actions, perhaps even amused. Or she can openly threaten or even hit any Misfit who dares to step out, with the foam bat. The players' job is to toy with the power play and the tension this creates between the Master, the Misfits, and the audience, to draw everyone into the play, as well as to manipulate who the crowd sympathizes with, and whose actions they most enjoy.

By the time the last player steps out, the taunt should be ludicrously nasty, pushing the Master and the Misfits to the limit of how they will react. The group improvises an exit as a clump: the Misfits run off defiant, terrified, chased off by the Master, or the Master runs off chased by the Misfits.

Note: The adviser can have the players improvise in front of class or let them work in groups to develop what each one will say—and the possible group reactions—as well as explore the play between them. After a short exploration and rehearsal, they play a rough sketch for the class.

Advice

- "Build the intensity of the play and the scene. Use this build to stay in the moment, not think too much about what you'll say or how you'll react."
- "The chorus's reaction is crucial to building up the intensity of the scene."
- "Misfits must continually monitor the reactions of Master and audience and play off them. What can you get away with, what will you be punished for saying or doing, what wins the crowd's sympathy, causes them delight?"
- "Enter into the heady mixture of confusion, simple mindedness and fear, contrasted with the desire to tease, intimidate and provoke. Let us see the struggle enliven you, encourage you to take risks, challenge the audience, despite your status as a misfit."

CHIPS AND STICK

Another exercise that explores status relationships on a more visceral and physical level.

Props: Stage flats or curtains, chair, a plastic or metal bowl with crackers or chips (Pringles work well), a small table or another chair to put the bowl on, objects to hide behind (mats, furniture, blankets, etc), foam bat (Master's stick).

Six players—five Misfits and one Master—wait backstage. The Master enters with a bowl of chips, sets it on the table, sits in the chair, and starts to nibble. By his chair rests his stick. The Misfits enter in a clump. They fear the Master and his stick, but they're desperately hungry; they all want a chip. The Master does not see them at first. They make fun of him, play games behind his back etc. The Master gives them something to make fun of by eating, standing, stretching, etc., in eccentric ways. At some point he picks up the stick either casually or to threaten the Misfits. They dash to various hiding places then regroup. The game continues with the Misfits trying to get a chip by daring to ask for one, sneaking out and stealing one, begging the Master for one, "Please give me just a lick, a smell—just let me touch it!" The Master provokes them, scares them, teases them: he knows they're starved and enjoys toying with them, and the fact that he can abuse them any time he wants. If a Misfit gets caught trying to steal a chip or is beaten by the Master for any reason, the others rush out to lead her away apologizing profusely for the indiscretion as they scuttle off to hide (all the while insulting the Master under their breath). Or they can cheer the beating hoping to win the Master's favor. The players improvise an ending or the adviser signals them to end the scene and exit.

Advice

- "Explore the conflict between the fear of the Master and the stick, and your starvation, the intense desire for food."
- "Enjoy making fun of the Master but don't forget who has the power and how much you fear getting beaten."
- "As the Master, your job is to intimidate the Misfits as much as possible, play the imperious, pompous ruler so they have something to play off of. Openly display your power in order to provoke a response from the Misfits. The Master can also allow things to happen—a chip to be stolen, not noticing Misfits ridicule him, etc.—to add variety to the play."
- "As the Misfits, how do you use the Master's role and their abuse to win sympathy from the audience? They are *your* allies, not the Master's."
- "For all players, the scene is a feisty game between the Master and the Misfits. The stakes are high: physical abuse, starvation, anarchy, or worse..."

THE RIDICULOUS ENSEMBLE

> In this exercise, the players perform improvised scenes from simple, absurd or abstract suggestions. It's good for getting them to loosen up and improvise using nonsensical scenarios. These could be developed into full routines, or act as a sudden illogical break within a more straightforward scene.

Props: Stage flats or curtains for entrances and exits.

Five players wait backstage. They enter in a clump, eager to please. They nod and pat each other on the back, full of humble self-confidence as the adviser praises their acting ability: "We're so excited that you're here today! We feel honored to welcome such an amazing group of thespians, known all over the world for their ability to act out *any* scene. So today we'd like to see, how do you pluck a chicken?" The group begins to act out plucking a chicken. They don't discuss it or spend time thinking about it: as soon as the question is asked, they begin the scene. This is a game of complicity, with the group finding the answer in the moment, seeing what develops as they use movement and gestures to play the scene. The players can vocalize but keep intelligible words to a minimum. The group stops when they're satisfied they've acted out an answer—or the adviser stops them—they acknowledge the applause, and the adviser suggests another scene or an addition: after plucking the chicken they act out gutting it.

Suggestions for scenes: How do you tame a lion? How do you train a monkey to sing? How do you train a fish to stand up? What is religion? What is chaos? What is war? What is death? What are politics? What is democracy? How do you eat a live octopus? What is Paradise? Show me the Warriors of Stupidville. Show me the High Priestesses of Vanity. Show me the Grotesques. Show me the Deeply Irritated Housewives.

Advice

- "Accuracy is not as important as revealing the delight of playing together in order to answer the question through movement, mime play and sound."

- "Keep a close eye on each other to see what your partners come up with. Work *as a group* to come up with answers on how to play the scene."
- "Let it be accurate as well as absurd, sensible as well as irrational. Turn the scene into a guessing game."
- "Keep a healthy sense of bafflement throughout, as in, *What is the answer? Is this the answer? Yes, this is the answer! Is it really the answer?*"

Summary

There is a saying, "like herding cats," which well describes working with a large number of clowns. Because clowning is a style that encourages individual expression and play, it can be hard to keep a clown troupe focused on a shared outcome; there will always be friction. This is one reason why this section includes ensemble movement: the cooperation and trust required when supporting and lifting one another physically, as well as paying close attention to the group to know when, how, and where to move, immediately creates complicity; the players are forced to focus on each other's needs. This creates a collaborative spirit even when the players compete or engage in status play.

We also looked at ways to allow individuals, duos and trios to step away from the group and have moments of play, while the chorus of clowns supported them, and how a group of clowns deals with a Boss or Master who, though alone, has the power to control the entire group. We ended with ensemble improvisations which encouraged the players to think together in the moment to create comic play. These exercises feed into the next section on devising material: all the exercises that follow involve ensemble improvisation and exploration as the players find ways to turn relationships into stories, a game into a planned performance.

Figure 10.1 Kate Brehm: The rules, the script, the game, the play. *Photo credit: Eric Gillet/Shoot That Klown.*

10

The Rules, the Script, the Game, the Play

Welcome to the Playroom

When I first started teaching clown I wondered what style of clowning I should teach—circus, cabaret, theater, street performance? But after less than an hour with the students I realized that style was irrelevant: what they needed first was to *relearn* how to play. The group ranged from nineteen to thirty-five years old, but they were all too caught up in looking good, acting clever, trying to get laughs, or pretending to be children. Some weren't truly engaged in playing, others were too self-conscious, and quite a few were thinking there was some secret to these exercises, and they were determined to figure it out and get it right. So, they ended up "playing at playing."

Figure 10.2 Clowns with drums—Joe Dieffenbacher with clown, percussionist, and juggler Fuman. *Photo credit: Toño Zarralanga.*

After that first class, I scoured a number of books on theater exercises, but my best finds came from books on games including a Cub Scouts book on children's games written in 1929. I developed variations on the games, forcing the students to think harder and more imaginatively about tactics, strategies, bending and breaking rules to gain an advantage for themselves and their partners, and to find more ways of collaborating through play. A good game demands a players' full attention—physical, emotional, and mental. When fully engaged, learning becomes dynamic, genuine, and insightful.

As I altered the games I had found and invented new ones, I understood them on a deeper level: they not only unified the ensemble in energetic ways, but they also helped them understand the development and performance of routines, scenes, and scripted plays. I began to see that the rules of a game were like the script of a show, and just like a game's rules, the script could be altered while playing (I'm speaking of devised work here). The rules were the introduction to the game, and as we played, the rules expanded in overt and subtle ways depending on how we used words, actions, props, costumes, scenic elements, status relationships, physical and visual play, and audience interaction. We agreed that anyone could bend, break or invent new rules in order to make the game a genuine experience of play and collaboration. The same was true of a devised act or scene: knowing that the script could be challenged, reimagined, and toyed with as we worked with it, kept everyone involved on their toes. They were eager to be part of the evolution, the construction—and deconstruction—of the play, to use it as a way to expand and deepen the connection amongst the players, and between the players and their audience.

This section takes some well-known children's games and uses the variations to create more complexity, inspire more inventive tactics, and get the players to use both the director's mind and the clown's to develop scenes that foster more dynamic play. This section also introduces one of the best games I know for understanding and experiencing how to utterly fail and be the fool.

THE EVOLUTION OF A GAME

This exercise is based on the well-known children's game Statues or Grandmother's Footsteps (I know it as Green Light, Red Light). The variations add obstacles: they make the game more complex in order to encourage more inventive and imaginative play and require

> the players to work together to achieve a shared objective (in Variation 1, it's every clown for themselves). Adding new rules and inventing complications helps turn the game into a scene and generates relationships between the players as they demand that they explore both solo and group strategies for "winning."

Props: Tape or rope to mark a line. Sheets of newspaper rolled and taped to make a soft, prop "knife," a large overcoat.

Variation 1—Green light . . . red light The adviser marks a starting line with rope. One player is chosen as the Leader. She stands at the other end of the room from the starting line with her back to the group. Everyone else gathers behind the starting line. The Leader turns away from group and says "Green light." This is the cue for the players to move towards the Leader until she calls out "Red light!" and turns. She can say the words quickly, slowly, or pause between the words but she must separate word and action: finish saying, "Red light!" *before* turning. The players must go still before the Leader turns. If she sees any player moving, she sends them back to the starting line. The game continues until a player tags the Leader. She then becomes the new Leader.

Variation 2—Freeze Same as above, but when a player gets caught moving for the third time (or twice or once), he must freeze in place until someone tags the Leader.

Variation 3—Yer dead Same as above but when a player gets caught moving, the Leader says "You!" the player says "Me?!" The Leader replies "Die!" The player acts out a melodramatic death complete with vocals. If the Leader catches more than one person, they move through the exchange quickly—"You!" "Me!?" "Die!" "You!" "Me!?" "Die!"—creating multiple death scenes acted out at the same time. She turns away and the game continues until someone tags the Leader.

Note: *When the Leader points at a player and says "You!" they reply and die; there's no discussion or debate.*

Variation 4—The knife, the peasants, and the leader Same as Variation 1, but the players are all Peasants and one of them has a rolled-up newspaper knife to stab their cruel Leader. One player holds the knife behind their back.

If any Peasant is caught moving, they're sent back. If they have the knife, they can hand it off but must do so without the Leader seeing the knife. The Leader has three chances to guess who has it. The Peasants work as a group to keep the Leader from guessing correctly by keeping the knife and the hand-offs hidden. Or faking hand-offs to get the Leader to guess wrong. If the Leader fails to guess on the third try, the Peasants surround her, pull her into the group, and replace her with the knife holder; he becomes the new Leader and the game begins again. The objective is for the group to work together to get someone close enough to stab the Leader with the newspaper knife.

Variation 5—Whisper The Group whispers the name of the Leader as a chant, or the players do it randomly as they move towards him with the knife.

Note: *Any of the variations—Freeze, Yer Dead, Whisper—can be added to Variation 4 to increase the drama and the need for advanced tactics.*

Variation 6—Overcoat Same as Variation 4, but with a large overcoat placed two meters from the Leader, between her and the Peasants. A Peasant must get the coat, put it on, and touch the Leader before she sees them move. Only the Peasant with the overcoat can tag the Leader. If a Peasant has the overcoat in hand or gets it on and the Ruler sees him move, he puts the coat down where he stands and goes back to the start. Or create the rule that he must take the coat back to the starting line: the players work together to hand off or throw it forward to a player close to the Leader.

A variation can be added as follows:

- A player cannot put on the overcoat himself; one or more of the other players must pick it up and hold it so he can slip his arms into it.

Variation 7—Combinations Combine variations: the player with the overcoat must also get the knife to stab the Leader; the players freeze or die if they get caught; the players whisper the Leader's name as they advance.

Each variation (obstacle) develops new layers in the scene, forcing the players to come up with more involved tactics, increasing their interaction, ensemble play, and group strategizing. Combinations of rules or obstacles could also be used when playing an exercise like *Chips & Stick* (pgs. 201–202), where the rule of the Master turning to look forces all the Misfits to freeze and stay that way until he turns away. Another option is to create an environment, where the players/Peasants must move as if walking on slippery ice, through mud, over hot coals, etc., as they make their way to the Leader.

Advice

- "The props, actions, obstacles, and complications are added to encourage you to find more inventive tactics and develop layers of comic and dramatic play. Don't let them frustrate you, let them inspire you."
- "How do the different variations change the dynamic of the play, its pace, and the tension within the group? How can you use these dynamics in a devised scene?"
- "Any number of things can be added before being able to kill the Leader, to the point of absurdity. For example, the players must pour a cup of water and give it to the player with the knife who must have the cup in hand when he stabs the Leader. Can you find both the dramatic and the comic play in what is added to make the objectives of a scene harder to achieve?"
- "There is the game and there is making a scene out of the game. Do you see the possibilities of transforming a game into an effective scene? Could you use variations of games from the early chapters of this book such as *Birds & Bees, Chase Me, Tag Me, Races, Chair Games,* or *In and Out* (entrances and exits) and create scenes out of the games?"

TAIL, TAG, SCENE

> I've had actors play this game underneath different scenarios and it always enlivens the scene and keeps the players on their toes. It shows the potential for using even the simplest game to bring a new level of play to any scene, even dramatic ones. For clown routines, it heightens the level of play and group interaction, and can lead to some highly creative tactics and physical interaction.

Props: Stage flats or curtains for entrances and exits, socks or handkerchiefs. A music player and a playlist with different styles of music.

Variation 1—Dance snatch Each player has one of their socks tucked in their back waistband with two-thirds of the sock protruding like a tail (this could also be played with handkerchiefs). The scene is a dance club, the atmosphere of the club is determined by the music that's played. Seven or more players enter (one at a time, as couples, or in trios). They check out the scene and begin to dance. As they're moving about the dance floor, they try and snatch each other's tails (after getting them, they toss them on the floor). The players can also team up in duos or trios and agree to get everyone else's tails first before going after each other's (they decide this backstage).

When a player loses their tail, they have to leave the club. They must find a reason to go (not just because they lost their tail). They can go right away or linger a bit before leaving but they cannot grab any tails once they've lost theirs.

The players should establish the scene and who they are, before starting in on the game. Play the tease and the tension, trying not to be so overly concerned about losing or grabbing a tail that the game becomes obvious; play the scene of a dance club and the characters that come there, let the game underly the scene and create dynamic tension. Turn the grabbing and the avoiding into a playful dance. Remember, the last one who grabs a tail wins, but then, they're all alone in the dance club . . .

A variation can be added as follows:

- When a player loses their tail, they stay onstage. They're out of the game – they can't grab anyone's tail – but still in the scene. This will generate some confusion as the players who are still in the game aren't always certain who is still playing (who might grab their tail) and who is no longer a threat. The last one left with a tail can choose to flaunt it or pull off his own tail and join the group.

Variation 2—Scene snatch Three players play a short scene or present a skill. Each player has a sock tail. They present the scene or skill while trying to snatch each other's tails. The main focus for the players should be on presenting the scene or skill, not the game of snatching a tail. As in Variation 1, the players don't rush to the game right away: they enter for a performance, set up the act, acknowledge or greet the audience, give them some idea of what they've come to do, show the preparation for the skill or task, all the while remaining alert to when the game starts.

Experiment with hiding the action, snatching the tail without the audience knowing it. Play the tension that the game elicits. Let it provide a dynamic subtext to the scene.

When a player's tail is snatched, they make an exit. The player should find a reason for leaving (e.g. they forgot something backstage; they're feeling sick; they become terrified of the audience, etc.). If a reason occurs to him right away, he goes. If not, he lingers before exiting. The player left onstage must then finish the scene.

Variation 3—The act, the game Same as either variation, but the players don't have socks, instead they tag each other out by placing their hand against the small of the back or other designated place on the body, such as the top of the right foot (putting the target in a hard-to-reach place forces the players to be creative in how they get close enough to tag a player out). The tagging spot should be known only to the players, not the audience. As above, the players can leave right away or delay the exit. They justify their exit according to the scene.

This game of tag could be played under any scene, whether it was a group performing a complicated task, presenting a skill routine, a love story, a serious, dramatic scene, etc. It forces the players to be in two minds: the director focuses on the scene, keeping the story alive for the audience. The clown stays aware of the game that is being played and how it keeps everyone in the moment, interacting in a more dynamic way. For example, the director's mind sees two players coming together to greet each other, shake hands or embrace; that's the scripted scene. The clown's mind is wondering if she will be tagged out, should she tag the other player out, or approach them with no other intent but to greet them. It's also possible to include this sort of game in a scene and not tag anyone out; the game will still add a dynamic tension to the scene.

Advice

- "Can you work the two objectives—playing the scene and winning the game—without having the game dominate, or making it obvious?"
- "Winning the game has an added consequence (or bonus): the last person onstage is left with the responsibility of finishing the scene (looked at this way, losing can be a good strategy for getting out of having to devise an ending)."

SCENE TRICKS

Some of these tricks are borrowed from film techniques, others from improv games. They are effective not only for creating comic moments but also for making an action or story clearer and better understood by an audience.

Props: Stage flats or curtains for entrances and exits and sound effects (see Variation 4 for suggestions).

Variation 1—Slow motion At any point in a scene everything goes into slow motion. Movements are slowed down (the group decides just how slow), vocal sounds are elongated, enunciation is exaggerated, the voice goes to a lower pitch, or a slowed down high-pitched voice, facial expressions are exaggerated. Slow motion is an effective way to change the dynamic or rhythm of a scene. Slowing things down may also help the players think faster: it gives them more time to see an action unfold, think ahead and be able to respond more quickly (but in slow motion). It can give the audience a rest, allow them to enjoy moments more fully, as you toy with time, movement, visuals and sound.

Variation 2—Rewind At any point in a scene, the players stop and rewind: they take the scene they've just enacted and play it backwards (keeping it physically accurate) so the audience can enjoy it in reverse. Or they do the rewind as a blur of movement and sound to get back to another point in time and go forward in a different way. The players can move in another direction—"We went that way and nearly fell off the stage. So, let's go this way!"—and they still fall off the stage. Or after the rewind, they play the scene with a new element added, as if the players forgot to include something or the audience missed some important action.

Variation 3—Fast forward At any point in a scene, the players fast forward the action and jump to a new point in time. This can be used to skip over "boring" parts, to leap ahead and give the audience information that might help them understand what's going on in the current scene (the players then rewind to the place they started from), or create suspense, for example, by fast forwarding to a later scene that shows a player strangling someone, then rewinding back; as the scene progresses towards the revealed moment, the audience waits with anticipation for the action.

Note: *In both Rewind and Fast Forward, the players can also explore speed and movement: actions can be done either in slow motion or as a speedy blur of sound and action. Or a mix of both.*

Variation 4—Sound effects A player—we'll call her FX—stands or sits to one side of the stage next to a table and provides sound effects. These can be made with the mouth, hands or feet, percussion instruments, whistles, bells, blocks of wood, trashcan lids, etc. The players improvise a task, an act or scene and FX adds sounds: they can pause for sounds to be added, or FX manages to hit them on cue with no prompt from the players, or FX interrupts the scene with an effect. Her job is to add to the scene as well as support what her partners are creating (and occasionally provoke an action by making a sound).

Variation 5—Sitting, standing, kneeling, lying To start, each player is assigned one of the four positions. The adviser creates a simple setting using props and furniture. The players improvise a scene or act out a task. As they play, there must always be one player sitting, one standing, one kneeling, and one lying down. If a player who is sitting stands up, the person standing must sit. Or the one kneeling might sit which means the person standing must kneel. This is played as a game underlying the scene: the players justify the changes in position. For example, they stretch their body upwards to stand, or drop to their knees, seized by a sudden urge to pray.

This can also be done with energies. For example, one player is happy, another angry, one is sad, another is lusty. When happy changes to angry, angry changes to happy. Or mix it up: angry changes to lusty, who changes to sad who changes to happy who changes to lusty. This can get confusing, but the players should enjoy the chaos that might ensue and keep their energies in play as they work to clarify who is using what energy.

Variation 6—Build Take any action, set it up and build it slowly. This can be anything from a sneeze, wanting to kiss someone, wanting to hit someone, etc. Find the initial movements that telegraph the action and use them to build anticipation: for a sneeze, the face starts to tremble, the nose wrinkles up, the breath comes in short gasps; for a kiss, the players make eye contact, touch their own mouths, their lips start to pucker; for a hit, one player starts to pace, clenching and unclenching her fists. The movements build up the suspense, the drama and/or the comic potential of a moment in a scene.

PROP JOURNEY

> This exercise builds on the work done in Section 4: Prop Play, combining an improvised journey with multiple partners, using props. These variations involve a single pass across the stage, but the ideas generated can be used to develop more involved scenes (any of the scene tricks in the previous exercise—Slow Motion, Rewind, etc.—can be used in this journey).

Props: Stage flats or curtains for entrances and exits, miscellaneous props.

Variation 1—Discover, play, move on Five or more players, each one chooses a prop. The players lay the props out across the stage, the first prop close to the entrance, the last one close to the exit. They step backstage and decide what kind of journey they're going on and what's the setting. For example, a bad section of town, a dark scary forest, a jungle full of wild beasts, a hike along a rocky, narrow mountain pass, a desperate walk across a brutally hot desert, etc. While they're backstage, the adviser lays a new prop amongst the others.

The players express the type of journey they're going on by how they enter and move towards the props (they could use the *Visualization: Environments* exercise pgs. 74–75. They can make vocal sounds or use gibberish but avoid intelligible words. Each prop they see and handle is used in such a way as to develop the journey: the player who chose it decides what it is in the scene and the others join in the improvisation with what that player decides. The prop can be used for what it is or transformed into something completely different: a stick could be a machete to cut a way through a dense forest, or a telescope to see further ahead. A hat could be a hat or a bucket to carry water, or the steering wheel of a jeep. The players enact a short scene with the prop, then lay it down and continue the journey.

At some point, the players discover the prop laid out by the adviser. This must be discovered *by the entire group, all moving to it together*. The group decides what it is and how to use it in a short scene. After a scene with the final prop in the journey, they find a finish for the scene and exit. All the props are left onstage.

Note: *Each prop creates a pause in the journey, a short scene that elaborates on the setting and develops the play between the group. Once this short scene is played out, the group leaves the prop behind and moves on. This allows each prop to have its moment of discovery and to be used in a scene.*

Variation 2—To each his own Five or more players count off; each one chooses a prop. In this variation they enter carrying their props. Crossing the stage, they each use their prop in some way to tell the story of their journey, player number 1 starting first and continuing in numbered order. The adviser sets one new prop onstage that the players must all discover and use together, at any point in the story. They find a finish for the scene and exit.

Note: The adviser can allow the players to explore all variations on their own, get a feel for the exercise and make some discoveries with the props before presenting to the rest of the class.

Advice

- "When a prop idea is introduced, develop it. Expand on the idea rather than get caught up in small clever bits or easy jokes."
- "Each player should aim to be clear about what their prop is once they pick it up. Once it's understood, the others commit to it and build a short scene around that choice. Don't bail out and suddenly change it: if you decide a bucket is a soldier's helmet, stay with that and build on the idea rather than switching it to something else."
- "Play with the prop's possibilities: let it be what it is; turn it into something else; make it come alive, manipulating it like a puppet; twirl it, flip it, juggle it, show off a skill. Fall in love with it, hate the damn thing. Fear it! Try to eat it. Dance with it ... How imaginative, absurd and surreal can you be with the props?"
- "Could you build the scene so that each prop creates an *escalation* in the journey, the story and the play?"

BLINDFOLDED EXPERTS

Crucial to good clowning is learning to play the scene, not the problem. The audience doesn't want to pity the clown but would rather, witness how imaginative, inventive, resilient, or lucky they are when they come up against an obstacle. This exercise creates real problems for the players which they cannot avoid; they must explore creative and playful ways of dealing with an obstacle rather than being totally flummoxed or defeated by it.

This is a great exercise for developing clown routines: I've had students film their blindfolded play then copy some of what they did without blindfolds to create an act. Blindfolds disadvantage the players in ways they cannot fake, makes them less self-conscious about failing, and generates material in an organic, unassuming way: no one has to try hard to be funny, it will happen naturally.

The basics: The players form groups of three to four depending on the scene. The adviser chooses a scene from one of the choices below and explains the scene first, *then* tells the players they must enact it blindfolded. The players go backstage and put on their blindfolds; the adviser hands them their props or sets them onstage depending on the scene.

Props for scenes: *Jugglers:* nine juggling beanbags or balls. *Paper planes:* sheets of paper for making airplanes. *Coat and hat:* three coats and three hats with a table or rack to hang them on, miscellaneous accessories such as a scarf, gloves, a handbag, a bra, etc. *The party:* table and four chairs, paper cups, a pitcher with one to two cups of water in it, a plastic tablecloth, a mop, and towels for clean-up. At least eight blindfolds (they can get a bit sweaty so have extras), stage flats or curtains for entrances and exits.

Note: *Please read all the way to the end. The Notes at the end of the scene suggestions are important for understanding the best way to prepare for the scenes and understand their objectives.*

Variation 1—The jugglers Three players wait backstage. The adviser informs them they are world-renowned jugglers who have come to show off their one, amazing, three-ball trick. The adviser explains the scene: "You enter together, come downstage and take bow. You move upstage and form a line facing the audience. The first Juggler moves centerstage, presents himself, acknowledges the audience, prepares for his juggling trick, executes the trick, gets the applause, takes a bow, and moves upstage to rejoin the line. The second Juggler follows the same sequence then moves back for the third. After the third Juggler completes the sequence, all three bow together and exit."

The players step backstage and put on their blindfolds. The adviser hands them their juggling props then cues applause: the players enter during the applause, take their bows and play the scene.

Variation 2—The paper airplane experts Three players wait backstage. The adviser informs them that they are paper airplane experts who have come to show off their amazing ability to make a perfect paper airplane with just five folds. The adviser explains the scene: "You enter together, come downstage and take a bow. You move upstage and form a line behind the table facing the audience. You each pick up a piece of paper. The first Expert presents herself, acknowledges the audience, then shows her method for making a paper airplane in five folds. She shows the finished plane. The expert prepares, throws the paper airplane, watches it fly, styles and takes the applause. She then gestures to the next Expert. He repeats the sequence, then gestures to the third Expert. He repeats the sequence. After the third Expert takes his applause, all three take a bow together and exit."

The players step backstage and put on their blindfolds. The adviser sets the table with three pieces of paper. The players wait for the applause to cue their entrance.

Variation 3—My coat and hat please Three players wait backstage. The adviser decides on a scenario: they're going to a party, a funeral, to the office, etc. They're entering in order to put on their coats, hats, and an accessory and go out. The adviser explains the scene: "You enter together or one at a time, make your way to the coats and hats and begin to put them on, making sure you get *your* hat and coat. You step downstage to check yourselves in a large (imaginary) mirror. When all have your coats, hats and an accessory, and have checked yourselves in the mirror, you exit, heading off to the party, funeral, or office, etc."

The players step backstage and put on their blindfolds. While they do this, the adviser sets the table or coat rack with three coats, three hats, and three accessories. The adviser cues the applause; the players make an entrance and play the scene.

Note: *The adviser can make the rule that all players must remain onstage until each one has a coat, hat, and an accessory on their bodies. Make it clear that there must be a sense of urgency in the scene: the players are late for wherever they're going and must get ready quickly.*

Variation 4—The tea party Four players wait backstage. One is chosen as the Host. The adviser explains the scene: "The Host enters first, prepares the space, arranging the table, laying out the tablecloth, chairs and cups, getting ready for her guests. I'll make a knocking sound to cue the first Guest to enter. The host hears the knocking sound, goes to the door. The first Guest enters. Host greets them, invites them in, and the party begins. I'll make a knocking sound to cue the next Guest. The sequence is repeated with the Host welcoming each Guest at the door. When all the Guests have arrived, the Host gets them seated, gives them each a cup, and pours water from the pitcher into their cups. They drink a toast. Play the scene—a lovely party on a lovely day—eventually finding an ending or I'll cue you to end it. The Guests exit, with the Host leaving last."

The players put on their blindfolds backstage. While they do this, the adviser sets the table and four chairs, four paper cups, and a pitcher of water (play with the amount, just be aware of how much may have to be mopped up). The adviser lets the group know when the stage is set. The Host enters.

Notes on the set up: *For Variations 2-4, The adviser can place things in a normal way—paper set neatly on the table; coats etc. neatly on the rack; chairs around the table, cups and pitcher laid out on the table—or in an unconventional way—paper set on the edge of the table so it falls off easily, hats stuffed in the sleeves of coats, chairs stacked on top of the table, placed under the table, cups placed so they might fall off the table when Host reaches for them, etc.*

Notes about the space: *Don't play Blindfolded Experts on a high stage and be aware of any areas in the space where the players may stub their toes, trip over, or run into (shoes can be worn if desired). The players should be challenged but not feel endangered. They should play boldly and with energy but stay aware of the challenges posed by the blindfolds and the space.*

Notes on all variations: *The adviser can decide how much she wants to explain regarding the things the players should focus on. It can be helpful to let them make mistakes so others can see what they are. For example, after a scene is played, the adviser asks the audience, "Who was playing the problem? What clues told you this person couldn't see? Did they constantly grope about, searching with their hands before doing anything? When others were doing their bit, did they watch them or just stand as if staring off into space, not present in the scene? When they bumped into things, did they react to it or did they ignore it, calling attention to the fact they couldn't see what they'd bumped into? Who took the mistakes and accidents and turned them into advantages? For example, groping about with the hands could be camouflaged by turning it into a dance or an eccentric way of moving." By playing the scene despite the obvious disadvantage, the players increase the comic possibilities, discover eccentricities, and the audience engages more with the play.*

Notes on the rules: *The adviser should set certain rules to keep the players in the scene and not let them take shortcuts. For example, in Variation 1, the Jugglers must do their trick with all three balls and leave with all of them in hand. In Variation 3, a player may drop a hat and not be able to find it. He may try to make it easy on himself and leave without it. The adviser should inform* *them they cannot leave without wearing a hat, a coat and with an accessory each. In Variation 4, all Guests must be served a drink.*

Advice

- "You can't see what you're doing but play as if you can. Don't grope about in space the way you might if you couldn't see or stand frozen not looking at what your partners are doing. *Look* at someone in the audience, even though you can't see them. *Look* at the place where you dropped the ball, even though it may be somewhere else. *Look* at your partners often, give them focus, even if – because you can't see – you're staring at the wall."
- "Your most important sense in this game is your hearing. Actively listen to the sounds of balls dropping, your partner's footsteps, paper being folded, chairs being moved, water being poured, etc. Listen for the audience's reactions: their applause can tell you when a trick is finished, their exclamations can tell you you're about to bump into something. If they laugh, find out why they're laughing. Make it an active search: 'Are they laughing at what I did? I'll do it some more! Or maybe it was someone else . . .' Work hard at listening, responding and building on what you hear and what you believe is happening in the scene."
- "No talking. Keep vocal sounds to a minimum. You can make sounds in other ways using the props, the space, etc."
- "Be cautious but at the same time play boldly! Coming out and playing with energy—damn those blindfolds—will generate more comedy and engagement with the audience, then coming out timidly, groping around the space. This exercise puts you on the sharp edge between relating energetically with the audience, while listening with great attention to your partners. Don't get lost in one or the other. Stay on that edge."
- "Why is it funnier when performers are disadvantage this way? It gives an audience a feeling of power. 'We're ahead of this guy—he can't see what he's doing!' But they also feel empathy: 'She can't see what she's doing, poor woman.' Because of the potential for imaginative play inspired by the disadvantage, the audience are eager to witness how the players solve problems and deal with limitations."
- "As you watch others, what are the tactics they use so as not to appear blind? Use them yourself and expand on them!"

- "How can you find the same level of mishap and comedy without the blindfold? What makes the scene work, why is it funny? Listen to the feedback and try to recreate the atmosphere and energy of the scene without the blindfolds."
- "A blindfold can also be internal: a person's pride, absent-mindedness, joy, lust, anger, fear, etc., can also act as a blindfold; it can disadvantage them in a way that can generate comedy (think of how Basil Fawlty's pomposity creates so many comic moments in *Fawlty Towers*)."
- "The audience doesn't want to see you groping about blindly, too timid to play; they know you can't see. The pleasure comes from watching you—the clown—deal with the problem in inventive and imaginative ways. Taking a disadvantage and turning it into an advantage—by cleverness, accident or luck—is one of the essential survival and performance skills of a clown, and one of the best ways to develop a scene, progressing from one obstacle and mishap, to another."

Summary

Devising new, original performance material from ideas and group improv is challenging. This is followed by the even more arduous task of making it all work in front of an audience. But when it does, it's a thrill like no other! To hear an audience laugh and applaud for something that grew out of a desire to collaborate, to share quirky ideas and individual passions, brings on a true feeling of joy and the delight of performing live. And when you see the pleasure you feel onstage mirrored by the audience, you know all the hard work has been worth it.

The exercises in this section further developed the trust and complicity needed for group collaboration, creating environments where individuals could share ideas and interact with one another in the moment, while offering ways to lay the groundwork for building comic acts and scenes. There were games that encouraged cooperation, others competitive status play. We explored how a game could be developed into a scene or used as a subtext in an existing scene. Groups improvised imaginative and absurd scenes as well as playing with props. It finished with an exercise that allowed the players to openly *be* a fool, as well as teaching the art of slapstick, which I define as the comic interaction with the physical world (more on this in Section 12: The Skillful Clown).

Figure 11.1 Devin Shacket: The mask of the clown. *Photo credit: Eric Gillet/ Shoot That Klown.*

11

The Mask of the Clown

Makeup, Nose, Costume

I've put this section at the end because I feel it's important for students to rediscover and manifest an honest, less inhibited, and fully engaged way of playing, before they consider putting on a mask (when I use the term "mask of the clown" I'm referring to makeup, nose and costume). While some players will forego a nose and makeup, most will choose some sort of costume (even if it's a t-shirt and shorts). I use all the elements of the mask as tools to help students in their explorations but discourage them from

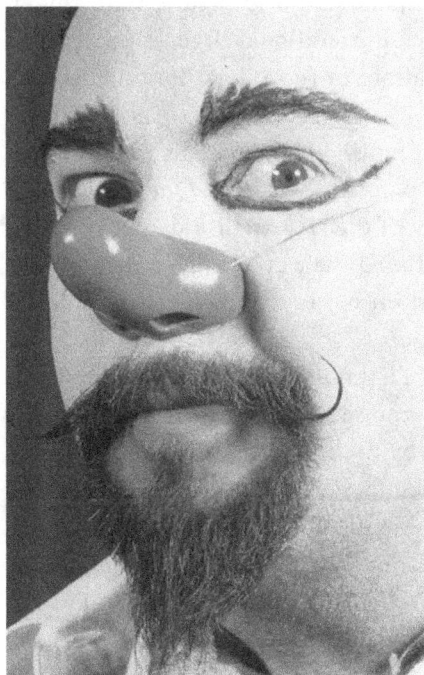

Figure 11.2 Paul Philion. *Photo credit: Eric Gillet/Shoot That Klown.*

designing a look right away: if the student tries to define the mask too soon, there's a risk they'll lock themselves into a way of playing based on how they look rather than how they truly play. Better to introduce a few bits at a time and let the students toy with various elements of the clown's mask so it evolves along with their understanding of true play. More on the costume later. First let's start with the face.

The Painted Face

As I stated in the Introduction, many people associate clowns with a certain look, and a big part of that look is clown makeup. But as I dug deeper into the history of clowning in the West, I discovered that the makeup had a source, there was a reason for its use. Here are a few theories cobbled together from many sources.

The authoritarian Whiteface clown grew out of the white makeup used by actors who played Death in the medieval mystery plays. The other characters were naturally afraid of him, but would also poke fun at him, much to the delight of medieval-era audiences for who had more firsthand experiences with death than we do in modern times. Because there was no escaping Death and his verdict, he was the ultimate authority figure. With this in mind, it's interesting how the Whiteface in traditional circuses became the high-status clown that everyone was afraid of (or at least intimidated by), but also made fun of.

The make-up of Joseph Grimaldi, English actor, comedian and dancer, was a major influence on how clowns painted their faces. One story is that his make-up was meant to be a parody of the way English dandies and the upper classes whitened their faces, outlined their eyes, rouged their cheeks and painted their lips. That joke is lost on modern audiences; to some, it's just face paint, to others, its scary makeup.

In the theater's early days, when stage lighting was minimal, actors would whiten their faces and accent the area around their eyes and mouth so their expressions could be read more easily by the audience. The white created a bright canvas on which to exaggerate their face with added colors and accents, more easily seen from a distance, in low light. Clowns took this further, especially in the early years of the circus ring before spotlights and high-tech lighting. It wasn't just a stylistic choice, it helped solve a real problem.

The invention of the make-up style known as the *Auguste* is usually credited to Albert Fratellini, of the Fratellini Brothers clown trio, one of the most popular comedy acts in Europe in the early 1920s. His look was a mixture of the Whiteface and the Tramp clown to which he added a red nose. Because of the group's popularity, their look influenced generations of circus clowns and is still in use today.

Emmet Kelly's Tramp clown, Weary Willie, was a reflection of the many poor people who were out of work or transient, when he first started with the circus. He was trying to make a connection to his audience with a clown who expressed their weariness over their struggles, while finding resilience through humor. The look, though exaggerated, was based on real people.

It's important to consider the source of things in any art form, why something was created, what it grew out of, how it was a transformation of an idea, an observation, or an attempt to solve a problem. Even the most exaggerated style grows out of something real. With this knowledge, the players can dig deeper into the source, try to empathize with it, to better understand its origins and perhaps use it in similar ways. They can keep it in the back of their mind as they explore: they should be conscious of it even if the audience isn't. It can give their play a greater depth and edge. For example, imagine playing the Fool to the authoritarian Whiteface while thinking of him as Death.

When I work with students, I use the makeup as a tool, not simply as a way of illustrating a clown. I've worked extensively with masks and witnessed first-hand the power they have to uncover the deeper potential in a student. I use makeup in the same way I would use a mask to help the students shed inhibitions, altering themselves visually and physically in order to expand their range and open up greater possibilities. We are identified and known mainly by our faces, the "social mask" we present to the world, so when this is altered—even a pair of glasses or facial hair can become a mask—it encourages the players to go beyond their ordinary, commonly recognized, social self. With the makeup as a mask, their usual expressions are expanded and transformed. And so is the player.

If they want to work with makeup, I ask students to keep three approaches in mind:

1 **Enhance:** Accent certain parts of the face with line and color, usually around the more mobile areas such as the eyes, the eyebrows, and the mouth to enhance their expressiveness. Most clowns who go this route use a flesh tone base (or none at all), a bit of red, black and white for accents. They avoid bright colors or use them minimally. The make-up is blended and softened, the lines between the colors less stark; this look is closer to stage make-up with strong accents.

2. **Fixed:** Decide on a particular look or expression and create a fixed look on the face. Paint on a smile or frown, draw the eyebrows high up on the forehead so the clown always looks surprised or confused. A painted-on smile makes it easy for a clown to always look happy, and when they really smile, it exaggerates it. Or if they frown, the painted smile creates a contrast between the mobile, frowning face, and the fixed, happy mask.

    The fixed style works well in the circus where a clown is usually playing in a large tent or arena and their expressions need to be read from a greater distance. When I first met the great American clown Lou Jacobs in makeup, I had to take a step back: up close, with his huge painted-on smile and the white highlights around his eyes drawn up onto the high prosthetic conehead he wore, it was a little scary. But when I sat in the arena and watched the show, he was the guy you noticed. His mask—especially the conehead which elongated his face, and the painted black area around his mouth which created a huge open grin—was exactly the sort of thing you wanted to wear in a three-ring circus because it read from even the furthest seats.

    So, when working with makeup, it's important for the players to consider the venue they'll be playing in. The amplified look of the circus clown may be too much up close (one reason this type of circus clown makeup scares some kids). In an intimate theater setting, it may come across as an unnecessary exaggeration (unless the objective is to create a hyperbolic world). A simpler makeup that doesn't distract from the expressiveness of the face but rather enhances it, may give a clown greater verisimilitude, the audience will be more willing to go with them if they play with deeper or weightier themes.

3. **Ornate:** Some call this style "Glitter Clown." Drawn-on stars, flowers, rainbows, curlicues, glued on glitter or rhinestones, lines and shapes that have no relation to facial expression. This style is mostly decorative. It's not often used in clowning outside the circus ring or in fashion shows, though it can be used if what a player is aiming to express is a vain, flashy, pretentious clown. The disadvantage is that it can get in the way of reading the clown's expressions.

The traditional circus evolved set ways of making up as a clown. Like any tradition that is adhered to strongly, it became a cliché, rote, restrictive. This is one of the reasons I believe it fell out of favor with the younger generation exploring clowning: to say the clown is open to play, to imagine and invent without limitations, and then restrict them to a set way of making up, felt like a contradiction. The form needs to be blown open now and then, traditions reimagined, the players free to explore in any way they choose—to enhance their face, to wear makeup as a mask, to decorate—even smudge it on like a child might and then, over time, shape it into a look, like a painter smearing colors over a canvas and then drawing out of it a face. Makeup is not mandatory for a clown: students should see it as a tool to help them expand their potential for play. They can continue to use it in performance, or take the insights gained from working with makeup and go onstage without the mask.

The Smallest Mask

At Jacques Lecoq's L'École Internationale de Théâtre, one of the most influential schools of physical theater in the world, one of his teachers, Pierre Byland famously said the clown nose is the world's smallest mask. Like a mask it conceals the identity of the player yet it has the potential to reveal and open up her inner life to an audience. Safely "hidden" behind the nose, she feels more secure to reveal her sinner elf—I mean, inner self.

Figure 11.3 The nose is a mask. *Photo credit: Eric Gillet/Shoot That Klown.*

Inspired by the idea of the nose as a mask, I rejected the one-size-fits-all red, ball-shaped nose and made a series of noses of various shapes, colors and sizes. It was interesting to see how the players became more discerning in their choices: they felt that each nose would bring out something different (and they did). It also allowed the clown work I was doing with the students to flow into commedia, a style of theater that has a lot in common with clowning. The emphasis on the nose as a mask made it much easier for the students to play with the commedia half masks I'd made (the masks I designed started with the nose, its shape influencing the sculpting of the rest of the features, and the final character). Understanding how clown and commedia overlap and influence each other is crucial to reclaiming them for the modern age. But that's another book.

As students develop their way of playing and the look they want to create, they then decide to nose or not to nose. Whichever choice they make, it's important for them to understand the significance of the red nose and experience its effect as a mask, as a tool to both conceal and reveal, and to see the red nose as a *symbol*. Most people are aware of clowns or have had an experience with one, so when they see someone wearing a red nose, that symbol creates an expectation of how this person will act. It's important for a player to keep this in mind: expectations are useful in clowning because most people will come to a clown show having already made a judgement about what they expect to see, which is usually something cute, mostly for kids, play that is exaggerated, silly, bombastic . . . Clowns constantly play with expectations, so a player who walks onstage as a red-nosed clown has plenty to work with: he can satisfy the audience's assumptions and play the way they expect him to; she can play to their expectations then go in a totally opposite direction; or they may do whatever they can to undermine any expectations about anything a clown supposedly does.

Like the makeup, the red nose can be used as a tool to help a player (and her audience) overcome inhibitions, but it's also a powerful symbol to play with if they keep in mind all that it represents and what people expect from a red-nosed clown. Thinking this way, the clown sees the nose itself as a game to be played with, the clown's energy defining the role and the mask from moment-to-moment.

Just as the nose can help a player reveal and open up her inner life, the clown can do the same for an audience. That kind of vulnerability can be downright scary for some people and players working in the form must respect that. Even if the clown plays with dark, uncomfortable, or weighty themes, they never lose their humanity, their desire to connect with the crowd. Their aim is never just to leave the audience feeling threatened, frightened or upset—this can be part of the play—but empathy is the essence of clowning and that affinity with the crowd—that understanding by the players that the clown is a part of the audience's world as well—is always at the forefront of the clown's interaction with the crowd. When it becomes only parody, anarchy, or agit-prop, it moves into the world of the satirist, the bouffon, the fool, or the jester. The clown shares a similar world to these comic types, but there is an openness, a deep curiosity, and a healing sense of wonder in clowning that is not always evident in more satirical work. What drives the clown is their intense interest in everything around them; this is manifested in how they play with the crowd. They may use critical comedy, lampoon, or barbed attack, but they do so to connect, not to simply comment, critique, or judge. Even in the clown's most difficult struggles or darkest moments, there is always the potential for play and resurgence.

The Body Mask

There is always that moment in the development of any show—clown or otherwise—when the costumes are brought into the room. Everyone lights up, eager to start putting on the clothes! The thrill of "dressing up" must be hardwired into us from an early age; it is one of those games that kids adore and brings out the kid in every adult.

The costume is probably the most significant element of clowning: everyone understands, on some level, how clothes work as a mask; we all know the expression, "the clothes make the man." Clothes have a greater visual impact and through movement—and the play with the costume—thoughts, ideas and emotions can be expressed, enhanced and expanded upon.

A costume can look like everyday clothes, have slight exaggerations, be too tight, too loose, or a combination of both (Charlie Chaplin's tight coat and baggy pants). The clothes may seem odd, the makeup bizarre (the Canadian clown duo, Mump and Smoot). The outfits can be dream-like, otherworldly (as in Slava's *Snowshow*). The players can juxtapose clothed parts of the body with parts uncovered: baggy shorts over skinny bare legs, a ridiculous looking shirt with no sleeves revealing muscular arms, a hat that covers a bald head or, when lifted, reveals a mass of curly hair.

Like the process of making up the face, the adviser should give the players a chance to evolve their look by bringing in racks of clothes and letting them try things on, to see what the bits and pieces of costume do to them physically and visually. Encourage them to try as many variations of the body mask as possible: find clothes that make them look good, and ones that make them look ridiculous. Clothes that impede their movement in some way—too loose or too tight, sleeves that are too long, a hat that's too small—thus creating conflict and comic possibilities. Sometimes the choice is visual or tactile: the players like the shape, the color, the way a costume hangs on their body, the way it feels against their skin. They should try clothes they feel uncomfortable in to see what that agitation does to their way of playing. Wearing an obstacle is one of the best ways to find comic play: a player is put off balance in a tangible way, the sense of being odd or awkward in their own skin is immediate and tactile.

The players should go wandering through secondhand clothes stores, the costume stocks in a theater, the closets of their friends, letting costume discoveries happen by chance. Put the players into groups of three and let them dress each other, the person being costumed is given little say in the choices made and is dressed completely before they can look in the mirror.

Like the nose, the costume is a teaching tool: it will make suggestions, offer ideas on how to move, play and relate to the world. It's also a mobile props case: clowns can literally wear their show on their body. A hat can be used to show off tricks, a coat can be turned into a lifelike human partner, shoes can be transformed into hammers or telephones, socks into hand puppets (comic and clown George Carl made a career out of playing with his hat, getting a microphone cord tangled in his coat and his thumb caught in the buttonhole). With this in mind, let's look at clowning and skills.

Figure 12.1 Sophia Knox-Miller: The skillful clown. *Photo credit: Eric Gillet/Shoot That Klown.*

12

The Skillful Clown

The Dexterous Fool

Due to their long history with the circus, clowns were exposed to a variety of highly skilled artists. From their fellow performers they picked up tricks they could use in their acts, either as a parody or presented to impress the crowd, who enjoyed the contrast between the clown's apparent clumsiness and a sudden display of first-rate skill. Many clowns started out as acrobats, rope walkers or trick riders, then moved into comedy after an injury or age limited their ability to perform more difficult tricks. Other skill artists discovered they had a natural talent for making people laugh and switched to clowning (the legendary Edwin "Poodles" Hanneford was a brilliant equestrian who became a clown).

Figure 12.2 Joe Dieffenbacher aka nakupelle in *Bon Appetit!* Photo credit: Matilda Dieffenbacher.

A lot of the training I've witnessed in circus spaces around the world is focused mainly on learning skills. The risk is that the more impressive the skills, the harder it is for the performer to connect with the audience: they're so concentrated on their tricks they have a hard time making a human connection with the crowd. Clowning offers a unique way to combine both skill and audience interaction because clown training creates an atmosphere that supports both competition and collaboration. It opens a player up to experimentation, bending the rules, flexing the imagination, not just the muscles. It embraces a high level of skill while it celebrates the inelegant, the inept.

Because I see the clown as a strongly physical and visual performer, training in any skill that teaches greater control of the body and provides the players with more options on how to use it, is encouraged.

Dance

Any form of dance will contribute to a more expressive body. Ballet will teach good posture and alignment, tap will teach rhythm and footwork, hip hop has elements of tap, mime, and acrobatics, while contact improv will open the players up to greater physical exploration, teach them how to base someone and to be comfortable with being lifted. It does wonders for ensemble work.

Music

Music has always been associated with clowns, whether playing an instrument, creating rhythms with props, or singing. Many clowns are also talented musicians, some play multiple instruments. Music speaks directly to the emotions in a way similar to clowning; the relationship to the music and the musician feels immediate for an audience, certain tunes make us want to tap our feet, sing along or get up and dance. Clowning should encourage the same desire to participate.

Mime/Movement

These are sometimes used interchangeably: they can involve illusion mime or silent acting, learning how to express thoughts and emotions with the body, the face, the limbs, the spine. They can help the players to discover the link between everyday movement, expressive gestures, and dance.

Tumbling

It's important for any player to be able to do basic tumbling moves such as a forward and backward roll, dive roll, aikido roll, back shoulder roll, cartwheel, round-off, headstand and handstand. Not only will the learning of these moves strengthen the body, but they'll decrease the risk of injury; rolls are some of the best ways to save oneself from a fall, intentional or accidental. These moves can be developed into pratfalls, used as dynamic entrances or exits, or to find eccentric ways for clowns to move across the stage. Tumbling teaches the players to let gravity have its way with them while acquiring techniques that keep them safe (e.g., how to use the hands and feet, as well as rolls, to spread out the impact of a fall).

Partner Acrobatics

Partner acrobatics will increase the ability of the ensemble to play together physically and help build trust. Moves should include partner balancing, lifting, and throwing. Many acrobatic moves that are difficult for the players to perform on their own can be accomplished safely with partners (such as a backflip). Partner work generates physical complicity which is essential for good clowning: partner acrobatics (and partner dance) encourages a more organic, visceral and immediate state of communication, which leads to a trust between the players that's impossible to achieve with words alone.

Slapstick

For the clown, all these disciplines serve the art of slapstick. It's much more than just silly knockabout or "comic" abuse: slapstick is how the clown relates to the physical world, how she responds to its attempts to defeat her, play with her, surprise her, and provoke her. And because everyone must deal with the physical world, it gives the clown a connection to any crowd anywhere in the world. This is why slapstick is universal.

Figure 12.3 The crowd in Ludwigsburg, Germany enjoying nakupelle's *The Trap*. *Photo credit: Matilda Dieffenbacher.*

In the most general sense, slapstick happens whenever you interact with the world, whether it's working with tools, furniture, office equipment, curtains, computers, walls, the floor—anything tangible. Any time the body moves—walking, sitting, lying down, standing up—there is the potential for slapstick; something will go wrong or, more accurately, not go as planned. You drop the thing in your hand, trip over a bump in the sidewalk, run headfirst into a glass door, have trouble articulating what you want to express and your body starts fidgeting and fumbling, you get your coat caught on a door knob, can't get the computer to function, etc. One can start to feel preyed upon, it's as if so-called "inanimate objects" have a mind of their own and have chosen you as their plaything. Slapstick turns this low-level paranoia into clown play.

Slapstick revels in all physical interaction, mines it for comedy, and uses it to find common ground between the clown and the crowd. It gets a player out of their head and forces them to engage with the physical world. Jacques Tati was a master of small, subtle slapstick, pulling a myriad of comic moments out of everyday life. Even the sound of a seat cushion or a swinging door, a person's way of walking or handling a broom, became part of his slapstick worldview, making us more aware of the physical world and the potential for play inherent in it (for a modern take on slapstick, physical and visual play, see the work of the UK-based Mischief Theatre).

Slapstick is about training your mind to inhabit the world of the clown, a world of obstacles, accidents, impact, and the tyranny of hard surfaces, especially in relation to status. For example, when you fall off a chair, that chair now has higher status. The comedy comes from how you recover, try to regain status, or lose it completely. It takes what is internal and makes it available to the audience by *showing the struggle* in physical terms, where grappling with a real object or an environment can become a metaphor and a visible expression of an internal state. For example, a man who keeps running into things because of his vanity, too busy trying to look good to pay attention to where he's going. A woman so full of frustration she can't carry out a task without getting exasperated, getting tangled in her clothes, her props, her own body.

There are three ways to present slapstick. I call them: Interruption, Intervention, and Invasion. The first level is interruption: the clown has a strong objective, "This MUST be done! By ME!" The clown is moving towards his objective, determined to make it happen, 100 percent focused on the goal! Then he's interrupted. The interruption opens him up, distracts and delays him. It's short—the clown is sidetracked by something he sees, someone stops him, he walks into a wall, he trips, etc.—then he gets back on course, continues to pursue his objective.

If an interruption delays the clown momentarily, an intervention steps in and alters her course. Something happens that moves her in a new direction, causes her to work towards a different objective. She sees one thing, then another, gets turned around by something behind her, then an object over to her left. She gets so distracted by all the looking about, she loses track of where she's going. Or someone stops her and demands she follow them, abandoning her original course. Or she walks into a wall and it dazes her to the point she forgets where she was going.

An intervention changes the clown's direction. An invasion destroys everything, creates chaos, making the clown forget their objective completely! A trip leads to a stumble, a fall, knocking over a chair, then a lamp, yanking out its plug, short circuiting the wiring in the room, causing a blackout in the house... Everything falls apart but somehow they bounce back or rise above it. Or they choose to dive into the chaos and revel in it, create more! They no longer have an objective; they simply try to survive (there are good examples of invasion between Cato and Inspector Clouseau in Blake Edwards' *Pink Panther* movies).

Because slapstick draws from many disciplines—acrobatics, dance, mime, martial arts, set design, object manipulation—and includes random, chaotic movements that challenge every part of the body—training in slapstick will increase a player's physical répertoire. And the more variety a player explores in their movement, the stronger and more protected their body will be: slapstick training will activate and build up a greater variety of muscles and strengthen joints, ligaments, and tendons. A diversity of movement training which includes slapstick, offers the players more choices when devising material, helps them express themselves physically, and creates more imaginative stage pictures.

Exercises that focus specifically on slapstick moves are difficult to describe in words, so I have not included them. The best discipline for getting started is tumbling, focusing on somersaults as well as front and back falls, learning to drop or faint safely, and any move that develops upper body strength such as planks or push-ups. Props and the physical elements in a scene—table, chairs, couches, beds, pillows, sheets, costumes, etc.—can be used to cushion a fall, support a player on their way to the floor, instigate a slapstick sequence, and add to the visual play.

Skills, Tricks, Feats, and Stunts

As mentioned earlier, circus clowns are often multi-talented, surrounded by any number of skill artists from acrobats and jugglers, to contortionists, aerialists, rope walkers, dancers, and animal trainers. When I was with the circus, I was always bugging the European acrobats to teach me something and, in between shows, went out in the ring to practice.

On an economic level, having a number of skills, tricks, feats, and stunts at your command can lead to more work: I've often been hired to do one thing in a production but while waiting around I would practice a different skill, the director would see me and get the idea to include that skill in the show. I've seen this happen to a number of artists (just make sure you're practicing in view of the director).

Presentation

Skills such as juggling, sleight-of-hand manipulations, acrobatics, slack rope etc., can be included in a performance in a number of ways:

- Present the skill as a display of tricks that garner applause in their own right.

- Integrate the skill into a performance in such a way that it helps the clown express who they are, what they're thinking and feeling (see Section 4: Prop Play).
- Skills can be used to enhance the playfulness and vitality of a scene. For example, the clown juggles everything they lay their hands on before climbing into the bathtub. He breaks out into a dance in order to overcome an adversary. The clown doesn't just run onstage to greet her partner, she does a handspring or a dive roll before saying hello.
- Skills training gives a player much more than tricks to show off: sleight of hand teaches misdirection which is particularly useful in comedy (especially slapstick). The concentration a player learns from controlling objects while juggling, helps her stay focused in scenes when there are many things going on at once (and does wonders for eye-to-hand coordination). Acrobatics not only gives a player a stronger body, but more choices in how they use it in a scene.
- The discipline required to learn a skill teaches the players to value focused work and dedicated practice. They begin to appreciate how time works on the development of expertise, and how long hours of practice and rehearsal contribute to the evolution of both the clown and their performance; it's not only about learning a skill but also exploring possibilities with the clown in relation to the skill, and how those skills can enhance and expand on the clown's relationship with the audience.

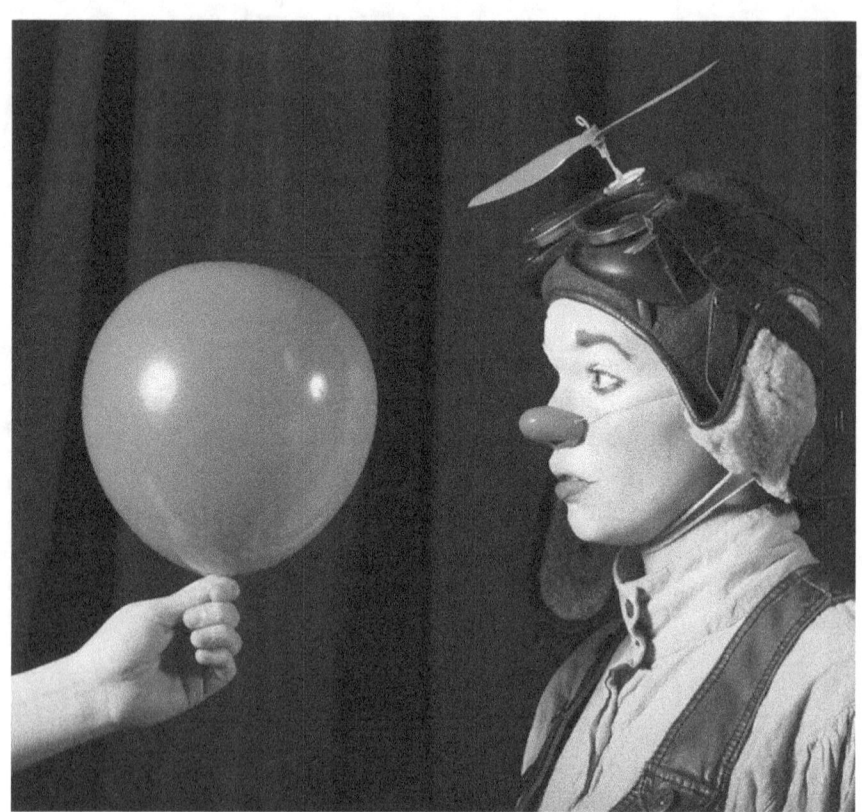

Figure 13.1 Get serious about your funny. *Photo credit: Eric Gillet/Shoot That Klown.*

13

Getting Serious About Your Funny

Begin to Begin

So, you've played games, explored exercises, and discovered new possibilities. You've been provoked and played with, challenged, and inspired. Now you're eager to create something you can call your own. You've got ideas for clever gags, hilarious physical business, jokes, and brilliant slapstick comedy! You also feel you have something important to say, deep and profound insights

Figure 13.2 Lars Adams and Carasue McClendon go on safari.
Photo credit: Eric Gillet/ Shoot That Klown.

into the human condition—you want to be a clown *and* a poet, a fool *and* a philosopher. But your head is so full of big ideas and lofty ambitions you feel overwhelmed! Where do you start?!

To make a routine or a devised play from nothing more than a few ideas is hard. You have to be honest about your weaknesses, and not rely solely on your strengths. You must give your ideas time to be accumulated, pondered, designed and built, tested, reworked, edited, and expanded. Your first performances for an audience will seem like an extension of the rehearsal process, as you stumble along trying to figure out what works and what doesn't. After that first presentation, you may end up with only a few insights into a new work, or you might make more discoveries than you know what to do with. The audience might respond to things you never imagined they'd respond to, sit blank-faced during scenes you thought would be hilarious.

It takes quite a few shows to feel comfortable with new material, get a consensus on what works and what doesn't, and a few more to build on what's discovered and refine it. Your first performances are opportunities to gather information, to discover more about your way of playing with an audience, how they respond to you and what you've created. You're trying to strike up a conversation, invite the public to collaborate on developing this new work, and expanding it further.

Below are notes that I've taken over many years of devising my own material and helping others do the same. When you're feeling stuck, I hope these words will help you move forward. Afterwards, I'll discuss practical things you can do to get started on devising.

Take Action

Make a rough outline of what you want to include in a particular show, gather the props and any costume bits you want to work with, get some music that inspires you, find a space to work, and get started. Don't spend too much time at the outset plotting every detail. Devisers will often try to include every single notion, skill, character, and comic bit they've ever thought of in their attempts to devise a show. Know that this is a tendency and be prepared to edit, to say no; you're searching for the main through line or story arc of the particular piece you're creating. Setting some ideas aside can make it easier to create a simpler foundation which you can then expand on and perhaps reintroduce the ideas you edited out, later on. Focus on what you want to say and how you want to play and include only the things that will help you do that. This will get you working your ideas on your feet as soon as possible.

Get Serious

Games played in class or when developing new work, shouldn't be looked upon as separate from devising. They're a way of understanding, evolving and refining how you play in front of an audience, a chance to rehearse a way of performing that is spirited and effective. If you play games in a distracted, half-hearted, or superficial way, you're reinforcing bad habits you'll carry onstage. If you play in a way that's engaged, provocative and inquisitive, then you'll be using the games to practice your approach to creating original material. You'll be trying out ideas, discovering comic bits, strengthening yourself physically, mentally, and emotionally. If you fully engage in the play, you'll be clowning and developing material every time you enter into a game or exercise.

Make Progress Through Play

Don't get caught up in long discussions or ponder or analyse objectives and motivations too soon. Take the games from this book and get moving: engage with one another. Use play to learn about yourself, your partners, and the way they clown. Use the exercises to discover and develop ideas. Take breaks, take notes, then get back on your feet and continue to relate and explore, making progress through play.

Own It

To call the clown a character is to create a separate entity into which you can dump all these things that actually belong to you. You have to learn to celebrate *your* foolishness, *your* pretensions, *your* desires, and *your* joys. The clown is you, opened up, elaborated, deepened, given greater dimension. The classroom and the rehearsal space should be an environment for self-discovery, a space to increase self-awareness, make you conscious of your habits, patterns, and tendencies. Not to analyze or judge, but to become mindful so the discoveries can be used to generate material, to develop and improve your art. There is no hiding, only acknowledging, accepting, and celebrating who you are in all your glory and all your floundering.

Stay Open

A clown show is *always* in flux: cause leads to effect which leads to another cause to another effect in the constantly evolving, expanding world which the clown inhabits. A clown show is never set, and you should seek opportunities to keep it open to new possibilities (e.g. audience participation—always unpredictable!). Combine this with a strong arc, structure or plot and you'll have a dynamic mix.

Make It Real

You may find yourself gravitating towards hyperbole when you begin to explore clowning: instead focus on keeping your actions and emotions grounded in reality. Do an action as you would if you were alone in your room just doing it, without feeling the need to perform it for an audience (see pgs. 124–128 *The Real Thing*). Once you can do something without pretense, then you can expand, amplify, elaborate, and embellish.

Tune In

Become like a hypersensitive radar, open to find inspiration and ideas in the rehearsal space, but also on the way to the space: from people on public transport, kids, dogs, billboards, construction workers, a falling leaf, etc. Stay aware, take notes, and develop the ability to recall anything that may be useful when rehearsing and performing. This is one of the defining skills of all great improvisers and devisers.

Find Ways to Connect

How does the clown develop her connection to the public? She might do it with her juggling, playing a ukulele, throwing a back flip, telling a story with movement, or inviting people onstage to act out a fairy tale. He might choose an energy that is strong in him—frustration, curiosity, fear, joy—and invite the audience to feel the same by his actions. They might have a social or political issue they want to share or discuss and through their play, find common ground with the crowd. The ideas, skills, and energies that make up a show should be seen not as ends in themselves but as bridges, connecting the clown to the audience.

Take Notes

Any act of creation helps you understand how *you* create: What is *your process* to take an idea in your head to a full-fledged performance onstage? Do you procrastinate, or do you dive right in and keep at it with a wild abandon? Are you focused, meticulous, pondering every step you take, or are you messy, your process chaotic? Take notes about your way of working without judging yourself: the notes will help you recall your process so that each new creation becomes less of an immense frustration; you can see by what you've written that you've been here before, and it's clearly part of your way of working. Taking notes can also help you break patterns, find new ways to progress. They'll help you get to know the Creator, Crafter, Clown, and Director within, to invite them all into the studio to talk, debate, argue, rant, and play together.

Accumulate

Any good clown act or scene is the end result of a long process—sometimes taking years. Any strong performance of original, devised material has come about through a long process of accumulation, the artists gathering together ideas, skills, bits of comic business, personal discoveries, their changing politics, an expanding social consciousness . . . all this is transformed in the crucible that is a rehearsal/creation space, and over many tryouts in front of an audience, forged into an entertaining/provocative/powerful/satirical/ moving piece of theater. That's why I encourage the players to learn as many skills as they can, hoard ideas, sayings, jokes, odd turns of phrase, eccentric ways of moving, finding play in everyday activities. Because the clown sees the potential in everything, they are the ultimate collector, one who is eager to share what they've hoarded with the crowd.

Figure 14.1 Los Payasos Mendigos: Devising for clown and physical comedy. *Photo credit: Matilda Dieffenbacher.*

14

Devising for Clown and Physical Comedy

Nuts and Bolts

I'd like to end this book with practical advice. Here are ways I've begun working on a piece (my own or when directing other artists), and the things that inspired me to explore in a particular direction. Often, they were combined: choosing a role also meant choosing props, choosing a task meant

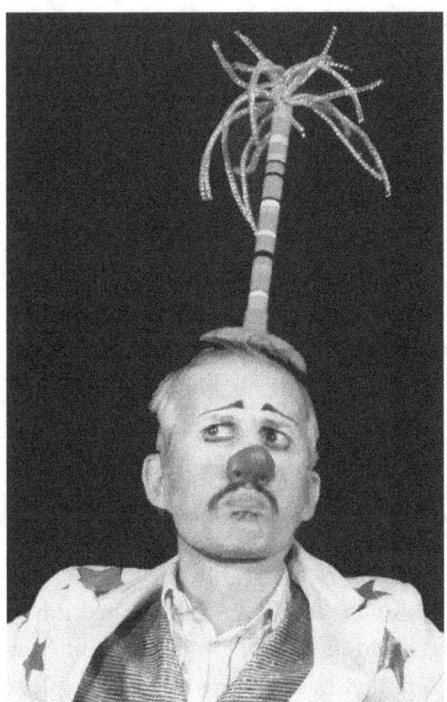

Figure 14.2 Michael Hayes shows off the emperor's new hat.
Photo credit: Eric Gillet/Shoot That Klown.

deciding how I would carry it out (what was the energy behind it). Choose any one and begin, and you'll discover how they all start to blend together and create a richer world to play in. These propositions can be used by solo players, duos or trios. Afterwards, I offer advice on ensemble devising.

Choose a Role

This creates expectations for an audience—they recognize the role. It could be a chef, a janitor, a doctor, an office worker, a waiter, etc. The clown can either play into the expectations suggested by the role or subvert them. The audience will enjoy the combination of role play that is recognizable, with actions that are eccentric, challenging, surreal or absurd.

When choosing roles also consider status: establishing a hierarchy can suggest actions, plot twists, comic play. This is true for solo artists as well: What is your status in relation to the audience? Are you there to serve them or show off? Do you see them as equals? Do you welcome them onstage and wait to see what they'll do, or do you require them to perform certain actions? And remember, status shouldn't be set in stone: as you play, stay open to the pecking order changing, a high-status clown doing something foolish, the fool taking the lead and establishing order.

Choose an Energy

When I created my solo show, *Bon Appetit*, one of the emotions I felt was frustration: I was touring all over Europe and every other weekend (sometimes every other day), I found myself in a new country having to learn a new language to use in the show. The frustration I felt in trying to communicate was translated into a way of speaking: the clown's language became a mix of all the words I learned on my travels, a "grammelot" of Euro-Asia-speak that allowed me to have fun with my frustration (and had the crowd wondering where the heck this clown was from).

Developing new work from an emotion or energy such as pride, confusion, joy, curiosity, etc., can help get a flow started; you then search for a role, a task, props, or a setting, that allow you to find degrees of that energy and ways to express it. The emotion creates an instant connection to an audience: they all know how you feel, and they'll delight in watching how the world you create heightens or alters that base energy. You can explore various levels of that energy—confidence turns to pride, pride becomes vanity, vanity becomes ridiculously pretentious—and how that base energy might transition to other emotions. For example, in my solo show, the frustration gives way to pleasure, then to a goofy pride as the clown manages to create a meal for the audience right before their eyes, despite all his difficulties.

Choose a Setting

Putting a clown in an office, a kitchen, a house that needs redecorating, a busy restaurant, a shop that sells clothes, etc., gives them not only props to play with, but an atmosphere that the clown's energy can alter and disrupt. A familiar setting will suggest actions everyone recognizes and will get the players acting out those tasks right away; variations and alterations are more easily discovered through play because everyone has something to do right from the start.

Choose a Prop

Working with an object can lead a player into a rich and playful world that she never knew existed. I once gave a student a mop and told her to go play with it for an hour. She hemmed and hawed, complained that it was just a mop: how was she going to discover how to clown with a cleaning tool?! But I refused to answer her questions until the hour of play was over. Fifteen minutes in, she began to make discoveries. After an hour, she wanted to keep playing. She added a bucket, she found a white bouffant wig that looked like a well-coiffed version of the mop, a dress that echoed both. We exchanged the wooden handle for a two-and-a-half-meter length of PVC: the mop head entered first, then the long white pole against the black curtain, building curiosity for her clown's entrance, with her high blonde hair, her billowy white dress, and her orange-tan work boots. She found play with the bendy pole, created a short dance, and found slapstick comedy as she mopped the floor. She even discovered an extended game that had the audience cheering her on as she stuck the handle between her knees and tried to lift the long bendy pole with the heavy mop head high into the air, drop it into the bucket, then lift both back in the air while crawling off stage on her back.

Props can be chosen because you want to display a skill—balance a broom, spin a plate, turn a plunger into a diablo, do acrobatics with a chair.

Figure 14.3 Windy Wynazz flexes her mop. *Photo credit: Eric Gillet/Shoot That Klown.*

Or a prop might solve a problem: I chose to play with a ladder for a solo street show because it allowed for large, standing crowds to see what I was doing as I climbed higher up the rungs. The ladder also offered me plenty of opportunities for slapstick-acrobatic play. You might choose to wear a coat because you realize you can turn it into a bed, a puppet, a magic cape to conceal and reveal a trick. Audiences are tickled, challenged, and inspired by how clowns transform mundane objects into something new, how they create imaginative play and whole new worlds out of props taken for granted or barely noticed. Props are excellent tools to start with when devising new material.

Narrative, Plot, Arc, Through Line

You've chosen a jumping off point—role, energy, setting, or prop—and you've played a bit. Now you have to find an arc, a through line, a story that takes the audience on a journey. Here are some things to consider as you try to shape your play into a performance that keeps the audience curious, intrigued, and engaged.

Find the Flow

The real work in creating a show for an audience is weaving all the elements together so they end up belonging to the same world, stylistically and energetically. It doesn't mean there can't be moments of absurdity, things that come out of left field; what you're aiming for is a flow so that even if there is an abrupt shift, the audience stays with you. Flow rarely comes right away: assemble what you need to tell your story, play with your ideas on your feet, decide on a structure or sequence, and try to get a feel for how everything flows together so you don't lose or confuse the audience in the transitions or shifts in energy and play. Whether your story is easily understood, is a series of odd, disconnected events, or a mash up of skills and comic bits, it all comes down to timing, pace, and changes in tempo. Find the flow.

Make it Personal

Connect your act to something you care about, a beloved hobby or activity. Or something that irritates, frustrates or angers you. Utilize the emotions that these things inspire: your personal investment will carry over to the audience. They will sense your passion and feed on it, they'll want to share in it.

Embrace the Struggle

Build a scene out of a series of obstacles and your interaction with them in order to develop suspense, tension, empathy. Get the audience rooting for you! Find out what the clown is good at and comfortable with. Now, throw the polar opposite at her. Challenge her. Make her uncomfortable. How does the clown respond? This helps give an act or scene dimension, depth.

Create a Map

Think of your act or scene as a series of pictures that show the beginning, the middle (a series of actions and obstacles, causes and effects), and the ending. What images or tableaux would you choose to tell the story, generate curiosity, excitement? Use these tableaux as a way to block out the scene physically and visually and get everyone moving right away. This is what I call mapping. It's not only for the sake of the story but for safety: physical comedy often includes movement that is athletic and, when working in groups, care must be taken that the players don't run into one another.

Mapping helps create safe traffic patterns: the players know where they enter from, how they move onstage, and where they exit to. They'll feel safer as they progress and start to develop the map; it gives them a structure to build on right from the start.

Bits and Pieces

Consider building the show in increments: find a costume you can play in, nose and makeup if you wish, gather a few props you can carry on you or in a bag, find an event with a meandering crowd—anything from a festival to people standing in line waiting—and do what's called a "walk act." You roam through the crowd, interacting with them, creating short moments of play then moving on. This allows you to discover your way of playing with a live audience, gives you a chance to develop comic business, and find what plays well between you and the public, without the pressure of presenting a show of all new material all at once. As you accumulate ideas and ways of connecting with the crowd, you can then incorporate these into a longer, stationary performance. I've used this way of working for many of my shows and most performers I know have explored a similar method, trying things out and building a longer show from an accumulation of bits and pieces they've worked in front of an audience.

Go with the Obvious

Get your obvious, lame ideas out in the open—verbalize them, act them out—and groan at them, enjoy the clichés, the easy answers. Keep at it until you exhaust the obvious: you might then find something original, or a way to twist the obvious to create an unexpected climax, a surprise ending; let the audience think they know where you're going and then throw a curveball.

Likes and Dislikes

What do you *not* want to do? Make a list. This may help with the flow of ideas. Better yet, you may find a gem in your pile of dislikes. Study a movie, a scene in a play, a clown act, stories you like, and ones you don't. Why do you like it? Define the reasons. How would you change what you don't like, reinvent it in your own way? Can you comprehend the *structure* of a piece, *how* it draws you in, keeps you engaged? Articulate and define how it moves you (and how it doesn't) and why. Something that provokes you in a positive or negative way can be used as a jumping off point to develop your own story while giving you an emotional connection to it.

Study

Become a student of comedy. Devour books about comedians, read anything with the words *laughter, funny, wit, humour, comic, clown, fool, jokes,* etc., in the title. Watch silent films and study how they use movement, gestures and facial expressions to tell a story. Or watch a talkie film with the sound off: can you follow the story through the visuals alone? Get into conversations with taxi drivers, lawyers, cops, bouncers and bartenders, housewives, truck drivers, nurses, etc. Could you create a clown piece based on their stories, their jobs? Study paintings and photographs: how do the pictorial elements cause your eye to travel around what's in the frame, how do they tell a story in a single image? Write down your dreams. Write down bits from random conversations. Open up to the rarely noticed world, the play of light and shadow when the sun comes through the trees, gives shape to clouds, dances across water. There's comedy happening everywhere: The clown desires to point it out and play with it (see Jacque Tati's *Playtime*).

Respect the Elders

When you study clowns and comedians from the past you're bound to find ones that you don't find funny at all. You may wonder why the audience is laughing when the clowns' antics barely raise a smile in you. This is when you must be a student not a critic: behind most every joke, comic bit or gag is a technique, a formula, a method that can be discerned if you study it closely. Watching as a student, ask yourself *why* is the audience laughing? Is it because the comedian surprises their audience with a sudden reveal of the punchline, or does the laugh come because they build up to it slowly, drawing the audience in bit by bit? Do the clowns get a laugh by playing broadly, satirizing through exaggeration? Or perhaps it's the contrast between two clowns engaging in acrobatic physical play, while one sits calmly watching and commenting. Is it the comedian's timing: compare the fast-talking frenzy of Robin Williams with the deadpan, near monotone, of Stephen Wright. Underneath all comedy—even humor that feels dated to you and not funny at all—are ways of playing with an audience that are universal and timeless. Look closely and you will find that modern clowns and comedians are using some of the same methods to generate laughs as people from the 16th century (take a look at the scenarios of the commedia dell'arte and those of TV sitcoms). Study and learn from the elders, the past masters. Adopt their techniques, formulas, and methods and see if you can use them to generate laughter from your audience.

Borrow, Purloin, Transcend

Every artist borrows and pilfers ideas and bits, but you should aim to *transform* and *transcend* never imitate. Someone else's idea can get you started but through your own efforts you apply your personal alchemy and make it uniquely yours.

Technique, Commitment, Tactics, Story

Create shows that combine all four in order to find a balance; don't let any one thing dominate but rather create a piece where they all work together to create a unique world onstage (see *Challenges and Obstacles* pgs. 20–23).

Use the Clock

Create a two-minute piece. Now do the same piece in one minute. Thirty seconds, fifteen (see *Speed Tasking* pg. 126). Get off the stage when your time is up. Use the clock to trim your piece down to its essentials, learn what's superfluous, stops the flow. Let the clock be a benign dictator. Use it to learn where you need to speed up and slow down, what needs to be emphasized, what needs to be cut. The clock is one of your most valuable allies. Respect it. Once you pare your piece down to its strongest moments, then consider expanding and embellishing. Or keep it lean, spare.

Build Bridges

In my early years devising new work I noticed the change in my energy as I went from hanging around with my fellow players in the green room to stepping backstage and getting ready, and then how different I was when I stood in the wings waiting to enter the stage. Accidentally stumbling on my entrance changed the way the audience perceived me when I hit my spot onstage to perform my act, and how I was suddenly a different person as I stood there in the spotlight. I'd go into my act, fully committed to what I was doing, the audience totally engaged! ... And then someone would drop something backstage and the crowd would turn their heads towards the sound.

Or a person in the front row would sneeze, distracting everyone. At first, I was put off by these interruptions, but the more experience I gained from playing in front of a crowd, the more I embraced everything that happened when performing live. The more attuned I became to the crowd's responses, the more I realized that each mistake, each distraction, was simply an attempt by other worlds, other realities, to join in the play. I could choose to ignore them, I could acknowledge the interruptions with a brief look, or I could integrate these offers into what I was doing and welcome them to join my show.

From these experiences, I understood how a clown could build bridges between realities: the person just hanging out, the person getting ready, the player waiting to go on, who he is as he enters, as he presents, as he exits (see *Backstage Butting In*, pgs. 113–116). And how to use the different realities of the audience as well: as they enter, get ready, engage with the players, get distracted... The playful mind of the clown stays attentive to all these worlds and seeks to build bridges between them. This means embracing accidents, mistakes, failures, the unexpected—even the annoying. In my own work—and in the shows of many performers that I know—at least 30 to 40 percent of their material came about because something didn't go according to plan either in rehearsal or in performance. So, if a player is determined to stick to the script come what may and ignore all unexpected "offers" that are bound to occur with a live audience, then they're cutting themselves off from a vast amount of great material.

Endings are Hard

Write out five (or more) endings. Get on your feet, play your act or scene, try an ending then start again from a different angle. End that and try another approach. Endings are rarely obvious. They require continuous attempts, feints, direct attacks, experiments, leaps of the imagination, searching for clues to the end from what has gone before. If you can't find a strong ending, perhaps you need to change your set up. Be willing to abandon even the most brilliant beginning if you can't find an equally brilliant ending.

Ensemble Devising: Developing Group Entrées, Scenes, and Routines

Ensembles can use some of the same starting-off points as solos, duos or trios, but a larger group will devise new work with slightly different approaches.

Games

One way to begin the development of group routines or scenes is by using games. This is better than simply assigning roles: the games can give the ensemble realistic insights into individual tendencies as well as the group dynamic, challenging the ensemble to be more honest in their play.

Roles

What roles or ways of playing do individuals naturally gravitate towards? What roles or ways of playing does the group naturally gravitate towards? When creating original material, consider using these discoveries rather than imposing roles. This will encourage the players to more fully express themselves. The group can then expand on this, lift it beyond the personal to the universal, while it remains grounded in, has its source from, the realities of a particular group of people.

Actions

Ultimately, it's not what the group does but *how* they do it that's most interesting. A skill can be impressive, a scene cleverly written, but it's living, breathing human beings—and the interplay between them—that's enticing to the audience. The games can help by making that interplay more authentic and dynamic.

Setting

Choose a setting—a bus stop, a restaurant, a laundromat, etc.—and play a game—for example *Tag, Racing,* or *Chair Games*—within this setting to see what it encourages. Add costumes, props, set pieces. In the beginning, keep the setting and props simple: what's most important is discovering the group dynamic within a particular environment (how they act in an office will be different from how they act at a sporting event).

Relationships

What's discovered when playing games may not only reveal relationships within the group, it can also determine the routine or scene; the devised piece becomes an expression of the group's relationships discovered through play. Utilizing skills, costumes, props, physical play, energies, alliances, oppositions, and obstacles, the group tells their story.

Switching

As roles are established, try switching the players to see how they might play a role differently. It will generate new ideas and new ways to approach a situation. Changing roles and status within the group can help your partners find new ways of relating to you; you can play the switched role as you perceive it or try imitating what your partner did when you take on their role. Help them see themselves through your eyes.

Writing

Let the piece evolve using the discoveries the group makes while on their feet, then use the writing process to develop the *structure* of the play. Writing helps give form to an act or a scene, can create an arc for the story, strengthening the plot as it evolves through ensemble play. If the story is non-linear, writing can help you find the best sequence, so the piece has a good build or flow and draws the audience in. Or a scene starts with a chaos of detail and, over time, reveals the narrative from within the mess. Writing can help the players see the bigger picture and how to weave together ideas and actions.

Editing

A piece borne out of the explorations of a group always starts off as complex; everyone wants their ideas included. Allow that, but let it be known there will be editing as the group works to simplify and clarify. Or the ensemble can embrace the complexity: as you explore and evolve, stay aware of the many threads you've laid out, and make the time to weave all the details together, find something that has a flow, a rhythm that the audience can connect with.

Respect

No matter how talented, creative, brilliant, or skillful you may be, recognize that an act or scene is always a *group creation* with each member contributing to a greater or lesser degree according to their strengths and their weaknesses; since the clown can turn a weakness into a strength, everything has potential. Dismissing someone you perceive as weak (in talent, ideas, or skills), can blind you to what they might offer. This doesn't mean everything should be altered to serve a less-experienced player—it's their responsibility to up their game whenever possible. If the players agree to work together, deficiencies must be acknowledged not ignored, and they must look for creative ways to incorporate them. If each member takes it upon themselves to help each other, it will deepen the connection and strengthen complicity within the group. Cultivate the ability to wait, to listen, to respect each person's process. Every "negative" dynamic should be seen as a greater challenge for learning.

That said, if the ensemble agrees that a player is dragging down the process to the point where there's no evolution, that must be honestly addressed, and actions taken; say your goodbyes and move on.

Questions

When developing an act or scene, each member of the ensemble should keep in mind the following questions.

- Who am I?
- Where am I?
- What do I want?
- Who do I want? What are my primary relationships? What are my secondary ones?
- Why do I want what I want? How will I get it? What stands in my way? What leverage do I have?
- What are my tactics for getting what I want?
- What will I do when I get what I want?
- What will I do if I don't get what I want, or get it and lose it?
- How do I imagine myself at the end of this story, how have I changed or not changed?

Ask these questions at the outset and keep asking them as the devised piece evolves.

When It All Gets Too Confusing

When you feel clueless, bereft of ideas, discouraged by your frustration—like you'll never find an end to the process! ... Stop. Breathe. Look around the room you're working in. Forget everything you've been struggling with; just observe the space and what or who is in it. Adjust your ears to all the sounds in the room, sounds that are distinct, and the general hubbub. Listen to

Figure 14.4 Sophia Knox-Miller: The balloon meditation.
Photo credit: Devin Shacket.

what's in between: the rests, the quiet. *Take it all in with no expectations whatsoever*. Practice this state of energized calm, this relaxed attentiveness. Don't be afraid to give the appearance of doing nothing but staring off into space, or with your head down, studying the patterns on the knotty wood floor. The answers are there. Sometimes you find them by not looking for them directly.

This is another way of saying don't limit yourself to what's in your head. Don't try to evolve your show or solve a problem with your thoughts alone. Look around: a prop can solve a problem, changing the color or size of something can open up new possibilities, a different costume, nose or style of makeup might alter how you affect the audience. For example, a long dress changes the way the audience perceives you (and you perceive yourself). It becomes a body mask that brings out a different energy. It alters—physically and visually—even the simplest move: doing a cartwheel in a long dress changes the nature and the visual of the cartwheel; it becomes a different move than if you were to do it in tights or a three-piece suit. It's simple, yet it has the potential to lead you in a direction you wouldn't have found if you tried to work out everything in your head. Look for solutions and evolutions through movement, objects, costumes, shapes, and colors, through play with the world around you, and all that's in it.

Not only is the creation of an original piece a process of discovering what makes it tick, but it's also a process of finding out what makes *you* tick. And then, how does what you discover play in front of an audience? We all have many dimensions, quite a few which we ourselves don't see. Diving into the creation of a piece will teach you about yourself, what you like and dislike, what intrigues you, what brings you joy, what provokes you, and pushes you into new territory, new worlds.

One of the reasons some clowns choose to work with tried-and-true gags or comic formulas is because it's easier, the process of discovery is quicker, and the audience responds to the piece more readily because they spot the clichés that formulaic work offers. There's nothing wrong with using formulas and indulging in the obvious; they make good jumping off points. But once you leave behind the formula, go beyond the obvious, you're on your own. If you keep at it, it will yield material that is unique and truly yours and you'll discover things about yourself that you wouldn't have if you relied only on the usual tropes. You'll grow as an artist and other players, afraid of trying something different, will see what you've created and how you've made your eccentric ideas work, see that it plays for an audience, and be inspired to take chances and indulge their own "weird" notions. This is how an art evolves, takes audiences in new directions, shows them that there is more to an art form than anyone thought was possible (especially with clowning). For these reasons, the headaches and heartaches are worth it for they seed and expand the imaginations of other artists, and more importantly, the audience.

I encourage you to indulge in and become fascinated by the creative process! Look upon the creation of new work as a mischievous friend that wants to draw you out to play, turn your struggles into a puckish game that demands you think, imagine, feel, indulge, and find your joy in the work. And that joy is the ultimate goal. Loving what you do is the source of all creativity. It keeps you going when things are difficult, blesses you with inspiration, and extends itself outwards to your audience, inspiring connection and complicity.

So, here's to your play and your joy.

Bibliography

Here are titles on the history of clowning, clowns in other cultures, comic archetypes, and critical analyses of various aspects of comedy and the comic spirit. These books have informed my own understanding and approach to clown and physical comedy.

Bakhtin, M. (1965), *Rabelais and His World*, Bloomington, IN: Indiana University Press.
Barker, C. (1977), *Theater Games*, London: Methuen Drama
Barron, F., Montuori, A., and Barron, A. (1997), *Creators on Creating*, New York: G.P. Putnam.
Bergson, H. (1900), *Laughter*, New York: Atropos Press
Berman, M. (1989), *Coming to Our Senses*, London: Unwin Hyman Limited.
Boal, A. (2002), *Games for Actors and Non-Actors*, London: Routledge Group/ Taylor & Francis.
Caputi, J. (1978), *Buffo*, Detroit, MI: Wayne State University Press.
Cline, P. (1984), *Fools, Clowns and Jesters,* La Jolla: Star & Elephant.
Conrad Hyers, M. (1973), *Zen & the Comic Spirit*, Louisville, KY: Westminster John Knox Press.
D'haeyere, H. (n.d.) *Dislexicon*, MER Paper, Kunsthalle Ghent.
Davison, J. (2013), *Clown: Readings in Theatre Practice*, London: Palgrave Macmillan
Disher, W. (1985), *Clowns and Pantomimes*, Boston: Houghton Mifflin Company.
Eastman, M. (1936), *Enjoyment of Laughter*, New York: Simon & Schuster.
Ehrenreich, B. (2006), *Dancing in the Streets: A History of Collective Joy*, New York: Metropolitan Books/Henry Holt and Company.
Erasmus, D. (2007), *In Praise of Folly*, London: Penguin Classics.
Fluegelman, A. (1978), *The New Games Book*, San Francisco, CA: The Headlands Press.
Harkonen, H. B. (1970), *Circuses and Fairs in Art*, Minneapolis, MI: Learner Publications,
Hugill, B. (1980), *Bring on the Clowns*, Exeter, UK: David & Charles Ltd.
Hyde, L. (2008), *Trickster Makes This World*, New York, NY: Farrar, Straus and Giroux Books.

Jenkins, R. (1989), *Acrobats of the Soul*, New York: Theatre Communications Group Inc.
Johnston, C. (2000), *The Improvisation Game*, London: Nick Hern Books.
Johnston, K. (2012), *Impro: Improvisation and the Theater*, London: Methuen Drama.
Keaton, B. (2015), *My Wonderful World of Slapstick*, Boston, MA: De Capo Press.
Kerr, W. (1990), *The Silent Clowns*, New York: Alfred A. Knopf.
Lane, L. (1972), *How to Become a Comedian*, London: F Muller Ltd.
Lee, J. (1996), *The History of Clowns for Beginners*, New York: Writers and Readers Publishing, Inc.
Madden, D. (1975), *Harlequins Stick, Charlie's Cane*, Madison, WI: Popular Press.
Mason, B. (1992), *Street Theater and Other Outdoor Performance*, London: Routledge.
McConnell Stott, A. (2010), *The Pantomime Life of Joseph Grimaldi*, Edinburgh: Canongate Books.
Miller, H. (1953), *The Smile at the Foot of the Ladder*, New York: New Directions Publishing Corporation.
Moore, T. (1994), *Care of the Soul* and *Soulmates*, London: Piatkus/Little, Brown.
Nisker, W. (2008), *Crazy Wisdom*, Berkeley, CA: Ten Speed Press.
Radin, P. (1972), *The Trickster*, New York: Schocken Books.
Rider Robinson, D. (1999), *The Physical Comedy Handbook*, Portsmouth, NH: Heinemann.
Spolin, V. (1999), *Improvisation for the Theater*, Evanston, IL: Northwestern University Press
Staveacre, T. (1987), *Slapstick! The Illustrated Story of Knoackabout Comedy*, London: Angus & Robertson Publishers.
Steinman, L. (1995), *The Knowing Body*, Boston, MA: Shambhala.
Tayor, R. (1987), *The Death and Resurrection Show*, London: Muller, Blond & White Ltd.
Towsen, J. (1976), *Clowns*, Boston, MA: EP Dutton.
Watteau, A. (1957), *Grock, King of Clowns*, London: Methuen
Welsford, E. (1935), *The Fool: His Social and Literary History*, London: Faber & Faber.
Willeford, W. (1969), *The Fool and His Scepter*, Evanston, IL: Northwestern University Press.
Wright, J. (2007), *Why is That So Funny? A Practical Exploration of Physical Comedy*, London: Nick Hern Books.

A lot of material can be found by looking up books or articles on play, games, circus, street theater, masks, and anything written by professional clowns or comedians. Look up your favorites.

Other fascinating studies include books or articles on Native American and aboriginal clowns/tricksters, sacred or holy fools, puppetry, the comic archetype in other cultures, religions and mythologies, circus, commedia dell'arte, and freak or sideshows. Besides giving you ideas for routines and ways of approaching new work, these books help you realize that in practising the art of clowning you are part of a long and global tradition.

Inspirations

The games and exercises in this book were introduced to me by various sources over a thirty-five-year period. Teachers or authors listed below may not be the originators of the games, but the person from whom I first heard about it. Games listed as "known theater games" have been used in various forms by a number of theater practitioners I've met over the years, so it's hard to say who's the originator. I've also been inspired by my students and fellow clowns whose play has helped develop many of the variations in this book.

1   Hello: A Pharmacist, Helium Balloons, and a Red Nose

Hello!: Some of these variations I developed, others were inspired by known theater or children's games.

Birds and bees: I came up with this game as a way to get the players moving and warmed up.

Group loco motion: I developed *Feet First* as a way for students to work their entire body while walking or running. *Walking the Dictionary* was inspired by the dictionary. The other variations come from known theater, dance or movement exercises.

Groups and agreements: These variations are known improv games with some tweaks added.

The five commandments: I first learned this from my Associate Director at Clown Conservatory, Dan Griffiths. I developed variations to add complexity and get the players to focus more acutely on listening and responding.

Wait, watch, jump, play: *Watch and wait* was inspired by director, dramatist, author, and teacher Augusto Boal. I developed *Hop HA!* as a variation on a movement exercise (source unknown). *Who's Got Game* was inspired by writer, director and teacher, John Wright.

2 Energy: The Telepathic Renaissance Fool

Walk this way: Inspired by a movement exercise I learned at the Dell'Arte school first shown to me by Bruce Marrs.

Chase me, tag me: These variations were inspired by known children's games.

The solo and the ensemble: These variations were inspired by Augusto Boal with some tweaks added.

Chair games: *Caller in the Middle* and *Numbered Chairs* were inspired by theater-maker and author Chris Johnston; I added variations to increase the level of physical play. I developed *Chair Race* with a group of Chinese clowns to get them working together physically without having to focus on acrobatic skill.

Races: Slow motion racing is a known theater game. I added the cheating and relay race variations. The races using paper were inspired by Chris Johnston.

Relax: Both variations were introduced to me by Ralph Hall at the Dell'Arte School.

3 The Talking Body: Silence on the Streets

Dance! I invented these variations as a way to get the players to improvise movement, warm up their bodies, and play together physically, inspired by music.

Playing with the breath: These variations were inspired by Augusto Boal with some tweaks added.

Where's my center? The first five variations are known movement exercises with some alterations added by me. *Stone Overhead* was learned from John Wright. I created *The Threat* to explore how using fear as a center outside the body would affect a player's actions.

Sculptures: These variations are drawn from known movement exercises with variations added by me.

The body mask: These are drawn from known movement exercises with clown-related variations added by me.

Visualization: Initially inspired by Ringling Bros. and Barnum & Bailey veteran circus clown Frosty Little, some variations are drawn from known movement exercises.

The five elements: Based on my reading of a number of theater and dance practitioners such as Vsevolod Meyerhold, Peter Brook, and Doris Humphrey, I developed the Five Elements to teach an awareness of space, movement and how to use that to reveal the clown and develop and enhance an act.

Looking out: I've had long conversations with various clown practitioners over the years about how to use the eyes. These variations were developed by me as a response to these debates.

4 Prop Play: The Prop Whisperer

Prop around: Some of these variations are known games for teaching circus skills, others I invented to get the players to use props to focus on ensemble play and movement.

Prop improv: I developed this list on using props to help the players clarify the ways they could use objects in both improv sessions and to create scenes.

Prop me: The inspiration for this exercise was Vanna White, who used to gesture with such poise and pleasure at the prizes contestants could win on the game show *Wheel of Fortune*. These variations were created to get the players to give value to their props.

Props and status: These variations were developed by me and are a combination of improv games, puppetry techniques and prop play inspired by my own performance work.

5 Curiosity: Odd Fellows

Space odyssey: These variations came out of my own explorations as a performer and director seeking to make use of spaces that were not designed as theaters.

Look, see, react: A "take" is a classic comic technique. I developed these variations as a way of exploring takes with students and helping them realize the potential of giving focus to something physically.

In and out: I'm a big fan of a great entrance and its potential for both introducing a clown as well as being used as a running gag (see Michael Richardson as Kramer in *Seinfeld*). This exercise was developed by me from known theater exercises to explore entrances and exits and how to use them effectively.

Listen: These variations were inspired by my experiences working in street theater where I had to listen with an almost radar-like intensity in order to stay on top of the sometimes uncontrollable environment of a street show.

Backstage butting in: I developed these variations not only to teach students how to use distractions, but also to explore the potential of the invisible spaces in any performance venue.

6   Clown Solos: Catching a Salad on Your Face

Pass it around: I created the variations, *Silly Sound* and *Silly Walk to* loosen up the players. *Big Gesture, Big Sound* was inspired by Keith Johnstone, author of *Impro*. The mirroring and reaction exercises were created to teach students clarity and truly sharing moments with their partners.

The real thing: I developed these variations as a way to get students to ground their actions in something real before expanding them into clown play.

The participating audience: *Reactions* was inspired by Chris Johnston; *Substitute* is a known theater game. *Love-Hate, The Fail,* and *The Bounce* were inspired by my own experiences with hecklers, and explorations into the effect failing in front of an audience has on their perception of a routine and the performer.

7   Clown Duos: The Wet Towel Intervention

Remember me: Some of these variations I developed, others were inspired by known theater games.

Pushers: Some of these variations I developed, others were inspired by Augusto Boal.

Mind leading the blind: *Blind Finger* was inspired by John Wright. The other variations are known theater games with tweaks added.

Followed: I developed *My Companion* after watching silent film comedians follow—or be followed by—their partners or their rivals. *Following Fool* is a classic bit of clown business. I created *Energies* as a way to explore the concept of the clown as energy. *Juxtapose* came about from watching two players rehearse their acts while standing next to one another, but totally focused on their own work.

Match my mood: I developed this exercise as a way of getting duos to work with clown as energy.

The big wind up: This was inspired by watching Jackie Gleason growing more agitated as Art Carney stalled and goofed around before carrying out a task on the classic TV show *The Honeymooners*.

Surprise, surprise: I developed this exercise as a combination of duo play and prop exploration.

Embrace: This was introduced to me by Ralph Hall at the Dell'Arte School.

8   Clown Trios: Boss, Negotiator, Fool

Get rhythm: I developed this exercise to increase the players' ability to listen to one another, to create movement and sound play, and to generate eccentric ways of communicating in scenes.

Paper and balloons: These are variations of known team-building exercises.

Thumbs: I developed this exercise as a way to get trios to improvise to solve a problem while listening acutely to the audience.

Follow your leader: When I first saw the Canadian clown duo Mump and Smoot, I enjoyed how the lower-status Smoot would constantly keep his eyes on Mump to see how he would react, like a puppy who pays close attention to his master for signs of affection, reprimand, or just out of curiosity. This exercise was partly inspired by them.

Status snapshots: I developed these variations based on known theater games to get students to include the use of props when exploring status relationships.

Get up: This is based on the old clown gag of clowns fighting over who gets to sit in a chair.

Top that: This was inspired by my work with Los Payasos Mendigos, the mock challenges we used to set up for each other, and the status play between us.

Down the line: This came from my studies of clown trios and their status play.

9 Clown Ensembles: Fractious Fun

All together now: These are known movement and acrobatic games with tweaks added.

Follow along: Some variations were invented by me; others are alterations of known theater games.

Follow me: These variations were inspired by Augusto Boal with some tweaks added.

Support staff: Source unknown.

Caretakers: Inspired by the work of director and author, Alison Hodge.

Eh? Oh: I developed these variations as a way of exploring group movement and status.

Add on: Inspired by known theater games.

Run, stop, relax: Some of these variations I developed, others were inspired by John Wright.

Revealing: I developed these variations to explore the solo artist within an ensemble.

Misfits and master; chips and stick: I developed these variations as a way of exploring group movement, improv, and status in relation to clown and bouffon.

The ridiculous ensemble: I developed this based on a game introduced to me by John Wright.

10 The Rules, the Script, the Game, the Play: Welcome to the Playroom

The evolution of a game: The starting point for this was a well-known children's game. The knife variation was introduced to me by former Pickle Circus clown Geoff Hoyle. I developed the other variations through my work with various students over the years.

Tail, tag, scene: I used a well-known children's game as a way to explore combining active play with a scene.

Scene tricks: These variations were inspired by my work editing films.

Prop journey: These variations were inspired by my work with students at Dell'Arte International.

Blindfolded experts: Originally inspired by a Violin Spolin exercise from her book, *Improvisation for the Theater*, I altered it to serve my explorations in clown, slapstick, and improv.

Index

Abbotts of Unreason xvii, 47–49, 63, 157–158
accidents, importance of 21, 24–25
acrobatics/tumbling 237, 240–241
Arlecchino 3
audience participation 111–113, 128–131, 165–166
auguste clown 3, 10–11, 226–227
Avner the Eccentric 3, 88

backstage, using the 113–116
balls, games with 89–91, 217–218
blindfolds, working with 142–144, 191–193, 217–222
body language 17–18
body mask/sculpture 5–6, 71–74
Boss Clown 11–12, 138, 159–160, 199–202
Boss, Negotiator, Fool 11, 157–161
bouffon 199–202, 231
breath, using the 67–68
Byland, Pierre 229

Carl, George 88
centering 68–70
chair games 54–56, 170–171
Chaplin, Charlie 21, 35, 88
character clown 3
child's play 5, 18
clown as energy 4–7, 20, 25–26, 30, 49–60, 146–150, 250–251
clown as storyteller 21–22, 195–196, 203–204
clown as troublemaker 6, 11–12, 196–197, 199–202
Clown Conservatory, San Francisco xx

clown costume 2–3, 231–232
clown dancing 65–67, 211–212, 236
clown, definition of 2, 16–18
clown duo 137–155
clown essentials 12–13, 19–26
clown groups/ensembles 181–204
clown makeup/mask 1–6, 30, 225–231
clown nose 229–231
clown partners 14, 137–155
clown routines writing/editing 13, 15, 19–26, 123–128, 259
clown skills 235–241
clown solo 119–134
clown traditions/history/influences 15–16, 226–227, 255–256
clown trio 157–178
clown/character walks 34–37, 49–50, 122
collaborating xx, 11, 24–25, 142, 208–213
commedia dell'arte 2–3, 255–256
commitment 20, 23, 256
competition 15, 25–26, 50–52, 54–59, 140–141, 163–165, 208–213
complicité/complicity 31–32, 40, 43–45, 48–49, 52–54, 59–60, 121, 204
curiosity, the importance of 4–7, 12, 23, 105–109

Dell'Arte School/International 101–104
devising xx–xxi, 6–7, 18–26, 60, 124–128, 195–196, 198–204, 207–232, 243–247, 249–262
Director and Clown 26
discovery moment 23, 105–109, 256

ensemble, developing of 32–45, 59–60, 181–204

Index

ensemble movement 33–39, 52–54, 64–68, 74–76, 182–186, 188–193, 195–199
entering/exiting 23, 76–80, 105–113
eye contact/using the eyes 80–84, 105–109, 173–174

face, using the 123–124
failure/accidents/obstacles 20–21, 23–26, 131–133, 217–222
Five Elements 76–84
following/shadowing 144–150, 166–167
Fratellini, Albert 3, 226

games, how to play 25–26
games, using in scenes 208–213
Gaulier, Phillipe 15, 229
Griebling, Otto 3
Grimaldi, Joseph 3, 226

Hanneford, Edwin "Poodles" 235

Irwin, Bill 3, 88

Jacobs, Lou 3, 228

Keaton, Buster 88
Kelly, Emmet 3, 227

Lecoq, Jacques 15, 238
lesson planning 13, 15, 31, 207–208
listening 111–113, 161–163, 193–195
Little, Frosty 74
Los Payasos Mendigos 63, 157–158, 181, 248

makeup 2–3, 225–229
mime 236–237
minimum-to-MAXIMUM 150–152, 215
mirroring exercises 71–72, 144–150, 154, 166–167, 185
Mischief Theatre 238
music 236

nakupelle 64, 87–88, 235, 238

personal clown 18
physical comedy/acting 63–85, 121–123, 193–204
physical warm up 33–39, 42–43, 49–59, 65–67, 140–142, 182–184
physical/visual play 17–18, 22–23, 87–98, 121–123, 235–241
play, definition of 4–5
playful mind xxi, 4–5, 7, 25–26, 207–232
playing it for real 124–128, 137–139, 157–159, 227, 246, 256
Polunin, Slava 3
prop play 87–99, 113–115, 152–153, 163–165, 171–177, 215–217, 251–252
props, ways to use 92–93
puppetry, techniques 87–98

realities, player's/audience's 256–257
relaxation 59–60, 154
rhythm games 161–163
Ringling Bros. and Barnum & Bailey 2–3, 11, 15, 74, 150, 157
rules, setting/bending/breaking 12, 15, 25–26, 31, 207–208

scene tricks 211–215
Shakespeare's Globe 120
skills 235–241
slapstick 21, 237–240
slow motion, using 57, 121, 214
sound, effects/using 214–215
space, using the 101–105, 109–117, 167–169
speed changes 214
stand-up comedy 17–18
status 12, 21, 96–99, 157–161, 167–169, 171–177, 193–195
street theatre 63–65, 120
success/the right way xx–xxi, 24–26, 207

tactics 20–21
takes, head/body 105–109
Tati, Jacques 88, 255
teaching methods xx, xxi, 10–12, 15, 31, 207–208
technique 20, 23, 64–65, 68–71
time, playing with 13–15, 124–128, 256
Tramp clown 3, 227
transformation 12

visualization 74–76
vocal/verbal games 32, 122, 193–195

Washerwomen clown gag 137–139
Whiteface 3, 10–11, 226–227
Williams, Robin 255
Wright, Stephen 255

zanni 2

www.ingramcontent.com/pod-product-compliance
Lightning Source LLC
Chambersburg PA
CBHW050135240426
43673CB00043B/1680